NEGOTIATING ON THE EDGE

NEGOTIATING
ON THE
EDGE

North Korean
Negotiating
Behavior

Scott Snyder

United States Institute of Peace Press
Washington, D.C.

The views expressed in this book are those of the author alone. They do not necessarily reflect views of the United States Institute of Peace.

United States Institute of Peace
1200 17th Street NW
Washington, DC 20036

© 1999 by the Endowment of the United States Institute of Peace. All rights reserved.

First published 1999. Second printing 2002.

Printed in the United States of America

The paper used in this publication meets the minimum requirements of American National Standards for Information Sciences—Permanence of Paper for Printed Library Materials, ANSI Z39.48-1984.

Library of Congress Cataloging-in-Publication Data
Snyder, Scott, 1964–
  Negotiating on the edge : North Korean negotiating behavior / Scott Snyder.
   p. cm.
  Includes bibliographical references and index.
  ISBN 1-878379-95-X (hdbk.) — ISBN 1-878379-94-1 (pbk.)
  1. Korea (North)—Foreign relations. 2. Negotiation. 3. Diplomatic negotiations in international disputes. I. Title.

DS935.65 .S69 1999
327.5193—dc21   99-048064

For

Ellis Haguewood,
Norman S. Thompson,
Richard J. Smith, and
J. Dennis Huston

teachers who challenged me to
broaden my horizons and to
express my ideas clearly

Contents

Foreword *by Richard H. Solomon*   **ix**

Preface   **xv**

Introduction   **3**

1. The North Korean Context   **17**
   Factors Shaping North Korean Worldviews

2. The Process of Negotiating with North Korea   **43**

3. Patterns in North Korea's Negotiating Style
   and Tactics   **65**

4. Comparing North-South and U.S.-DPRK
   Negotiating Patterns   **97**

5. The U.S. Negotiating Experience Compared with KEDO   **117**

6. Conclusion   **143**
   North Korea on the Edge

Appendixes

    I. Interviewees   **159**

    II. Chronology of U.S.-DPRK Negotiations, 1990–97   **163**

Notes   **169**

Selected Bibliography   **191**

Index   **197**

Foreword

"North Koreans are crazy!" is a familiar response to the threatening behavior of the Democratic People's Republic of Korea (DPRK) that has so long characterized the enduring confrontation on the Korean Peninsula. In fact, they are not crazy; they are not even unpredictable. Their use of threats or violence is disorienting to Americans, and highly disturbing. But such behavior has an internal logic and repetitiveness to it. Dismissing the North Koreans, or other international actors, as "crazy" limits our ability to deal with their threatening behavior effectively. We need to understand their way of looking at the world and use the predictability of their behavior to better manage what are often difficult and crisis-driven confrontations with the DPRK and other such "rogue" states.

There is a special challenge in assessing the mindset of a leadership that, by its own choosing, has isolated itself from the outside world. It is with good reason that Korea has traditionally been characterized as a "hermit kingdom." In this tradition, North Korea for decades has attempted to close off the country and pursue policies of "self-reliance" that keep even "allies" of the North such as China or the USSR at bay. During the depths of the Cold War, when the iron curtains of communist rule were drawn tightly around vast areas of Eurasia, no nation was more cut off from the rest of the world than North Korea. Today, in a world of economic and communications openness that even countries like China have joined, North Korea's self-imposed isolation is all the more pronounced.

Very few outsiders are allowed to enter the heavily guarded state that Kim Il Sung built after World War II on the ruins of the Japanese occupation. Still fewer North Koreans are permitted to travel outside the restricted borders of their homeland. The current North Korean leader, Kim Il Sung's son Kim Jong Il, is especially reclusive. His voice has been heard only once by the people he rules. Nonetheless, as son and heir to "the Great Leader," Kim Jong Il's grip on power is, it seems, as all-encompassing as was that of his father. I say "it seems," for next to nothing about North Korea can be known with high confidence. We know that the country suffered from a terrible famine in the mid-1990s, but we do not know its full geographic extent, how many people have died, or the effects of malnutrition on an entire generation of North Koreans. We know, too, that North Korea has a missile program and that it sells its weaponry to several other countries, but we do not know the full capabilities of Pyongyang's weaponry, or if and how North Korea plans to use them. We know also that North Korea has nuclear capabilities, but we do not know how close it is to assembling a nuclear bomb, or to developing chemical or biological weapons.

Our ignorance of so many facets of life in North Korea and our uncertainty about the intentions of its government make the job of negotiating with North Korea highly problematic. This difficulty was not overly troubling for most of the forty or so years between the end of the Korean War and the end of the Cold War, simply because, with Kim Il Sung adamantly opposed to rapprochement with South Korea, there was little basis for negotiations with North Korea on other than a crisis management basis. In the 1990s, however, as nonproliferation climbed to the top of the U.S. government's international agenda, North Korea's announcement of its intention to withdraw from the Nuclear Non-Proliferation Treaty provoked a strong U.S. response and began a process of diplomatic engagement with officials from Pyongyang that has broadened to more fully include such players as Japan and the European Union. Diplomatic encounters with North Korea have also been spurred by the election in 1997 of a South Korean president prepared to seek a more cooperative North-South dialogue. Another, although decidedly less positive, reason for increased contact with North Korean representatives has been the need to defuse crises engendered by one or another of their inflammatory acts—missile tests, for example, or incursions into South Korea by North Korean commandos. This is a regime that seems to thrive on self-created crises. Perhaps sensing the possibility of its imminent demise, the leadership appears to think it has little to lose by confronting its adversaries. For all these reasons, as well as its economic crisis, North Korea in the early 1990s became interested in dealing with the outside world, especially the United States.

Since then, U.S. and other Western negotiators have dealt with counterparts from a country about which they know very little except that it has a reputation for behaving aggressively, recklessly, and apparently irrationally. U.S. diplomats seem to have performed creditably in these challenging circumstances. Even so, missteps have inevitably been made, miscalculations or miscommunications have sometimes hindered the pursuit of U.S. interests, and North Korea has on occasion been able to use its military capabilities and reputation for violent behavior to gain negotiating leverage far beyond its political, military, and economic capabilities. There is much reason to learn about the negotiating tactics and behavior of the world's most idiosyncratic, least penetrable country.

Negotiating on the Edge is an important contribution to this learning process. Recognizing the shortfall in our understanding of how North Koreans negotiate, and recognizing, too, that much of what we do think we know is based on outmoded or misguided assessments made during the early years of the Cold War, Scott Snyder has sought to capture the essence of North Korea's negotiating behavior as exhibited in the 1990s in bilateral and multilateral encounters involving the United States and other countries. He has produced a remarkably insightful assessment.

Snyder studied Korean language and society during a year in Seoul conducting research through the Thomas G. Watson Fellowship program and subsequently spent time as an intern in the economics section of the U.S. Embassy in Seoul. He has visited North Korea four times, most recently in July 1999. With the existing literature on the subject conspicuously thin, Snyder has supplemented his direct exposure to Korean society and the existing written record by conducting scores of interviews with negotiators from the United States, South Korea, Japan, and KEDO (the multilateral body created to oversee implementation of an agreement to furnish North Korea with proliferation-resistant nuclear reactors). He has also spoken—off the record—to North Korean diplomats themselves. Snyder's study also draws on the conceptual framework of the United States Institute of Peace's Cross-Cultural Negotiations project, of which this book is one in a series of country studies of states important to U.S. interests.

Drawing on all these resources, Snyder has written a clear, succinct, and highly readable analysis, one that supplements the lessons learned through hard experience during this decade with insights into recognizable patterns in North Korean negotiating style, and an assessment of this experience in terms of Korea's history and culture. As the reader will discover in the following chapters, Snyder carefully dissects the North Korean approach to diplomatic encounters: objectives and expectations, tactics and strategies, strengths and weaknesses. As the reader will discover, "crazy" North Korean negotiators do not operate according to the same logic and rules that guide Western negotiators: actions that may seem to westerners to be irrational or reckless have their own internal logic and purpose.

The key findings of this study are the degree to which North Korean diplomats are skilled in converting weakness, through threatening behavior, into leverage so as to gain favorable outcomes to negotiations with outsiders. That said, their tactical skills reflect an isolated society and a political leadership whose policies have led to great strategic failures, most notably in their international isolation and the associated failure of their economy (most evident in the great famine of the years 1995–98, as described in Andrew Natsios's *The Politics of Famine in North Korea,* a Special Report recently published by the United States Institute of Peace).

That said, the North Koreans persist in creating for themselves and the world the myth of "self-reliance" (when in fact they are heavily dependent on outside aid), the pretension of "genius" leadership, and a worldview of undiminished threats from all outsiders. This is a regime that finds it difficult to sustain itself without enemies. The challenge for Amerian diplomats and other outsiders is to deal with North Koreans without getting drawn into their mythology and pattern of crisis-driven brinkmanship as a framework for negotiations. Despite their unique political culture and self-imposed isolation, the North Koreans demonstrate very Korean characteristics of exceptional discipline, will power, and the determination to survive on their own terms and to overcome all challenges.

With its carefully balanced and nuanced assessment of the extent to which cultural factors affect North Korean negotiating behavior, *Negotiating on the Edge* is an excellent addition to the series of studies undertaken by the United States Institute of Peace on cross-cultural negotiation behavior. Designed to help diplomats and other negotiators better understand their counterparts, and thereby be prepared to reach mutually satisfactory political solutions to issues that might otherwise escalate into armed confrontation, the Cross-Cultural Negotiation project supports both wide-ranging research into the impact of culture on international communication and more tightly focused studies of specific countries. The former category of research is reflected in such Institute books as Raymond Cohen's *Negotiating Across Cultures: International Communication in an Interdependent World;* Kevin Avruch's *Culture and Conflict Resolution;* and Chas Freeman's *Arts of Power: Statecraft and Diplomacy.* In addition, three country-specific studies have now been published by the Institute: a revised edition of my own book *Chinese Negotiating Behavior: Pursuing Interests through "Old Friends";* Jerrold Schecter's *Russian Negotiating Behavior: Continuity and Transition;* and the volume at hand. Two more country-focused studies, one on Japan and the other on Germany, are underway, and more will follow.

As we move ahead with the Cross-Cultural Negotiation project, we also intend to turn the spotlight on ourselves: to see how diplomats from other cultures regard the negotiating behavior of their American counterparts. In all these future endeavors, as in the projects we have supported to date, the Institute's intention is to provide both practitioners and scholars of negotiation with materials and training experience they can use to bridge cultural divides and so reduce the mutual incomprehension that can foster violent conflict. With books such as *Negotiating on the Edge*—packed with reliable information, astute observations, and practicable recommendations—we are, I believe, helping to realize that intention.

Richard H. Solomon, President
United States Institute of Peace

Preface

This book is truly an interim assessment, a snapshot of a work-in-progress. The subject of the book—the effort by the United States and North Korea to negotiate with each other following the end of the Cold War—is the result of a sustained endeavor by official and unofficial U.S. and North Korean interlocutors to bridge an enormous gap of distrust following more than four decades during which there was no direct political dialogue. The effort to overcome that distrust continues; in May 1999, for example, former Secretary of Defense William Perry visited Pyongyang to present ideas that may lead to a broadened process of negotiation between officials from the United States and the Democratic People's Republic of Korea.

This book could not have been written without the help of Americans, Japanese, and South Koreans who have negotiated with North Korea and who have given generously of their time to the author. I hope that this compilation of experiences and lessons learned from the U.S.-DPRK negotiating process will be useful to future officials who find themselves building on this interim assessment by expanding our understanding of the nature of the negotiating process between these two very different states. A full list of those interviewed appears in appendix I.

This study is part of an ongoing project to develop a series of studies examining national negotiating styles, a project inspired and led by the president of the United States Institute of Peace, Richard H. Solomon. I have benefited enormously from Dr. Solomon's encouragement and advice and from the example of his earlier study of Chinese national negotiating behavior, as well as from periodic sessions held at the Institute designed to grapple with the key variables that should be catalogued as part of any effort to explore the relationship of culture to national negotiating behavior. Needless to say, this book would not have been conceived, executed, or published without Dr. Solomon's unstinting support.

This book is a work-in-progress in terms of my own personal study of the Korean Peninsula, which began in 1987, when I was a senior at Rice University in Houston, Texas. Although I did not begin to focus my attention on patterns in North Korean negotiating behavior until 1995, my efforts to develop an understanding of the two Koreas extend back to my time at Rice University. The Thomas G. Watson Foundation provided me with my first opportunity to travel to Seoul following my college graduation, where I was introduced to Korean history and culture by Professors Lew Young Ick and Kim Key Hiuk. Professors Carter Eckert and Edward Wagner sustained my academic interests in Korean history during two years at Harvard University following my year in Korea. At the Asia Society in the early 1990s, I was able to travel to North Korea twice with K. A. Namkung and Professor Robert Scalapino, whom I am pleased to count along with so many others as a mentor and friend. While at the United States Institute of Peace, I worked closely with research directors Alan Romberg, Stanley Roth, and Patrick Cronin, who have provided unfailing encouragement and support to my professional development and who directly supported my work on this project. The final stages of this publication were finished while I was conducting research as part of the Abe Fellowship program of the Social Sciences Research Council, for whose support I am deeply grateful.

I have benefited during the course of my study from the advice, comments, and encouragement of many colleagues in the fields of Korean studies and international relations. Although it is impossible to name everyone who has provided me with deeper insights on North Korean negotiating behavior, several individuals have made concrete contributions by reviewing and making comments on parts of the manuscript as it has developed over time, including Bob Carlin, Victor Cha, L. Gordon Flake, Roy Richard Grinker, Katy Oh, David Kim, John Merrill, C. Kenneth Quinones, Don Oberdorfer, Donald Gregg, Robert L. Gallucci, J. R. Kim, Steve Noerper, Stephen Linton, Moon Moohong, Park Chan Bong, Hajime Izumi, Kunihiko Yamaoka, Yang Chang Seok, Samuel Kim, Charles Armstrong, Joel Wit, and Philip Yun. I also benefited from assistance in setting up interviews in Seoul from Ahn Chung Shi, Kim Young Ho, and Chung In Moon and in Tokyo from Hajime Izumi and Shuji Shimokoji. And I have benefited from the encouragement of a wide range of experts on aspects of negotiation and inter-Korean relations, including Lee Chae Jin, Kihl Young Whan, Han Sungjoo, Ahn Byungjoon, Chas Freeman, Choi Kang, Kwon Jong Rak, Cho Tae Young, Chung Oknim, Paik Haksoon, Han Shik Park, Mark Barry, Ezra Vogel, Dong Wonmo, Paul Evans, Aiden Foster-Carter, Nicholas Eberstadt, Larry Niksch, Bates Gill, Ralph Cossa, Jim Kelly, Bruce Han, Hyun In Taek, Kim Kyung Won, Hyun Hong Choo, Kil Jeongwoo, Kim Changsu, Kim Djun Kil, Kim Joochul, Masao Okonogi, Tetsuo Murooka, Lho Kyungsoo, B. C. Koh, James Lilley, and David Timberman, among others.

I owe a debt to all the North Korean diplomats with whom I have had the opportunity to interact during the past eight years, many of whom have gone on to play central roles as part of the U.S.-DPRK negotiating process. Although I am not listing their names here, they know who they are, and I look forward to the day when I can read their own assessments of patterns in the U.S. negotiating style.

The United States Institute of Peace has provided an excellent intellectual atmosphere in which to conduct this project, and I owe a debt to the entire staff for their kind collegiality and friendship. Research and Studies colleagues Patricia Carley, William Drennan, and Lauren Van Metre provided excellent advice and suggestions, as did Lewis Rasmussen and Timothy Sisk. I am also indebted to Amina Khaalis, Jodi Koviach, and Donna Ramsey Marshall for a wide range of assistance. Although I knew the Institute's Publications Staff and occasionally saw them around the building at very odd hours, it was a pleasure to work with them firsthand. Publications director Dan

Snodderly and all of the publications staff have been a pleasure to work with, and I am truly fortunate in my first publishing experience to have worked with Nigel Quinney, a true professional whose editorial instructions imposed clarity and discipline on any red herrings I tried to pursue on the way from first draft to final.

Finally, I thank my family, Buck, Carol, and Joy Snyder, for their indefatigable support, love, patience, and occasional nagging to hurry up and get this book done. No one will take greater pride in this work or be more generous critics than they, even if others argue that I got it wrong after all!

NEGOTIATING ON THE EDGE

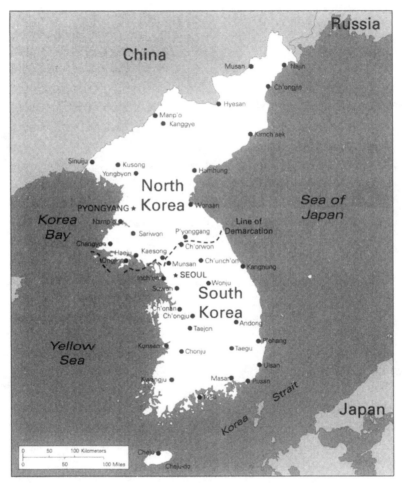

The Korean Peninsula

Introduction

On June 4, 1993, Vice Foreign Minister Kang Sok Ju of the Democratic People's Republic of Korea (DPRK) and his delegation arrived at New York's John F. Kennedy International Airport to participate in negotiations stemming from North Korea's decision to withdraw from the Nuclear Non-Proliferation Treaty (NPT). The delegation was greeted by the State Department's desk officer responsible for North Korea, C. Kenneth Quinones, and an armed customs official, who escorted the delegation to a special area for questioning and immigration processing. Having arrived in the United States for diplomatic negotiations at a time of high crisis that could possibly lead to war, the North Korean delegation regarded momentary detention by an armed official of the U.S. government with alarm.[1] At this moment of high tension, it was not a greeting that inspired trust among Kang and his delegation, who had come to New York for high-level political talks as part of a last-ditch U.S. effort to convince North Korea not to follow through on a March announcement to withdraw from the NPT, a decision that was scheduled to take effect the following week, on June 12. If these talks failed, the United States threatened to lead a drive at the United Nations for international economic sanctions, a measure that North Korea had announced it would regard as an act of war. The stakes could not have been higher in these negotiations between two countries with no diplomatic relations and little previous official contact.

North Korea, an isolated and seemingly impenetrable state that had managed somehow to survive the collapse of communism in the rest of the world, sought to achieve its diplomatic objectives and maintain the survival of its regime by engaging the United States, a distracted superpower with a new president who had been elected on a domestic agenda and had little experience in foreign relations. Moreover, U.S. negotiators had almost no idea of what to expect from North Korean officials. With the exception of a single high-level meeting the previous year in New York between Arnold Kanter, the Bush administration's under secretary of state for political affairs, and Kim Yong Sun, secretary for international relations of the Korean Workers' Party of the DPRK, the U.S. and North Korean governments had not been involved in high-level political negotiations since the 1951–53 armistice negotiations that ended the Korean War.

When Minister Kang arrived at the door of the U.S. mission to the United Nations the following day, he was again greeted by the State Department's Ken Quinones. It was only after Minister Kang was escorted inside the mission that he finally met his negotiating counterpart, Robert L. Gallucci, assistant secretary of state for political-military affairs. Although Kang may have perceived the low level of his initial greeting as a slight, it was politically impossible for the State Department to conceive of the American media reporting a live, public greeting between Kang and a senior administration official at the doorway of the U.S. mission to the United Nations, particularly given the perceived audacity of North Korea in announcing that it would flout the international regime designed to prevent nuclear proliferation. The atmosphere inside was initially tense and uneasy as long-time adversaries shared coffee before sitting down to a make-or-break negotiation with serious implications for war or peace in Northeast Asia. There was little allowance for small talk between delegations on either side, and there were virtually no previously existing relationships or common experiences between delegation members on either side that might have helped break the ice. Yet the task of the two delegations was to find mutually acceptable areas of agreement that might lead away from confrontation over the future of North Korea's nuclear program.

Decades of distrust and miscommunication between the United States and North Korea had created a difficult atmosphere for dialogue before official negotiations had started. In the eyes of the U.S. public, the North Korean government was irrational, "crazy," violence-prone, and unpredictable, precisely the type of adversary that is not amenable to negotiations.[2] Such images had accumulated over the decades since North Korea initiated the Korean War in 1950. Subsequently, American images of North Korea were shaped by aggressive terrorist acts such as the capture and yearlong ordeal of the crew of the USS *Pueblo* in the late 1960s; the "axe murder" and other incidents at the demilitarized zone (DMZ) during the 1970s; the North Korean assassination of over half the South Korean cabinet in 1983 in an attempt to kill President Chun Doo Hwan; and the downing of KAL flight 858 in 1987 in retaliation for Seoul's successful bid to host the 1988 Olympics. At any mention of North Korea in the news, there was also the TV file footage of a million-man army goose-stepping in lockstep formation across the vast public square in Pyongyang. At the height of deliberations over the proper response to the grisly axe murder incident in 1976, for instance, then Deputy National Security Adviser William Hyland is reported to have described the North Korean leadership as "wild people."[3]

This assessment of the North Korean leadership as irrational, violent, and unrestrained was still typical in Washington almost two decades later, throughout the U.S.-DPRK nuclear negotiations and during the nuclear crisis of 1994. Paul Wolfowitz, under secretary of defense during the Bush administration, remarked, "I'm more profoundly skeptical of North Korea than of any other country—both how they think, which I don't understand, and the series of bizarre things they have done." In a similar vein, another senior official recalled that "the basic assumption in the intelligence community and in Defense was that these people are liars, they dug tunnels and you couldn't trust any agreement that you reached with them."[4]

Assistant Secretary Gallucci's objective in the nuclear negotiations in New York was to convince the "irrational" North Koreans to refrain from fulfilling their publicly announced plan to withdraw from the NPT. Furthermore, Gallucci had to convince North Korea to return to full compliance with treaty obligations, including International Atomic Energy Agency (IAEA) demands for special inspections of North Korea's undeclared facilities suspected of being storage areas for reprocessed plutonium that could be used for making nuclear weapons.[5] In return, Gallucci had "nothing to trade," and concrete institutional experience in political negotiations with North Korea was practically nonexistent. "It was the thinnest briefing book I ever had in my life," Gallucci said of instructions given to him in advance of the June 1993 meetings in New York.[6] According to one State Department official present at the talks, the experience of negotiating directly with the North Koreans in the context of an impending confrontation was "sort of like learning how to fly while you are rolling down the runway."[7]

The negotiations with North Korea were an on-again, off-again sixteen-month ordeal for the Americans that eventually resulted in the Geneva Agreed Framework of October 21, 1994, a complex agreement between the United States and North Korea to freeze and eventually dismantle North Korean nuclear facilities that could be used to manufacture fuel for nuclear weapons in return for the provision of technologically superior, proliferation-resistant light-water reactors (LWRs) and of 500,000 tons per year of heavy fuel oil (HFO) to North Korea. Given the context and atmospherics surrounding the negotiations and the bitter history of military confrontation between the two nations, it is surprising that the United States and the DPRK—two nations with very different historical perspectives and perceptions of their relationship to the international community—were able to come to an agreement at all. In June 1994, almost everyone—including some members of the U.S. negotiating team itself—was privately predicting failure, if not for the negotiations themselves, then for the process of implementation, which has survived for over five years following the negotiation of the Agreed Framework in 1994.

These two nations of vastly different size, power, ideological persuasion, and historical experience were separated not only by intractable negotiating positions but also by very different experiences and ways of looking at the world—differences that were exhibited by the negotiating strategies and tactics of both parties. What can be learned about patterns in North Korean strategies and tactics as a result of the American negotiating experience? And to what extent do both the cultural context of decision making and the expressions of particular national negotiating patterns influence the process and outcome of a negotiated settlement? In what ways do differences in background, experience, and culture influence the negotiation of an agreement, and how is it possible to reconcile differing approaches to problem solving with the respective national interests of the United States and the DPRK? How might understanding such patterns enhance the ability of American negotiators to understand North Korean negotiating strategies and tactics and respond effectively to them?

OBJECTIVES OF THIS STUDY

This effort is one of a series of case studies published by the United States Institute of Peace that analyze the influence of cultural factors on negotiation through the identification and comparison of discernible patterns in national negotiating styles. There is a growing body of literature analyzing the characteristics of Russian, Chinese, German, and Japanese negotiating styles.[8] Other studies have also been conducted on characteristics of Saudi Arabian, Nigerian, Mexican, and French negotiating behavior.[9] This study will identify and analyze patterns in North Korean approaches to political negotiations with the United States from 1992 through 1997. A special emphasis of the study is on recurring patterns in the negotiating style of North Korean officials that might be considered unique to North Korea's negotiating behavior, to the extent that such patterns can be isolated and identified as influencing negotiations.

The negotiation process between the United States and North Korea provides an excellent case study by which to test a wide range of issues in the theory and practice of negotiation: how weaker states can seemingly enhance their negotiating leverage against stronger states; the dynamics and impact of a crisis atmosphere on negotiations; the "Toughness Dilemma" (whether "toughness" or "softness" yields a better negotiating strategy under certain circumstances); and the influence of cultural factors on negotiation approaches and outcomes, among others. To the extent possible, this analysis of North Korean negotiating behavior should shed light on each of these issues.

The primary objective of this study is to analyze North Korean diplomatic negotiation strategies, style, and tactics in their broader cultural and historical context—that is, to show how North Korean choices in negotiations shape and are shaped by North Korea's unique historical experience. This study will examine the influences of North Korea's national identity, values, and socialization processes on North Korean negotiators. The study will also compare the North Korean negotiating process with that of South Korea, the United States, and the Korean Peninsula Energy Development Organization (KEDO). This comparative approach should reveal differences in North Korean negotiating strategies and tactics with a range of counterparts over time. Such a comparison may help to "bridge the gap" of understanding, not only between scholars and practitioners but also between different theoretical approaches to negotiation.[10]

The primary data for this study have been gained through interviews with American officials who participated directly in negotiations with North Korean counterparts and through analysis of media reports about U.S. negotiations with North Korea. Interviews were also conducted with Japanese and South Korean diplomats who have engaged in negotiations with North Korean officials both in bilateral negotiations and in multilateral settings, adding a comparative perspective on North Korean negotiating styles. The experiences of unofficial interlocutors with North Korea have also been drawn upon, as have academic studies and, to the extent possible, relevant observations gained from North Korean officials themselves, although the near-impossibility of gathering frank assessments through interviews with North Korean negotiators and the lack of access to the written record of diplomatic negotiations between the United States and the DPRK constitute major limitations in carrying out this kind of research.

This analysis of patterns in North Korean negotiating behavior with the United States, the Republic of Korea (ROK), and KEDO reveals six major themes in North Korean negotiating style during the post–Cold War period.

- The decline in North Korea's relative power position after 1990 has required Pyongyang for the first time to achieve tangible negotiated outcomes as necessary components of a strategy for survival, unlike in Cold War negotiations, in which the objective of reaching a negotiated agreement was secondary to the propaganda value to be derived from weakening or distracting the negotiating counterpart.

- North Korea's unique historical experience has ensured that "stubbornness" (or resolve accompanied by guerrilla tactics), "self-reliance," and a strong defense of sovereignty are major characteristics of North Korea's strategy and tactics in international negotiations.

- The dynamic of negotiations with Pyongyang follows a distinct pattern in which hard-line and bellicose opening statements are followed by a period of quiet flexibility away from the official negotiating table and then a return to hard-line positions as part of an end game designed to wring additional concessions from the counterpart prior to reaching a final agreement.

- Brinkmanship and crisis diplomacy have served North Korea well in pursuing its objectives during negotiations over nuclear issues, at least initially. However, as time has passed, the effectiveness of such strategies has diminished as they have become predictable elements of North Korea's negotiating style.

- North Korean negotiators seek equivalency and observe reciprocity in negotiations with the United States while continuing to be trapped by a zero-sum dynamic of one-upmanship in negotiations with South Korea, even if such a strategy requires Pyongyang to forgo potential benefits that outweigh the "costs" of agreement.

- Pyongyang's brinkmanship and crisis diplomacy are muted in multilateral negotiations and in negotiations in which North Korea has "something to lose" if it fails to honor the letter of its obligations in agreements with outside parties, including the United States.

In his study *Negotiating across Cultures,* Raymond Cohen presents a three-point definition of culture that attempts to bridge apparent differences between negotiation theory and practice: "[Culture] is a quality not of individuals as such, but of the society of which they are a part; it is acquired—through acculturation or socialization—by the individual from that society; each culture is a unique complex of attributes subsuming every area of social life."[11] In addition, Cohen argues that depending on cultural influences within various societies, there exists a range of stylistic approaches to negotiation that might be placed along a continuum from individualist-oriented approaches on one end to collective-oriented approaches on the other end.[12]

This analysis of patterns in North Korean negotiating style will be conducted at two levels: (1) the identification of major influences in the formation of the DPRK's national cultural identity that might shape the way its negotiators perceive negotiating choices, and (2) the identification of recurring methods employed by North Korean negotiators to express their strategies, tactics, and preferred outcomes in a negotiation setting.

THE COLD WAR NEGOTIATING EXPERIENCE WITH NORTH KOREA

Although the U.S.-DPRK negotiations over North Korea's nuclear weapons program in 1993 between Assistant Secretary of State Gallucci and Vice Foreign Minister Kang initiated the first sustained political negotiation process between the two countries in over four decades, various negotiation channels and venues with North Korea have existed since the armistice negotiations to end the Korean War in 1951–53. In fact, rather extensive source materials are available on the armistice negotiations involving the United States, the People's Republic of China (PRC), and the two Koreas.[13] Regular low-level technical contact between the militaries has been consistently maintained through the Military Armistice Commission (MAC), the vehicle through which military violations of the Armistice Agreement itself have been discussed and resolved. After two decades of silence during the fifties and sixties, a historic step to reinitiate inter-Korean political dialogue was taken by Kim Il Sung and Park Chung Hee with the signing on July 4, 1972, of the South-North Joint Communiqué, which laid out three principles for national unification.[14] This first step toward inter-Korean rapprochement opened the way for significant further communication, and there is now a rich record of intermittent crisis-focused contacts, dialogues, and negotiations between the two Koreas stretching back to the early 1970s.[15]

Initial perceptions of North Korean negotiating behavior were shaped primarily by the experience of negotiating the Korean armistice with Chinese and North Korean communists at Panmunjom during 1951–53. The landmark study of the armistice negotiations that has shaped American perceptions of North Korea's negotiating style is *How Communists Negotiate*, by Admiral C. Turner Joy, the lead negotiator in the armistice talks. Turner Joy's first-person account identifies and magnifies the negotiating strengths of his counterparts while simultaneously vilifying their motives and intentions. Most notable among the tactics Turner Joy describes are attempts to "load" the agenda in order to create a context for one-sided concessions, psychological warfare conducted through incidents away from the negotiating table, delaying progress in order to wear down the opponent, making minimal commitments while extracting maximal concessions, dishonoring commitments already made, maintaining a veto in practice over the enforcement of agreements, raising "red herrings" in the course of negotiations, denying or distorting the truth, pocketing concessions instead of offering an equal concession in turn,[16] and agreeing to an item in principle and later applying a different interpretation to its content or significance. "Communists are not embarrassed in the least to deny an agreement already reached," says Turner Joy; "[they] simply state your interpretation is an incorrect one."[17]

A recent study by Chuck Downs analyzing the implementation and maintenance of the armistice through negotiations between the DPRK and the United Nations Command (UNC) via the MAC underlines many of the patterns in North Korean negotiating behavior observed by Admiral Turner Joy. Although intended as a temporary mechanism for maintaining the peace, the MAC has now been in place for almost fifty years, during which time it has often served as the only vehicle for international negotiation with North Korea, usually during periods of crisis. Following negotiation of the armistice, the MAC quickly devolved into a venue for competition by peaceful means, with adversaries "acting out" aggression for propaganda purposes and testing each other through limited provocations. When tensions came close to reaching their breaking point during the *Pueblo* incident of 1968, periodic border helicopter incursions, and the axe murder incident, the MAC was by default the only diplomatic vehicle through which such incidents could be settled and thus provides a reservoir of experience with North Korean propaganda tactics. At the same time, the MAC's technical negotiations have been restricted in their purpose to issues related to the implementation of the armistice and are limited in their scope.[18]

The 1972 Red Cross negotiations between North and South Korea marked the first direct inter-Korean contact since the end of the Korean War and the initiation of an on-again, off-again series of negotiations between North and South Korea over economic matters, sports exchanges, and political issues. The sporadic but growing negotiating record of North-South dialogue that has built up in the past quarter century on economic, cultural, political, and sports-related issues is characterized by a zero-sum approach—the perpetuation of North-South competition for legitimacy through means other than war. This quarter century of interaction between North and South Korea has reinforced Cold War perceptions of North Korean negotiating behavior among Americans, since the United States and South Korea have regularly shared viewpoints, experiences, and lessons learned from their negotiating experiences with North Korea.

Kim Do Tae of the Korea Institute of National Unification, in a study that analyzes over two decades of inter-Korean dialogue, concludes that North Korean negotiating objectives are related to its effort to "safeguard its political system and to attempt, together with physical force, to achieve unification on Communist terms."[19] In typical negotiations with South Korean counterparts, North Korea's real agenda is not reflected at the table; rather, the purpose of negotiation, or "pseudo-negotiation," is to allow North Korea to pursue ancillary objectives separate from those of the negotiation itself, such as positively influencing North Korea's international standing or denying potential benefits to South Korea. Also, North Korean pursuit of "incidental effects from the negotiations" rather than a negotiated settlement itself is usually designed to prevent South Korea gaining any benefit from a negotiated outcome, even if such an agreement might also be of benefit to the North.

These studies of North Korean negotiating behavior during the Cold War emphasize the communist approach to the negotiation process as "war by other means." Although this approach may indeed characterize some aspects of North Korean negotiating behavior even today, its wholesale application as a model for understanding current North Korean negotiating behavior is limited in several respects. First, the armistice was negotiated and implemented while hostilities were in progress, creating a very different context for negotiation than that which exists today, after over four decades of stalemated confrontation punctuated by occasional episodes of violence. Second, Turner Joy's analysis reveals that aspects of the negotiating behavior he encountered have more to do with Chinese and Korean cultural styles than the influence of communist ideology, yet this fact is unacknowledged in Turner Joy's narrative.[20] Third, the Korean armistice negotiations were led in large part by the Chinese and thus are not fully reflective of patterns in North Korea's negotiating style.[21] Fourth, Soviet records regarding the Korean War that were released in the mid-1990s have shown that the prolongation of armistice negotiations was influenced significantly by Stalin's desire to take a hard line as a means by which to drag out the war and thus weaken the capacity of the United States to build its capabilities in anticipation of a broader global conflict. Despite an increasing desire on the part of North Korean and Chinese leaders to end the war as the conflict dragged on during 1952, it was only after Stalin's death, in March 1953, that the Soviet Council of Ministers advocated a rapid conclusion of the Armistice Agreement, which was finally accomplished only four months later.[22]

Finally, patterns in North Korean negotiating behavior during the Cold War were influenced by the extent to which North Korea was able to project its power vis-à-vis the South. Chinese and Soviet backing put North Korea into a powerful position in the armistice negotiations in which the cessation of hostilities and the end of confrontation arguably would be of greater advantage to the opponent than to the North Koreans themselves. However, the end of the Cold War has

significantly changed the structural environment of a now abandoned and isolated North Korea. Under current circumstances—in
which the North Koreans must attain concrete objectives that can be
realized only through a negotiation process—North Korean negotiation
strategy cannot simply be "war by other means"; rather, North Korea
must pursue negotiations in order to attain benefits of agreement
necessary for regime survival. However, one-upmanship and intense
zero-sum competition in inter-Korean negotiations have made it difficult
for both sides to achieve breakthroughs even after the end of the Cold
War, with significant progress in inter-Korean dialogue thus far occur-
ring only during periods in which dramatic external changes have
affected the relationship between Pyongyang and Seoul.

STRUCTURE OF THIS STUDY

The 1993–94 negotiations over North Korea's nuclear weapons program pitted the United States, a superpower with global security
interests in defending against potential threats to the safety of the
global order, against North Korea, a weak and isolated state driven to
desperation in its search for survival but unwilling to admit defeat.
The two sides differed in almost every respect, including their fundamental approaches to problems that had been shaped by vastly different national values and perceptions of national identity. Yet the
differences between the two sides did not mean that their respective
interests and needs were contradictory in every respect, since it was
possible to reach an agreement that appeared to meet the fundamental needs of both sides. Although culture is not the decisive factor in
negotiations between states with conflicting national interests, empirical observation of the U.S.–North Korean experience plainly shows
that cultural factors are not insignificant influences on the negotiating process.

   To identify variables in negotiations that might be traced to uniquely
Korean experiences and cultural origins, I will examine patterns in
North Korean negotiating strategy and tactics in chapter 1. This examination will draw on key aspects of North Korea's history, including
the political, sociological, and cultural formation and development

of the North Korean state. This examination should shed light on the environment in which North Korean negotiators are socialized and the influences of North Korea's historical experience on its behavior in political negotiations with the United States.

Next, I will identify and interpret patterns in the American experience of negotiating with North Korea in chapters 2 and 3. Chapter 2 will examine each phase of the negotiating process with North Korea, including prenegotiation, opening moves, middle phase, end game, and implementation of agreements. Chapter 3 will explore patterns in North Korean tactics of crisis diplomacy, brinkmanship, and attempts to create leverage and maximize concessions from the negotiating counterpart and will identify facilitating tactics used by North Koreans to speed up the pace of negotiations toward a final settlement.

Chapter 4 will contrast U.S.-DPRK and North-South negotiating patterns and dynamics. It will explore stylistic similarities in North and South Korean approaches to negotiation despite the vastly different social structures and systems that form the basis of their continuing confrontation, and it will examine how those similarities in perception, style, strategy, and tactics may actually contribute to stalemate and inhibit compromise rather than facilitate cooperation. I will also compare U.S. and South Korean experiences to isolate factors that contribute to differences in American and South Korean approaches to dealing with North Korea.

Chapter 5 will examine negotiations between KEDO and the DPRK to compare the similarities and differences between South Korean indirect and direct influence on American-led negotiations with North Korea. The differing approaches to negotiation that have developed within KEDO will be compared with the experiences of the U.S. and ROK governments. Finally, chapter 6 will offer concluding observations on North Korean strategies and tactics as demonstrated through patterns of behavior in international negotiations and will draw lessons for U.S. negotiators and policymakers to consider as they manage future negotiations with North Korea.

The North Korean Context

Factors Shaping North Korean Worldviews

Almost all of the select group of foreign visitors to the Democratic People's Republic of Korea have found that their itinerary includes a mandatory pilgrimage to Mangyongdae, the birthplace of the "Great Leader." The focal point of the neatly kept grounds is a small, thatch-roof house with a few simple rooms adorned with family pictures and a shed for agricultural implements, a symbol of the peasant origins from which Kim Il Sung rose. The tour guide provides the official version of Kim's early life, emphasizing his departure from home as a young adult to lead a guerrilla revolutionary movement based in northern China and the Soviet Far East. These small guerrilla bands struggled to liberate Korea from Japanese colonialist oppressors who ruled Korea from 1910.

A walkway to the top of a small ridge leads to a pagoda overlooking the Taedong River, where a young Kim Il Sung is reported to have meditated on his plans for Korea's liberation and subsequent socialist revolution. The skyline of the city of Pyongyang extends to the other side of the river, and the tour guide points out another monument, this one celebrating the (perhaps fictitious) bravery of Kim Il Sung's great-grandfather in turning back an invading force that had attempted to open the "Hermit Kingdom" in 1866. In that year, an American warship, the *General Sherman,* steamed up the Taedong River with plans to open Korean society much as Commodore Perry's "black ships" had done some years before when they had arrived in the Bay of Tokyo to initiate contact and trade with an equally inwardly focused Japan. However, the invasion of the *General Sherman* was repulsed by the Korean garrison forces defending Pyongyang, reportedly led by Kim Il Sung's great-grandfather.

A visit to Mangyongdae is a visit to the DPRK's foremost national shrine, a symbol of the nation and of the role played by its founder, the Great Leader. Today, even the calendar of the DPRK, "*juche* time," starts with the birth of the Great Leader, thereby implicitly merging concepts of state and family by focusing on the founder's birthday as the defining marker of the North Korean calendar. One result is that Kim Il Sung's personal biography before liberation appears to merge with and extend the historiography of the North Korean state backward to before its actual creation in the aftermath of World War II. As founder of the DPRK, Kim Il Sung has put himself on a par not with Korean kings of the Koryo or Yi dynasties, but with Tan'gun, the mythological founder of the Korean people. Kim Il Sung's history, including his childhood and guerrilla experiences before the founding of the DPRK, is intertwined with and indistinguishable from the history of the nation.[1]

Likewise, the eulogizing of Kim Il Sung's great-grandfather emphasizes the influence of history on the formation and development of nationalism of the DPRK through a revolutionary ideology that has its roots not only in socialism but also in the Japanese colonial period and even in traditional Korean governance and polity. The DPRK's claim to have discovered the bones of Tan'gun and Kim Il Sung's order to build a tomb to house those bones in the early 1990s further manipulate aspects of Korean tradition in an attempt to fortify the all-encompassing role of the North Korean state and in turn have become components of the education and socialization process of the North Korean people, including North Korean diplomats who represent the state in international negotiations.

Within dynastic Korea, negotiations to resolve conflicts were shaped to a large degree by hierarchical and collectivist patterns characteristic of traditional Korean society. These historical influences are today shared by both North and South Korea, despite the fact that the two Koreas are now governed by drastically different political systems. The only recourse for those oppressed by unjust or wicked local officials under Korean dynastic rule was to travel to Seoul to make a direct petition to the king. The king would occasionally send censors to the provinces to secretly check up on local practices, but a strict vertical hierarchy of power relationships limited opportunities for protest. The social order was based on a strict patriarchal hierarchy of the landed, educated, and privileged upper class, or *yangban,* who ruled over the disenfranchised and uneducated commoner or slave. The order was reinforced by neo-Confucian conceptions of virtue, which justified the privileged, landowning, scholar elite's superiority over the masses who faced an existence without hope of social mobility and with little opportunity for financial gain. Occasional local peasant rebellions erupted in response to circumstances of extreme inequality,[2] but in general, conflicts were resolved consistent with the respective power relationships of those directly involved, and "negotiations" primarily involved ratification of those hierarchical relationships and of the social expectations resulting from the relationships.

Opportunities for public protest to bring attention to social injustices were even more limited during the early part of the Japanese colonial period (1910–45), with Korean peasants at the mercy of the unchecked power of local authorities. However, a limited tradition of social protest and state response continued in some form, as Japanese authorities responded to mass Korean independence protests in 1919 with violent countermeasures but also with a relative accommodation and liberalization of rights of association during the 1920s. This liberalization and the accompanying dilemma every Korean faced of whether to accommodate the Japanese overlords or risk death by instigating full-fledged resistance against the repression of Japanese colonial authorities are part of the pattern of challenge and response that extended throughout the colonial period and set the stage for the civil component of the Korean division that followed World War II.[3]

At the level of the state, survival, endurance, and resistance against foreign forces who seek to dominate or subjugate the Korean people are recurrent historical themes that extend back to the successful defense of the Korean Peninsula against Chinese challengers during the T'ang dynasty, and to the successful repulsion of an invasion by the Japanese warlord Hideyoshi at the end of the sixteenth century. By the end of the nineteenth century, Korea's weakened position forced it to attempt to play one great power off another as Korea became the staging ground for a series of military struggles for hegemony among China, Japan, and Russia. Even since the end of World War II, leaders of both Koreas have attempted to play great powers off one another in order to enhance legitimacy, gain leverage, and avoid overreliance on outside forces. The precarious geographic position of Koreans, who have endured at the vortex of great power confrontations, is expressed in the old Korean proverb that describes Korea as "a shrimp among whales."

These historical traditions have influenced both North and South Korean self-perceptions and attitudes toward self-identity and negotiation. Byung Chul Koh's comparative study of North and South Korean foreign policy formation shows that there were significant parallels in the psychological, historical, and even ideological foundations of the two countries' foreign policy outlooks through the 1970s. For instance, the concept of *juche* (self-reliance) not only was a guiding force in Kim Il Sung's political philosophy, but also played an important role in Park Chung Hee's expression of the national self-identity of South Korea, and the vestiges of traditional collective and hierarchical relationships in postcolonial South Korea remained and were reinforced by a strong authoritarian state structure borrowed from the Japanese colonial model.[4] At the same time, the psychological disjuncture caused by Japanese colonial rule has led the governments of both North and South Korea to emphasize the "recovery" of national cultural forms, in the process redefining for their own purposes certain national values and social structures.

To discern the experiences and influences that shape the worldviews held by negotiators from North Korea, it is necessary to identify primary themes in North Korea's history. Within any community, the socialization process consists of shared experiences, values, and ideals that make up the experience of representatives from that community and provide a reference for their view of the world. The challenge of identifying the major themes that shape the worldview of a negotiator from North Korea is that outsiders have few opportunities to explore or analyze the internal social and political structures of North Korea (a situation that calls to mind the moniker for traditional Korea, the "Hermit Kingdom"). Much literature about North Korea carries with it the prejudices and distortions that reflect the country's history of troubled dealings with the outside world.

Major influences on the North Korean socialization process include a mixture of historical experiences and new elements that are part of the DPRK's process of state formation: the role of the partisan guerrilla tradition in shaping the modern DPRK; the adaptation of the socialist system to North Korea; the residual influences of Confucian-based traditionalist thinking and practice and the experience of the Japanese colonial period on the relationship between the ruler and the people and on conceptions of national sovereignty; and the development of *juche* ideology and the personality cult of Kim Il Sung. By examining these historical and social influences that have shaped the national identity of the DPRK, we should find it possible to better understand the experience and approaches of North Korean officials as they engage in international negotiations.

THE PARTISAN GUERRILLA TRADITION

State building and national identity formation in twentieth-century postcolonial societies of Asia and Africa have often been closely identified with the charismatic experience of a national founder and ruler; the revolutionary role of the national leader has been particularly emphasized in socialist traditions, including those of Joseph Stalin in the Soviet Union, Mao Zedong in China, and Ho Chi Minh in Vietnam. In the case of Kim Il Sung, the unique qualification on which he based his original claim to leadership was as a partisan guerrilla leader who had persevered in continuously opposing Japanese colonial rule. Kim drew from, added to, and eulogized his nationalist credentials as a guerrilla patriot, and the formative experiences of his guerrilla days had a real impact on Kim's leadership style and understanding of power. The roots of Kim's guerrilla experience—and the suffering of the struggle for independence from Japanese colonial rule—have been idolized as part of North Korea's historical record.[5] Ironically, however, even Korea's liberation and Kim Il Sung's return to his home town at Mangyongdae following World War II were dependent on foreign forces, not self-reliance. Such facts seem only to have hardened Kim Il Sung's will to weave for his nation a new history, a mythic identity that would erase past humiliations and failures, replacing historical reality with national mythology.

Two clearly identifiable themes represent critical aspects of the psychological character projected through Kim Il Sung's—and therefore the nation's—historical experience: (1) the will to persevere despite tremendous odds for the sake of redeeming the nation, and (2) defiance of fate and assertion as the actor, or subject, as the creator of history rather than as the passive object shaped by historical experience—the essence of the *juche* idea. Commitment, solidarity, and unconventional tactics are the core resources of a guerrilla fighter who has nothing to lose and yet faces the prospect of losing everything. There is little benefit to be gained and much danger to be faced if one plays strictly by the opponent's rules.

The roots of Kim Il Sung's nationalist ideology have been planted deeply in the mythology of the guerrilla tradition, and Kim Il Sung's own experiences are presented as prototypes for how North Koreans should respond in difficult situations, including negotiations. No matter what obstacle is placed in front of the guerrilla troops, they survive, and survival is turned into eventual victory. The will to survive and to sustain oneself in the face of overwhelming odds is an important lesson for current North Korean negotiators, who have little to trade away in a negotiation and therefore little to lose in pursuing a strategy of obtaining maximal concessions while offering few concessions of their own. North Korean brinkmanship tactics and willingness to challenge conventional rules are derived partially from Kim Il Sung's own experience as a partisan guerrilla fighter against Japanese colonial rule.

The guerrilla experience taught Kim Il Sung the value of maintaining a united front and of using unconventional tactics against a stronger opponent. A constant refrain of Kim's descriptions of the resistance movement during the Japanese colonial period was his disappointment in factional rivalries among competing Korean nationalist groups. His autobiography, *With the Century,* describes a negotiation session Kim held with a Chinese National Salvation Army contingent under Commander Wu Yi Cheng, a Chinese nationalist who supported Chiang Kai-shek. This negotiation represented one of Kim Il Sung's early efforts to build a "united front" against his chief opponents, the Japanese military occupation forces in Manchuria.

First, Kim Il Sung used prenegotiation contacts with Commander Wu's subordinates to lay a favorable groundwork for a negotiation (similar to prenegotiation contacts pursued in negotiations with the United States). Second, despite contrary advice from his confidants to play it safe, Kim Il Sung sought a direct face-to-face meeting with Wu to discuss the issue of cooperation. Third, he established bonds with his counterpart by (a) offering to *give* Commander Wu precious rifles in response to Wu's request for an *exchange* of equipment, and (b) building a personal relationship in an attempt to dispel doubts regarding differences between the social practices of communist forces and Chinese nationalist forces. Finally, Kim insisted that cooperation occur on an equal basis (neither subordinate nor superior) by focusing on limited cooperation toward the common goal of fighting the Japanese while promising to subordinate communist revolutionary practices and ideology.[6] Kim's pursuit of a united front showed pragmatism, even if this alliance between Chinese nationalists and Kim's communist guerrilla fighters was short-lived. Several of Kim Il Sung's maneuvers as a guerrilla fighter, including prenegotiations and focus on equivalency and reciprocity, stand out particularly in the North Korean strategy in negotiations with the United States to be explored in subsequent chapters.

Guerrilla tactics were applied by Kim Il Sung not only to warfare but also to statecraft. Bruce Cumings traces the influence of the guerrilla tradition on the operation of the state to documents by Kim Il Sung's official biographer from as early as 1946, in which "the officer went on to recommend the guerrilla [track] as a good principle for party and mass organizations; he might have added that it would be the principle for the organization of the entire North Korean state."[7]

Kim's guerrilla instincts—inherited from centuries of Korean historical strategies maneuvering as a "shrimp among whales"—proved to be of particular value in managing relationships with the Soviet Union and the People's Republic of China throughout the Cold War.[8] During rising tensions in relations with the USSR and the PRC, Kim Il Sung never made direct responses or frontal attacks, even when he was attacked personally during the Cultural Revolution by the Chinese Red Guards. Rather than pursuing the central confrontation and risk being destroyed, Kim or a representative would pick a fight over a smaller issue on which the opposing party might give in. Even as North Korea's paramount leader, Kim sought symbolic victories in negotiations with China to press his point in low-level skirmishes while avoiding direct confrontations over intractable issues.[9]

Because Kim was isolated and without strong friends, conventional tactics and direct confrontations with the enemy—through either military or diplomatic means—were likely to have counterproductive outcomes. However, the threat even from a small and unpredictable force would cause the enemy to hesitate. Likewise, if the negotiating table can be used as a means to procure new resources without jeopardizing the fundamental organizing principles on which one's resistance is based, one should use negotiations as long as one is not drawn into the enemy's trap or forced to suffer humiliating defeats.

The traditional historical strategy in dealing with the threat from foreign oppressors has been essentially "divide and survive," a strategy that is clearly evident in North Korea's management of relations with China and the Soviet Union during the Cold War. The same strategy applies in North Korea's management of its relations with South Korea and the United States, and its management of potential post–Cold War competition between China and the United States. The case of the *Pueblo* and other aggressive incidents and unorthodox interactions with the outside world are representative of North Korean guerrilla tactics.[10] Always probing for weakness, avoiding frontal attacks, maintaining endurance while using tactics of diversion to disguise potential weaknesses, pocketing concessions without reciprocating: these are the tactics of a guerrilla state that has little reason to confront stronger adversaries head-on except on particular core issues and only on its own terms.

STATE FORMATION, ORGANIZATION, AND STRUCTURE: IMPORTING THE SOCIALIST REVOLUTIONARY MODEL

Because the DPRK was established as a revolutionary state with revolutionary leadership, the initial emphasis of North Korean authorities following liberation from Japanese colonial rule was on consolidating power by rooting out traditionalism and other old forms and importing socialist government structures that would overturn reactionary ways. Among the commonly recognized structural features of the DPRK political system are Marxism-Leninism as an all-encompassing official ideology, socialist rules of conduct and organization of the economic system, the "dictatorship of the proletariat," the leadership of the Communist Party, and the principle of democratic centralism.[11]

This does not mean, however, that the DPRK should be seen as a carbon copy of other Soviet satellite states, but rather that socialist organizational forms proved useful (perhaps even unavoidable, given the apparent influence of Soviet advisers in Pyongyang immediately following World War II) to Kim Il Sung in achieving power and that the structure of leadership was adaptable to the North Korean situation. The Soviet military was unprepared as an occupation force. Soviet advisers were active in reforming North Korean legal and cultural institutions but took a cautious approach toward encouraging social revolution in Korea, preferring to influence North Korea's foreign policy and trade and to encourage a leadership that would remain pro-Soviet.[12]

The structure of the DPRK government was set up prior to the Korean War with the assistance of key Soviet advisers, including Soviet ambassador T. F. Shtykov and Soviet military personnel. Without experience in governing and dependent on Soviet support during the initial stages of his return to Pyongyang, the young Kim Il Sung appears to have been in no position to ignore his Soviet advisers regarding structure and functions of government; indeed, the adoption of Soviet institutional forms in North Korea probably well suited Kim Il Sung's needs and objectives because such a process helped Kim to consolidate his rule and eliminate factional rivals who might challenge his policies. During a six-month period in 1946, Kim Il Sung introduced land reform, labor laws, the nationalization of heavy industry, an agricultural tax-in-kind system, equality of the sexes, and a new election code with the help of his Soviet advisers. The creation of the Korean People's Army, led by fellow guerrilla partisans with proven loyalty to Kim, and the Public Security Bureau provided Kim with the enforcement mechanisms by which to consolidate his power.[13]

Australian scholar Adrian Buzo has suggested that the influence of Stalinism on state formation in the DPRK has been underemphasized and that too much attention has been paid to the role of Korean traditionalism.[14] There is little reason to dispute that the first-generation leadership of a new state—at a revolutionary moment in global affairs in which opportunities for change supersede continuities—might well be eager to introduce new forms, structures, and methods of organization in an attempt to repudiate traditionalism, and it is clear that Kim Il Sung himself remained a steadfast admirer of Stalin even after de-Stalinization campaigns in the Soviet Union. Furthermore, a number of elements of North Korean state building clearly were not in keeping with Korean traditional influences, including many related to the cult of personality that developed around Kim Il Sung—such as on-the-spot guidance and emphasis on Kim's military background, charisma, and all-embracing ideological and philosophical role in North Korean society. These are characteristics that derived primarily from the Stalinist model but also appear to have been influenced by adaptations undertaken by Mao Zedong.

However, such an analysis underscores that many aspects of Stalinist leadership, ideology, and social structure (which had already been adapted to a Russian traditionalist context) that proved to be most easily adaptable to North Korea were elements that resonated with Korean social traditions and structures. In his study of influences on North Korea's state formation, Charles Armstrong emphasizes the transitional nature of the period immediately following liberation from Japanese colonial rule, during which the North Korean people played the major role in initially establishing their own local governmental structures, many of which welcomed socialist practice and readily laid the groundwork for Marxist-Leninist influences. "Soviet influence and Korean nationalism were not necessarily incompatible," as Soviet advisers promoted a "cultural renaissance" in North Korea, the architectural and cultural expressions of which were influenced significantly by the adaptation of Soviet cultural forms.[15]

While North Korea's smaller size made the application of socialism to North Korean society more manageable in some respects, size and other factors were variables that affected the success or failure of socialist innovations and practices. North Korea scholar Yang Sung Chul notes an "echo effect" between Mao's and Kim's approaches to leadership, in which either leader might borrow techniques from the other in order to achieve his own revolutionary aims. For instance, the Chollima movement in North Korea paralleled the Great Leap Forward, but with less disastrous results; the Chongsanri model of collective farm mobilization in North Korea preceded Mao's Dazhai model; and there were parallels between the development of Kim Il Sung's *juche* idea and Mao's doctrine of self-reliance.[16]

While acknowledging the central role of Soviet leadership as the vanguard of the communist movement, Kim Il Sung is careful in his autobiography to distance himself from dependence on Soviet leadership. While Kim expresses great faith in the Comintern, he also expresses exasperation with lack of attention and assistance from the Soviet Union. The origins of Kim's frustration date to his guerrilla days, when he made a request to Moscow for assistance to build a hand-grenade factory in the guerrilla zone. "But the Soviet Union sent no reply to our request, neither a promise to comply with it, nor notification that she could not do it or was not in a position to assist us. It was at this time that we resolved firmly to rely only on ourselves. The silence from the Soviet Union confirmed us in our belief that self-reliance was the only way to live, that the decisive factor in promoting the revolution was to enlist our own forces to the maximum and assistance from others was an auxiliary factor."[17]

Despite Kim Il Sung's cautions regarding overdependence on the Soviet Union, the influence of the Stalinist institutional structure of government on North Korean negotiating behavior is revealed through "salami slicing" tactics (in which symbolic progress is made at the expense of the substance of agreements), which are widely regarded as standard issue for many communist negotiators. But more influential has been the influence of the decision-making structure as an element that reinforces the rigidity of North Korean negotiating positions. This vertical reporting chain and the overarching position of the top leadership shorten the distance between the negotiator and the top of the command chain but also distort the negotiation process. Such a negotiating structure makes it more likely that negotiation may be used for dual purposes and that formal sessions may be used for propaganda purposes. It also carries the danger that the information flow to a single decision maker, the totalitarian leader, might be distorted by underlings unable to challenge the leader's presumptions or manipulated so that the leader himself does not have an accurate understanding of his own negotiating situation, stakes, or objectives. The tactical use of negotiation for purposes other than to reach an agreement may be another characteristic of North Korea's approach to negotiations during the Cold War that demonstrates Stalinist influence.

LIBERATION FROM JAPANESE COLONIAL RULE AND THE RECOVERY OF NATIONAL SOVEREIGNTY

As a Korean nationalist, Kim Il Sung had several paramount objectives following Korea's liberation at the end of World War II. Clearly, the foremost goal was to fulfill the prospect of liberation and reunification of the Korean Peninsula. In the process, Kim also hoped both to remove the negative influences of the Japanese colonial dictatorship and to obliterate the old, traditional Korean ways that had so weakened his country that an outside power had been able to subdue it.

The humiliation of having lost national sovereignty to outside oppressors—even after centuries of heroic resistance and maneuvering to maintain a semblance of sovereignty against more powerful foes—is a significant component of the contest for legitimacy between the two Koreas. The influences of the Japanese colonial experience are often overshadowed in contemporary analysis by the emergence of Cold War rivalries between the United States and the Soviet Union, widely seen in modern North and South Korea as the authors and perpetuators of Korea's national division.

The most immediate influence of the Japanese colonial legacy was to discredit nationalist competitors to Kim Il Sung who had remained in North Korea and cooperated, even indirectly, with the Japanese government. Korean nationalist leaders who had stayed in Korea during the Japanese colonial period—such as the widely respected Cho Man Sik, leader of the patriotic "Buy Korean" effort in the 1920s designed to resist Japanese economic domination—were subject to this charge. Despite the near impossibility of engaging in oppositionist activities within Korea under Japanese colonial rule (the Japanese had effectively wiped out Korean Communist Party activities on Korean soil in the 1920s), those who had stayed in Korea were automatically marked as collaborationists and attacked mercilessly by Kim Il Sung. Most were eliminated even before the start of the Korean War.[18]

In his autobiography, Kim emphasizes his family's nationalist roots and recounts the vivid memories of his youth.[19] "The Japanese, whenever they had a chance, would slander our nation, calling it an 'inferior nation.' They claimed that, therefore, Japan should 'protect,' guide, and 'control' the Korean nation." Kim recalls one role model who said, "The Korean people, even if three of them get together, must unite to fight against the Japanese imperialists."[20]

Despite the strongly anti-Japanese sentiment expressed by Kim Il Sung in his memoirs, the Japanese colonial experience also provided continuities that influenced the formation of the Democratic People's Republic of Korea following liberation. Charles Armstrong describes the conceptual approach to governance of the Japanese state as "paternalistic and persuasive, strict but not brutal," but the Japanese colonial government took on a much more authoritarian hue, particularly in the area of public security and policing functions in Korea and Manchuria. As for public security, the Japanese state applied modern organizational functions to the self-policing functions that had traditionally existed within the Korean village, often using Koreans to carry out most policing duties at the local and village level, while ensuring that, for the first time, the central government directed and controlled these self-policing functions.[21]

Following liberation, Korean localities initially organized themselves through local self-governing committees in the absence of the state apparatus. Where the institutional void remained as the state began to establish institutions, particularly in local policing roles and in the legal system, there was little choice but to rely on the same villagers who had already developed appropriate expertise under the Japanese colonial system to play similar roles in the new state structure. One result is that the influences of Japanese colonial rule, particularly the functions of the modernized state, were incorporated as part of the new North Korean state as it gradually reasserted centralized control by 1948. A primary legacy of the Japanese colonial state was a disciplining experience that was effectively adapted for use in exerting control over society. "While it is true that the North Korean regime eliminated many high-ranking colonial personnel from the Japanese administration, many in the lower ranks seem to have been retained, and the legal system itself remained in place for a time. In the end, the North Korean legal system combined features of both Japanese colonial law and Soviet law, with certain elements reflecting a particularly Korean revolutionary experience."[22]

After South Korean and U.S. authorities, the Japanese government is arguably the third favorite target of vituperation by North Korean propagandists at the Korean Central News Agency (KCNA). North Korean concerns about the "revival of Japanese militarism" have been a recurrent theme in the North Korean press. Kim himself editorializes on Japan's history of aggression against Korea in his memoirs: "The rulers of Japan are under a moral obligation to reflect upon the crimes they have committed in Korea and Manchuria. Repentance implies neither shame nor humiliation. It is a process of self-reform by means of reason in the effort to approach perfection. They may close their eyes, but time will never erase the facts of history. Japan must remember that her high rate of growth, the economic bed of roses in which she glorifies, is stained with the blood of the Korean nation."[23]

North Korean negotiators continue to show particular sensitivity to perceived threats to North Korean sovereignty, no doubt partially as a result of the historical legacy of Japan's colonization of Korea. Like Chinese negotiators, North Korean negotiators put a strong emphasis on the principle of noninterference with a state's internal affairs, a principle that underscores state sovereignty and is designed to resist perceived hegemony or external pressure from outside forces.[24] In negotiations with South Korea as well as with the United States, North Korean counterparts often go out of their way to demonstrate their independence, even if such demonstrations appear to run counter to North Korea's immediate or long-term national interests. Suggestions that the North Korean government may be pressured into accepting a weak or undesirable position or might be forced to make a concession on a sovereignty-related issue have usually resulted in strengthened rhetorical or physical demonstrations of resolve through delay in the negotiating process.

SOCIAL RELATIONSHIPS: THE INFLUENCES OF CONFUCIAN NORMS

If Kim Il Sung utilized the combined legacy of Japanese colonial and Stalinist organizational structures to mobilize, control, and "discipline" society, perhaps the post–Kim Il Sung period in North Korean politics has witnessed the resurgence of Korean traditionalism. The dominant feature of governance in the post–Kim Il Sung era has been the submission by the Great Leader's successor and son, Kim Jong Il, to Confucian expressions of loyalty and filial piety, themes that have deep roots in Korean traditional society and in the mythology of the nation presented by Kim Il Sung.

The neo-Confucian philosophy that influenced the Korean Yi dynasty from the fifteenth and sixteenth centuries was based on what had been developed in Sung-dynasty China, including concepts of strict order and a clearly defined social hierarchy existing under the "mandate of heaven," an emphasis on *li* (righteousness) and *yi* (principle) as central concepts for ordering social relations, and the importance of maintaining order within patriarchal family relationships through filial piety and fulfillment of duty, with the ruler taking on the role and duties of "father" over those subject to him. Social position determined one's role within society, and challenges to the carefully balanced social order were punished severely.[25]

The vestiges of Confucian thought—reinforced by the vertical structure of North Korea's socialist bureaucratic organization, Kim Il Sung's personality cult, and the philosophy of *juche* (discussed later)—are primary influences shaping North Korean approaches to individual relationships and relationships at a national level. Although an empirical analysis of the role of relationships within North Korean society is still not possible, there is a growing database of information available for consideration, including the declaration by Kim Jong Il of a three-year national "mourning period" to show respect for the leadership of Kim Il Sung.

Confucian roots were skillfully manipulated by Kim Il Sung in establishing the nation as family and himself as the patriarch of the nation. In the process, Kim Il Sung honored his own pantheon, including his father, Kim Hyong Jik, a revolutionary martyr, and even his great-grandfather, said to be the leader of troops that had repelled the "American imperialists" of the *General Sherman*. His mother also has been treated with special respect, and Kim Il Sung's own filial relations are handled very carefully in his autobiography. His mother gave him over to the revolution, releasing him from the duties of the first son in order to pursue a higher calling, even though she was on her deathbed. Likewise, his mother's last words excuse Kim Il Sung from his filial obligations in order to meet a higher call: his mother tells a neighbor that if her son returns after her death, "if . . . the Japanese are still in our country and without having achieved Korea's independence, you must not allow him to open my grave. You should not even let him into the yard. It is not that I am boasting of my son, but Song Ju [Kim Il Sung] will not return before the battle is won."[26] By narrating this story, Kim Il Sung not only exemplifies his voluntary and self-sacrificing action in placing nation before family but also combines it with an act of filial piety in obeying his mother's wish. At the same time, the story provides a clear message regarding the type of behavior Kim Jong Il must assume in order to be worthy of honoring and succeeding his father as North Korea's leader.

Russian scholar Alexandre Mansourov has analyzed features of the "politics of filial piety" under Kim Jong Il, exemplifying the continued emphasis on Confucianism in North Korean society. Kim Jong Il's legitimacy hinges on his filial piety and reinforces the power of Kim Il Sung's legacy from beyond the grave. One way for Kim Jong Il to place his father in the pantheon of Korean rulers (an effort that has implications for inter-Korean legitimacy struggles) is to equate him with Tan'gun, the mythical founder of the Korean nation, whose tomb was reconstructed in the mid-1990s.[27] A second way of demonstrating filial piety was for Kim Jong Il to observe the longest mourning period in modern Korean history, placing himself on the right side of any possible challenge to his authority.[28]

The hierarchical structure and the ritualistic aspects of Confucianism, although influenced by socialist interpretations, are important determinants for understanding and interpreting modern North Korean behavior on both personal and national levels. For instance, the North Korean population has been divided by the state into three classifications, "core," "fluctuating," and "antagonist," and there are reportedly fifty-one categories within each classification.[29] A North Korean's classification may determine the relative freedom of action, privileges, and types of opportunities or goods he or she might receive from the state and can't help but be a reminder of the traditional "bone rank" hierarchical structure of *yangban* society dating back to the Shilla dynasty.[30]

As in South Korea, hometown and school ties and intermarriage and family relationships may be important factors in determining the structure of the North Korean political and social hierarchy.[31] However, since we know little about these sorts of ties within North Korean society, it is much more difficult to use them to predict the behavior, loyalties, or effectiveness of individuals within that political system, or the likelihood that individual actors will conform strictly to externally imposed "moderate" or "hard-liner" labels. The relative success of individuals who have blood ties to Kim Il Sung and Kim Jong Il or who have strong revolutionary credentials or relationships to the "first family" reinforces the impression that an essentially traditional social structure (with socialist factors such as class background playing a primary role) remains a fundamental aspect of North Korean social organization.

Confucian influences on the behavior of North Korean negotiators are demonstrated most clearly through emphasis on an unyielding adherence to and protection of "principle" in negotiations and an insistence on the moral rectitude of one's own position at all costs. Both of these characteristics might be drawn from the core concepts of *li* (principle) and *yi* (righteousness) at the core of Confucian thought. In addition, Korean sensitivity to symbolic issues that connote hierarchy (superiority or inferiority) might be drawn originally from the vertical social and political structures of Confucianism, reinforced by Japanese colonial influences as well as by the overwhelming leadership role of the Communist Party as the vanguard of the masses.

THE INFLUENCE OF *JUCHE* THOUGHT AND THE CONCEPT OF SOVEREIGNTY

Another primary element that influences North Korean concepts of identity, relationships, and negotiating behavior is the concept of *juche* (self-reliance). Much has been published by North Korean scholars on the intricacies of *juche* thought; in fact, a significant portion of North Korea's institutions for higher learning and propaganda organs has been devoted to developing, elucidating, and propagandizing the *juche* ideal around the world. The central concept as it applies to North Korean national behavior is best illustrated by defining *juche* in opposition to *sadaejuui*, another concept that was part of the behavioral pattern of traditional Korea when confronting larger, more powerful neighbors. *Sadaejuui* (serving the great) was a term used to describe the tributary relationship between Korea and China during the Yi dynasty, but it has also taken on the connotation of fawning, flattering, subservience, and doing whatever was necessary to survive in the context of the Chinese tributary system and Japanese colonial rule.

The oppositions between the concepts of *sadaejuui* and *juche* extend to the traditional practice whereby Korean kings offered tribute to the Chinese emperor; from the foundation of the DPRK, gift giving has been for visitors to Pyongyang a significant component of relationship building with Kim Il Sung, and their gifts are on display in a special museum at Mount Myohyang to underscore the tribute that has been paid to Kim. Defined in opposition to *sadaejuui,* the fundamental *juche* concept takes on connotations of independence and freedom of action that are central to North Korean existence.[32]

The originator of the concept of *juche* was Sin Chae Ho, a Korean nationalist of the early twentieth century who has influenced historiography and Korean conceptions of identity on both sides of the DMZ. In fact, Sin himself defines *juche-ui chongsin* (autonomous spirit) in opposition to *sadaejuui* as an antidote to centuries of bowing to more powerful neighbors. Sin defines history as a function of race *(minjok),* not as a function of space.[33] This conception is strongly influenced by the fact that he lived through the period during which Korea was deprived of its nationhood.

Why might a guerrilla fighter like Kim Il Sung be familiar with Sin Chae Ho's work or even subscribe to his thought? First, Sin was a nationalist, although while in exile in China he supported a movement of anarchists. Sin and Kim Il Sung were both devoted to retrieving and restoring Korea's dignity and independence. Second, both Sin and Kim Il Sung spent time in exile in China.

Regardless of whether or not Kim Il Sung was the originator of *juche,* it is clear that he successfully appropriated the concept and applied it even before liberation as a powerful idea that eventually would become the unique basis for the existence of the North Korean state. It is ironic that Kim might use Sin's concept of *juche* as a foundational ideology for the North Korean state because one of Sin's primary intellectual contributions was to define the nation as apart from the state, not confined by space but rather defined by the presence of a Korean community that threatened to eliminate or disregard state boundaries.[34] It is also ironic that, according to the testimony of North Korean defectors, Sin Chae Ho's intellectual contribution to the struggle against Japan—like that of many others from whom Kim Il Sung borrowed or with whom he is associated—has been expurgated from the North Korean historiography.[35]

The precursors of *juche* are referred to early and often in the autobiographical accounts of Kim Il Sung as he retells the story of his youth. As he begins his search for the right way to approach the task of national recovery, Kim Il Sung projects themes of autonomy, stubbornness, and independence, which are all to varying degrees components of the *juche* idea: "I decided that in order to work out a correct guiding theory suited to the Korean reality it was necessary to take an independent view of all problems and settle them in an original way that was suited to our own specific situation, instead of holding classic works or the experiences of other countries supreme."[36] Further confirmation of the practical influence of Kim Il Sung's application of *juche* is provided by a former Soviet official posted in the Soviet embassy in Pyongyang, who described Kim Il Sung as "a flexible and pragmatic politician, an Oriental Talleyrand. He would agree with our leaders and give a lot of promises, but afterward he would pursue the same line, his own line."[37]

The influence of *juche* can be seen most strongly in North Korean attitudes toward sovereignty—attitudes that are repeatedly expressed in North Korean media and official rhetoric. This May 5, 1995, release by the KCNA regarding the impasse in the implementation of the Geneva Agreed Framework is indicative of North Korean attitudes toward sovereignty that are grounded on the philosophy of *juche:*

> If the United States withdraws its unjust position even now and assumes a position of trying to solve the question, we will stand face to face with them in good faith; however, if on the contrary, the United States continues to insist upon its unjust position, we will inevitably go our own way as we have made up our mind to do. The DPRK-U.S. framework agreement is good for us; however, what is more important is sovereignty.[38]

Although the concept of self-reliance seems to be directly at odds with Confucian influences, they may play complementary roles in defining North Korea's relationship to the world, particularly when viewed through the lens of Korean nationalism. The hierarchical control of North Korean society emphasizes internal unity, while the doctrine of self-reliance underscores independence and freedom from domination by external enemies. Likewise, Koh Byung Chul describes the similarities in the use of *juche* as an expression of South Korean nationalism, particularly in the speeches of Park Chung Hee during the 1960s and continuing during the Yusin reforms period.[39]

Such similarities are underscored in the transcript of Korean Central Intelligence Agency (KCIA) director Lee Hu Rak's conversation with Kim Il Sung in Pyongyang on May 4, 1972, in which Kim Il Sung states, "Our position is to oppose reliance on external forces on the issue of reunification. This is where I agree with Park Chung Hee . . ."[40] This striking shared viewpoint at the height of inter-Korean confrontation indicates that self-reliance is a component of Korean nationalism that is likely to be expressed both north and south of the DMZ.

The fundamental question of "sovereignty"—as interpreted based on the philosophy of *juche*—has critically influenced North Korean policy decisions in the international arena, sometimes to the detriment of North Korean material interests. For instance, public South Korean "humanitarian" offers of rice—a gift that carries symbolic overtones related to national conceptions of self-sufficiency in Japan and South Korea—have been routinely rejected by the North, even in times of critical need. Likewise, offering and accepting rice in times of difficulty may pave the way for cooperation, but only if the gift does not convey with it suggestions that the receiving state has failed to provide for the needs of its people. North Korean conceptions of sovereignty may also prove to be a key stumbling block as Pyongyang haltingly seeks an economic opening while maintaining political control over its population.

KIM IL SUNG'S CULT OF PERSONALITY

Perhaps the most unique, pervasive, and—for the outside observer— incomprehensible aspect of North Korea's socialization process is the all-encompassing role played by Kim Il Sung, who arguably continues to be the ruling figure—the "Eternal President"—in North Korea even after his death. Of course, Kim Il Sung followed in the footsteps of Stalin and Mao in developing a cult of personality, but no other society has sustained such a cult following even during a leader's life, must less after his death. A 1995 *Economist* report on a visit to Pyongyang notes, "To the student of communist regimes, the Kims' personality cult may seem as hollow and fragile as that of Romania's Ceausescu, felled in a popular uprising six years ago. Yet Kim Il

Sungism may have more in common with religions than with other communist regimes. And, like many strong faiths, it feeds on a form of aggrieved nationalism."[41]

A former diplomat in Pyongyang reports, "Once said by Kim, it is said forever. Nobody is allowed to change anything; the smallest sign of deviation means the system has developed a dangerous crack."[42] My own private conversations in Pyongyang in 1991 with North Korean officials reflect a similar adherence to the Kim Il Sung line; when asked if Kim Il Sung had ever made a mistake or if he was perfect, the official replied, "The Great Leader hasn't made any mistakes yet."

The relationship between the hagiographic portrayals of Kim Il Sung and the project of nation building in North Korea is clear, but perhaps the element of the cult of personality that is unprecedented is the extent to which Kim Il Sung was able to merge traditional roles, images, and relationships of the Korean family with a broader set of relationships between the people and the nation. Charles Armstrong describes North Korean metaphors connecting family and state relationships as the key concept in North Korean nationalism. "The images of family and body are among the most common metaphors of nationalism everywhere; both appeared frequently in North Korea, coming together in the dual metaphor of 'blood' as both vital fluid and signifier of kinship. The party was initially metaphorized as the 'veins' (chongmaek) of society, later as the 'mother party'; the transition from blood to motherhood, body to family, expressed the party as a metonym for the nation as a whole."[43]

Kim Il Sung's cult of personality draws on a diverse set of cultural influences, including the indirect influence of the Japanese imperial tradition, the Stalinist cult of personality, Confucian tradition, Korean shamanist practice, and, ironically, symbolism from Western Christianity, to which Kim Il Sung was exposed as a child before his family moved from Mangyongdae. In his book, *The Two Koreas,* Don Oberdorfer relays the exchange between a Soviet party official and Kim Il Sung in the late 1960s, in which the official asked Kim, "How is it possible there is this cult of personality in your country?" to which Kim replied, "You don't know our country. Our country is used to paying respect to elders—like China and Japan, we live by Confucian culture."[44]

Borrowing from each of these traditions, Kim Il Sung's cult of personality has taken on a palpable religious aura that is omnipresent in Pyongyang's public representations and in the pervasive propagandizing of the Great Leader. It should not be surprising that citizens who have known nothing else but an unrelenting exposure to propaganda in praise of Kim Il Sung might genuinely feel loyal to him, as evidenced by the outpouring of grief upon his passing. Intellectuals had faith in Mao even during the Cultural Revolution, but Kim Il Sung's cult is long-standing, without the uncontrolled violence or generational and cultural confrontation that marked the height of Mao's cult of personality.[45]

Kim Il Sung is omnipresent in Pyongyang through his image in houses, in public places, and even on the lapel of every North Korean citizen. "In front of a statue of Kim Il Sung in Pyongyang a child cries; its mother smacks it, for this is a place of worship . . . The chant of 'Comrade Kim Il Sung will be with us forever' is not intended to ring true to secular ears. It is a religious incantation . . . [Kim Il Sungism] may impose asceticism upon its flock, be ridden with intolerance and myths, and involve a leap of faith; but so do many religions that show no sign of disappearing."[46]

Kim Il Sung's religious and political roles are intertwined in his position as the savior and founder of the Korean nation, notwithstanding the failure to fulfill the long-standing promises of a paradise in which every North Korean would live in a house with a "thatched roof, silk clothing, and meat soup," the heavenly goal held out as reward for those loyal followers who were willing to pursue dreams of a revolutionary paradise. "All were combined into the symbol of Kim Il Sung, whose emergence as a leader was marked by a brilliant star, whose return to Korea was equated with the coming of the sun, and who shed his 'precious blood' for the sake of national salvation."[47]

The durability of Kim's cult of personality even after his death is so powerful that it cannot be discarded lightly; rather, there was no choice, no foundation for legitimacy within North Korea other than to embrace the cult and allow it to envelop the son, the "Dear Leader," the second person of North Korea's trinity, along with the flame of the *juche* ideal. The religious quality of the relationship between

Father and Son could not be missed in Kim Yong Nam's eulogy to Kim Il Sung, the first public statement at a moment of high drama and grief in North Korean history. The eulogy declared Kim Jong Il to be the personification of his father, and the personality and leadership qualities of father and son were intentionally merged: "Equipped with both literary and military accomplishments, and both loyalty and filial piety, Comrade Kim Chong-il is another great leader *[ttohanbunui widaehan chidoja]* who has completely inherited the fatherly leader's ideas, leadership traits, and noble virtues. . . . As long as we have the dear comrade leader, we will not fear any difficulty or big enemy *[taejok]* but will always be ever-victorious."[48]

In analyzing the significance of the cult of personality in North Korean history, Charles Armstrong identifies a critical factor with significant implications for our study of North Korea's negotiating style and tactics: "The maintenance of this cult has been justified partly by North Korea's ongoing siege mentality, as a defensive focus of unity against the constant threat of imperialist subversions, for nearly half a century. In maintaining the cult of Kim Il Sung at such a level of intensity for so long, without lapsing into the disruptive terror of Stalinism or the anarchy of the Chinese Cultural Revolution, North Korea has achieved the seemingly impossible: a stable state of permanent crisis, an institutionalized, continuous emergency."[49]

Kim Il Sung's cult of personality is tall enough to cast a shadow over North Korean negotiation tactics even during negotiation sessions themselves, particularly if there is any comment by negotiating counterparts that fails to connote proper respect to the Great Leader. Perceived insults to Kim Il Sung are "hot button" issues for any North Korean negotiator, who will break off discussions on a negotiating agenda to vigorously defend the honor of Kim Il Sung if he is insulted during talks. There have been several instances during negotiations between the United States and North Korea when unintended comments were perceived by the North Korean side as derogatory to Kim Il Sung, resulting in a spirited response and defense of Kim Il Sung's honor. Another example of such behavior outside a negotiation is represented by incidents caused when American personnel have accidentally thrown papers containing the image of Kim Jong Il into the garbage or have set objects on top of newspapers showing Kim Jong Il's image, result-ing in temporary breakdowns of cooperation until the offender has shown proper regret for having accidentally insulted the Dear Leader.

Perhaps more significant, Kim Il Sung's leadership and the empha-sis on "single-hearted unity" derived from his unitary philosophy and rule of North Korea mean that unity is interpreted as a key component of national strength and diversity is interpreted as "national weak-ness." The disciplining and structuring of North Korean society are the core elements of North Korean unity, in contrast to the factional-ism and division of traditional dynastic history.[50]

THE NORTH KOREAN DIPLOMAT: INFLUENCE OF ENVIRONMENT AND HEREDITY ON STRATEGY AND TACTICS

The complex mix of influences that may shape the thought processes and approaches of North Korean negotiators certainly go well beyond the primary formative influences on North Korean society that have been identified and briefly described in this chapter. The extensive propaganda effort described earlier is used constantly to reinforce, justify, and internally legitimize the North Korean state, so we have a relatively straightforward picture of the ideals of North Korean society and the central elements of what the North Korean negotiator is *sup-posed* to be thinking. The more difficult task is to discern the private reality of a negotiating counterpart who must reconcile three worlds: the world of the North Korean ideal represented by the official pro-paganda line of the DPRK; the real, unarticulated situation in North Korea; and the potentially hostile, mysterious, and even enticing out-side world in which the North Korean negotiator must work to repre-sent and defend his country's national interests.

Individual experiences and the personalities of North Korean nego-tiators, even coming from a society as highly structured and rigid as the DPRK, may emerge as primary influences on particular decisions and approaches represented in North Korean tactics and styles. How-ever, the primary themes identified here may shape the intellectual, social, and systemic structures through which decisions are processed and determinations are made.

In sum, the mix of these influences suggests that North Korean negotiators should be highly aggressive and protective of their society's prerogatives and defensive about limitations that might be placed on North Korea's sovereignty or freedom of action. Issues related to sovereignty or criticisms of the DPRK's internal structure may invite particularly strong reactions, because such issues are sensitive and might easily be seen as threatening. Tactics may be unconventional but are also subject to the inflexibility and rigidity of the institutional structure within which North Korean negotiators must work. However, even within such a rigid structure, compromise appears to be possible on certain issues if it can be justified by direction of the top leadership or if it reaps sufficient concrete benefits that the rules can be ignored without sacrificing core interests. Whether North Korean negotiators believe their own propaganda or recognize the limitations of their own system becomes to a certain extent irrelevant. Self-preservation requires skillful recognition, acceptance, and manipulation of one's system to achieve a satisfactory outcome without taking missteps that would directly undermine one's system or subject oneself to suspicion or doubt.

Having identified the major formative influences in the unique socialization process through which the philosophy and the approach of any North Korean negotiator are shaped, we now turn to an analysis of the primary patterns of interaction observed by Americans who have negotiated with North Koreans.

The Process of Negotiating with North Korea

Contrary to the views of many external observers who evaluate North Korean behavior on the basis of their own expectations, North Korea's approach to negotiations is not characterized by "irrationality" or craziness but rather is highly regularized and internally consistent.[1] North Korean negotiators have shown remarkably consistent style, behavior, and objectives in their interactions with American officials. Indeed, American negotiators describe a recognizable pattern of "drama and catastrophe." North Korea's crisis-oriented negotiation style has grown increasingly familiar as the agenda has expanded from the nuclear issue in 1993 and 1994 to negotiations over missiles, prisoner-of-war (POW)/missing-in-action (MIA) missions, terms under which the Department of Energy might encase North Korean fuel rods, initiation of the KEDO project, and preliminary negotiations leading to the Four Party Talks (which included North and South Korea, the PRC, and the United States and were designed to replace the Armistice Agreement with a permanent peace agreement formally ending the Korean War).

Although each negotiation between the United States and the DPRK has differed according to the nature of the issues and personnel involved, the personalities of the lead negotiators, and changes in the external environment, the process of negotiating with North Korea itself has developed its own rhythm and ritual characteristics that are different at various stages in the negotiating process and serve to define the possibilities for progress, expectations for agreement, and the likelihood of deadlock, pause, and revitalization of the dialogue process. The stages of the negotiation process may be signaled by the strategies and tactics employed by North Korean negotiators themselves but may also be signaled by public pronouncements, specific types of media comments, and attempts to employ brinkmanship and unconventional, crisis-oriented "guerrilla" tactics to foster an atmosphere designed to weaken the opponent's position and extract concessions. Inflexibility in the initial stages of a negotiation is often used as a tactic to induce concessions and to demonstrate to superiors in Pyongyang that negotiators are strongly pursuing the DPRK's maximum interests; however, it may also signal an unreadiness to negotiate or a determination that the atmosphere is not favorable to the DPRK. Following an initial "hard" stance, indications of flexibility signal that North Korean negotiators are looking for a deal. However, their position will harden again in the end game of a negotiation as a tactic for extracting additional concessions. North Korean negotiators may even appear to jeopardize the entire negotiating process by walking away, but such breakdowns may also presage an eventual agreement.

U.S. negotiations with North Korea, rather than being a linear process with a discrete beginning, middle, and end, also have cyclical characteristics, as issues are revisited, points reexamined, and interpretations redefined. The expansion of the negotiating process itself to include new issues, although often painstaking and usually frustrating, has supported the development of limited cooperation and deeper mutual understanding of how and when the United States and the DPRK can work together in practical ways and where unbridgeable differences remain. This chapter will explore the now-familiar process of negotiating with North Korean counterparts, and the next chapter will highlight patterns in the style of North Korean negotiators, as observed in the U.S.-DPRK negotiating context.

THE NORTH KOREAN NEGOTIATING TEAM

The DPRK Ministry of Foreign Affairs has intensively trained a small group of experts on American affairs, including those responsible for negotiations with the United States. Members of this team have played the primary roles in managing negotiations across the whole range of issues that are part of the U.S.-DPRK negotiating agenda. Although the lead negotiator appears to have little flexibility at the negotiating table, some observers have suggested that North Korean negotiators are on a "longer leash" than their American counterparts.

The rigidity of the North Korean bureaucratic structure that manages negotiations, combined with stubbornness and an unwillingness to engage in a negotiating process requiring concessions from one's own side, is highly frustrating and wears down negotiating counterparts. Stephen Linton has described the North Korean bureaucracy as a "highly compartmentalized institutional structure [which] often evokes the image of a bicycle wheel with thin spokes radiating out from a small hub at the center and extending all the way out to a narrow rim."[2] Within this highly centralized and hierarchical bureaucratic structure, information travels from the contact point to the center but is not disseminated to other parts of the bureaucracy, even if sharing of knowledge might strengthen the North Korean position.

North Korea has often used a dual-track negotiating strategy in order to take full advantage of opportunities to exploit weaknesses of the other side. The 1994 Berlin negotiations between Gary Samore, deputy assistant secretary of state for politico-military affairs, and Kim Jong U, chairman of the External Economic Affairs Commission, were part of an effort by a "second team" of negotiators from Pyongyang to wring concessions from the United States—namely, the provision of heavy fuel oil and an undertaking that a light-water reactor to be constructed in the North would not be of South Korean origin. A dual-track approach to negotiations is also evident in North Korean negotiations with Japan and South Korea, in which public negotiations may be backstopped or facilitated by secret channels of negotiation and in which informal contacts are often initiated or "trial balloons" are floated between the two sides by unofficial private emissaries.

Likewise, DPRK negotiations with Japan over normalization have attempted to exploit party and bureaucratic channels on numerous occasions, with the most notable success being the negotiation initiated with Liberal Democratic Party president Shin Kanemaru in 1989. An inebriated Kanemaru went beyond his authority to issue a joint statement apologizing and compensating the DPRK for Japanese occupation of North Korea and for the period of abnormal relations following World War II. North Korea has on various occasions continued to attempt to exploit party and bureaucratic differences in talks with Japan in order to facilitate resumption of normalization talks on positive terms.[3] The DPRK also uses party channels as a counterweight to government channels as it probes for differences in the senior leadership of foreign countries. Some U.S. diplomats see North Korea's efforts to open private channels of communication with senior U.S. specialists and former officials as an attempt to employ the same dual-track strategy.

American negotiators describe their working-level counterparts as paying strong attention to detail and having a good understanding of the internal logic of phraseology in the structure and meaning of agreements. At these meetings and at plenary negotiating sessions, North Korean negotiators have been assiduous note takers and are thoroughly immersed in the past record of negotiations on specific issues. North Korean negotiators are reported to refer regularly to the past negotiation record to check the consistency of individual or official statements on a particular topic.

Given the relative rigidity and hierarchy of the North Korean political system, the North Korean chief negotiator's main opportunity to influence the course of a negotiation lies in his ability to report back to his capital the positions of the opposing side in ways that will facilitate agreement, or to find ways to put into his counterpart's mouth the words he needs to influence his own higher-ups back in Pyongyang. In some cases, this may involve using private or informal sessions to explain directly the practical restraints of Pyongyang's position or even to coax counterparts into using language necessary to bring closure to a particular deal. The most skillful North Korean diplomats are aware that they have more influence in shaping the perceptions of their superiors in Pyongyang than in persuading their negotiating counterpart to adopt their government's position.

Representatives from the Ministry of Foreign Affairs have led most policy-oriented negotiations, while other DPRK agencies may be involved in technical talks aimed at the implementation of broader agreements.[4] For instance, the Bureau of Atomic Energy has been involved in technical negotiations on implementation of the Geneva Agreed Framework, while representatives of the Korean People's Army have been responsible for implementation of U.S.-DPRK agreements to conduct joint recovery operations of POWs/MIAs in North Korea. In some cases, combined delegations from the DPRK have suffered from internal divisions, though these divisions have usually been bridged by the Ministry of Foreign Affairs representatives, who have participated even in the most technical negotiations to ensure that outcomes conform to North Korean policy objectives.

The United States has held political negotiations of various types and at various levels with North Korea in New York, Geneva, Berlin, Kuala Lumpur, and Hawaii. Primary considerations for North Korea have been to avoid holding political negotiations in locations where the North might be perceived as dependent (for instance, Moscow and Beijing) and to choose locations where North Korea has sufficient infrastructure and communications capacity to keep the costs of supporting a negotiating team to a minimum. (Thus, the North Korean government has shown a preference for cities with existing North Korean facilities where the delegation can be housed without additional expense, such as Kuala Lumpur, Berlin, Geneva, and New York.)[5]

MESSAGES IN THE NORTH KOREAN MEDIA

Because the North Korean media are highly controlled by political authorities in Pyongyang, they are more than simply propaganda instruments. In fact, the media are used both to influence the psychological atmosphere surrounding negotiations and to signal the onset of a new stage in the negotiating process by delivering targeted messages, usually through comments by officials of the Ministry of Foreign Affairs or briefings for the foreign press at the ambassador level.

There is a clear hierarchy of internal relationships and purposes among various organs of the North Korean press, with media statements being targeted to multiple audiences at different levels, and different types of programming being designed to reach different sets of ears. Some messages are designed for mass broadcast; others are intended for consumption by party elites. Some messages are designed explicitly to carry disinformation and propaganda to the South; other messages are targeted for international ears and may carry different levels of authority, depending on who is delivering the message and the audience to whom it is addressed. One implication of this hierarchy of authority and capability to direct media messages to different audiences is that contrary to popular belief, North Korea is not a black hole—it is possible to use analysis of North Korean media to gain an understanding of the outlines of internal political processes, despite the lack of transparency in North Korean society at large.[6]

The most common and lowest form of channel is probably the organs for dissemination of propaganda intended to mobilize the North Korean masses. Newspapers such as *Minju Chosun* and *Nodong Sinmun* disseminate propaganda in support of North Korean party, military, and government objectives and are designed to guide the people in determining behavior patterns and choices and to build public support for their positions. As propaganda designed for purposes of mass mobilization, the content of these newspapers can differ widely from messages intended for upper echelons of the party, who have a deeper context for interpretation of party direction, to those for foreign audiences, to whom quite different messages might be sent. The primary mass message delivered through *Minju Chosun, Nodong Sinmun,* or state TV or radio may be designed for both mobilization and information dissemination. The content of these media channels unmistakably indicates in the broadest possible terms the foundation and the limits of public discourse within a tightly controlled society.

Certain international media outlets, including the English service of the Korean Central News Agency, may be used by the North Korean government to send a message—for instance, that it desires to improve relations with the United States—but authorities in Pyongyang may also find it convenient, both in the context of a maximalist negotiation strategy and in terms of domestic political mobilization, to simultaneously emphasize the evils of "the American imperialists" or to portray U.S. military exercises as aggressive and threatening to North Korea.

Close readers of the North Korean media may discern differences in position between the government and the party on various policy issues. Unattributed comments, which provide room for maneuver and deniability to the author or to the party or government, may reflect policy positions that are under consideration or debate but have not been adopted as official party or government positions. Such trial balloons may be intended to elicit reaction or support from elite members in the bureaucracy, party, or military.

Editorial comments on various issues may reflect the party view but may not wholly reflect the view of the government. "Voluntary" statements may reflect official policies and are made at the instruction of the government. Those who analyze the North Korean media on a daily basis emphasize that one can distinguish elements of a political dialogue being played out in North Korea, even if it is more opaque than in most countries. A historical knowledge of the major influences in North Korean society and culture is critical to interpreting North Korean media trends, and often the most significant discoveries relate to "the dog that didn't bark"—that is, things that one might have expected to appear in the North Korean press but didn't. For instance, North Korea's omission of its objections to special inspections in formulating its position in plenary sessions of the Geneva negotiations signaled a North Korean willingness to compromise on that critical issue. This observation parallels that of those involved in negotiations with North Korea who note that a change in a North Korean negotiating position is often signaled by the absence of an objection to a particular policy direction, rather than by an admission or declaration of a new course in policy.[7]

Foreign ministry statements may be made at a variety of levels and may be intended to attribute relative degrees of significance to a position of the North Korean government. A statement by a foreign ministry spokesman in response to a question may be a device for clarifying the government's position on a particular issue or for signaling a change or clarification of the government's position to a foreign audience.

Such statements may differ significantly from material being carried in mass media organs and may be intended to respond to a specific issue that has been raised regarding North Korea's foreign policy.

An official statement from the Ministry of Foreign Affairs may be even more authoritative, as it reflects the foreign ministry's position on a particular issue, providing negotiating counterparts with a clear statement of North Korean objectives and intentions in a negotiating process. In order to signal a government position in a less authoritative way, North Korean ambassadors may hold press conferences and make comments on particular issues, although occasionally the choice of ambassador may seem to be unrelated to the issue on which the comment is made. During the Geneva negotiations in 1994, North Korean ambassadors to Egypt and Thailand occasionally made public comments, although the ambassadors in Beijing and Moscow are the more common choices for issuing such statements. One analyst suggests that ambassadors in Beijing and Moscow occasionally have gone beyond the instructions of their government in making comments on particular issues, so it is important to be careful in interpreting the significance and accuracy of their statements.[8]

A more careful reading of the North Korean press may give a very different picture of the North Korean government's official position than simply taking North Korean propaganda at face value; however, mixed or conflicting messages do have an impact on each other and must be studied carefully for their significance. Given the level of control over the North Korean press, awareness that there is a hierarchy of importance in North Korean media statements is useful in discerning some aspects of the North Korean decision-making process and their significance.

THE NEGOTIATING PROCESS

Prenegotiation

Before engaging in the give-and-take of an actual negotiating process, North Korean negotiators first size up the positions and potential flexibility of the negotiating counterpart. Such a process may take place at the table itself in the first rounds of a negotiation, or it may take place during informal meetings held before the initiation of official talks. In unofficial, private discussions with negotiating counterparts, North Korean representatives may test propositions in an informal environment in which statements or proposals may be subsequently retracted in the absence of agreement in more formal sessions, but the primary purpose of such meetings is to gather information on the negotiating position and points of weakness of the negotiating counterpart. North Korean diplomats may compare information gathered in prenegotiation meetings with information received from diplomats and an informal intelligence network of overseas Koreans, but on balance, North Korean analysts may be unable to effectively interpret and use such information because of their limited knowledge of the outside world. In the initial stages of official negotiations, North Korean officials may sometimes remain in a prenegotiation phase, in which North Korean positions will remain inflexible and uncompromising while weaknesses and possible concessions in the counterpart's negotiating position are explored.

North Korean officials began prenegotiation contacts in preparation for the initiation of political negotiations with the United States as early as 1990, simultaneous with the initiation of North-South prime minister–level talks.[9] During this period, a wide range of senior American policymakers, academics, and former officials were invited by Deputy Permanent Observer Ho Jong to visit Pyongyang under the auspices of the Institute of Disarmament and Peace (IDP), a quasi-official think tank closely associated with the North Korean Ministry of Foreign Affairs.[10] North Korean diplomats on loan from the foreign ministry also came to the United States under IDP auspices to attend academic conferences, developing new informal relations with American counterparts. Direct, low-profile contacts had been maintained on an increasingly frequent basis through working-level contacts in Beijing and New York.[11] Through these interactions, IDP officials gathered detailed information regarding American views and positions on key issues. During this period, IDP was a training ground for those North Korean officials who became the primary interlocutors with American officials, and who are even now the primary representatives in most negotiations with the United States.[12] These dialogues provided an opportunity for direct contact with experienced American interlocutors, including private contacts with analysts from the Department of State. They provided a context for interpreting media coverage and confirming other information gathered in diplomatic channels and pro–North Korean networks.

To determine whether the international environment is favorable for pursuing official negotiations, North Korean diplomats have regularly activated contacts with the United States through government representatives who have traveled under unofficial auspices of the IDP and other organizations. Vice Foreign Minister (and acting director of the IDP) Kim Byong Hong traveled to the United States in November 1995 to have discussions with American counterparts on a range of issues in U.S.–North Korean relations; two months later he traveled to Hawaii as the leader of a North Korean delegation to resume negotiations over the issue of American POWs/MIAs from the Korean War.[13]

In the spring and summer of 1996 Ambassador Ri Jong Hyok of the Korea Asia-Pacific Peace Committee and Director Ri Gun of the IDP (and deputy director of the American Affairs Division of the Ministry of Foreign Affairs) came separately to Washington to hold detailed, informal discussions on the Four Party Talks proposal made by Presidents Clinton and Kim Young Sam on Cheju Island the previous April. Indeed, informal discussions between Ri Gun and American counterparts reportedly set the stage for a visit by Congressman Bill Richardson in September 1996 to outline a concrete package of steps that might lead to North Korea's acceptance of the Four Party Talks proposal. This visit was suddenly called off as a result of the discovery of a North Korean submarine grounded in waters off South Korea's eastern coast, an incident that created a three-month crisis in inter-Korean relations.[14] The submarine incident itself required informal prenegotiation in October 1996 in New York between American Affairs director Ri Hyong Chol of the North Korean Ministry of Foreign Affairs and counterparts in the Department of State. Director Ri returned to New York in November and December for a series of eleven official negotiating sessions to codify the outlines of a proposed solution that had originally been discussed in previous informal discussions.

Prenegotiation contacts may have several purposes as part of North Korea's management of the negotiating process. First, they provide an opportunity for North Korea to gain information regarding the flexibility and parameters of the thinking of policymakers in the United States. This information is necessary to assess the favorability of the negotiating atmosphere to North Korean objectives and may be used to shape North Korean positions and expectations regarding a negotiated outcome. Second, they provide an opportunity for North Korean negotiators to influence the views of potential counterparts, in some cases by suggesting areas of flexibility in North Korean policy through a channel that may later be denied if the proposal does not achieve North Korea's objective. Such a process may represent a willful attempt to portray flexibility or mislead the other side into having unrealistic hopes for a negotiation, or it may be an external manifestation of the rigidity of the North Korean structure, in which there may be risk in going ahead with a formal negotiating process without some assurance of success. Third, such contacts may be used to establish personal relationships with potential counterparts that will subsequently enhance prospects for a successful negotiation.

Opening Moves

The first operational issues to be settled in any negotiation relate to the protocol of the meetings themselves. When initiating negotiations with the United States, North Korean officials have dispensed with protocol matters relatively quickly, without significant regard for procedural issues. The primary protocol concern has been to reinforce perceptions of equivalency between the United States and North Korea as negotiating partners on the same footing.

North Korean officials have rarely stood on ceremony in interactions with U.S. officials, welcoming and even aggressively seeking the opportunity to engage on various issues in informal, private settings. Despite differences in level that might have created protocol problems, Foreign Minister Kim Yong Nam appeared genuinely surprised and pleased to make his first informal contact with an American State Department official, North Korea desk officer C. Kenneth Quinones, at an unofficial public gathering in New York in September 1992.[15]

Ambassador Ho Jong did not hesitate to call Ken Quinones at the State Department to suggest high-level negotiations to settle the North Korean nuclear crisis in the spring of 1993.[16]

However, if the North Korean government perceives itself as unready for a negotiation or if concerns regarding face or relative negotiating strength vis-à-vis a more powerful negotiating counterpart enter the picture, protocol or other procedural matters such as location of talks, size of delegation, level of delegation represented, and so on may become a pretext for stalling or delay. Protocol issues might also be used to press a symbolic advantage or to advance North Korea's own political or propaganda objectives. For instance, the United States and the DPRK haggled over protocol following the breakdown of talks in Berlin between Kim Jong U and Gary Samore over LWR type in April 1995.[17] The United States proposed the resumption of higher-level talks between Robert Gallucci and Kang Sok Ju in Geneva. The North Korean counterproposal called for talks at the Gallucci-Kang level to be held alternately in Washington and Pyongyang. This alternative was unacceptable to the United States because the North Korean intention appeared to separate the United States from its ally in South Korea by maneuvering the United States to accept a concession that would yield to Pyongyang a symbolic political advantage over Seoul.

Plenary Sessions

The initial plenary session marks the formal kickoff of the negotiating process, and as such plays a more ritualistic than substantive function. Opening plenary statements by North Korean negotiators have generally consisted of expansive and rigid formulations of negotiating demands designed to gain maximum leverage for subsequent negotiations.[18] The strategy of presenting the most uncompromising and maximally advantageous position possible is designed both to intimidate one's counterpart and to facilitate a settlement as close as possible to one's bottom line.

The plenary provides the lead North Korean negotiator an opportunity to show toughness to his negotiating counterpart, to his colleagues representing various organizational affiliations in the room, and to his hidden audience back in Pyongyang, which receives full reports on such sessions. Reporting of plenary sessions may be more comprehensive if the session is hosted on North Korean premises, where full session transcripts might be made available to higher-ups in Pyongyang. This has resulted in a noticeably more aggressive presentation by North Korean negotiators at sessions held on their own "home court."[19] Some American negotiators have described such presentations as "very greedy," "provocative and truculent," full of stubbornness, brinkmanship, rhetoric, and "baldly propagandistic" threats, perhaps designed to delay and wear down the opponent by presenting an unyielding position. American negotiators have also described these presentations as ineffective and easily dismissible.

Despite the formulaic, prescribed restatements of maximalist positions characterizing an opening plenary session, such meetings do have important uses. For instance, opening plenary session statements set the parameters for measuring progress by providing a baseline for comparison with statements made at subsequent plenary sessions. North Korean negotiators might embed hints of their real position in long, boring exegeses on apparently unrelated issues. One American participant in the Geneva negotiations over the nuclear issue suggests that it took time for American interlocutors to "break the code" of North Korean negotiating patterns. "They were sending signals that we didn't understand."[20] Until those signals were deciphered, negotiations remained deadlocked. Changes in argumentation or omissions from subsequent plenary statements may provide a measure of the direction and pace of the negotiating counterpart's thinking as negotiations proceed. Needless to say, breakthroughs rarely occur at plenary sessions.

North Korean officials involved in plenary sessions are thoroughly familiar with the negotiating record and listen carefully to the opening U.S. official position to identify inconsistencies or changes from previous statements. Any differences that the North Korean negotiating team identifies are sure to be raised in later negotiating sessions. Japanese analysts involved with the Japan-DPRK normalization talks confirm the North Korean strategy of probing carefully for weak points or divisions among negotiating counterparts.[21]

Informal Sessions

While formal negotiating sessions are used to consolidate one's position, establish "toughness," signal continued difficulties in disputed areas, and manipulate the record in order to obscure concessions or compromises made away from the negotiating table, informal discussions are much more likely to be the venue for negotiating progress. As with many other negotiations, the real work in negotiations with North Korea is done at working-level or informal technical meetings to discuss the concrete details of the negotiations.[22] These meetings, in which working-level negotiators sit down with counterparts to lay out the technical business of drafting statements indicating areas of mutual agreement and differences, are much more constructive venues than the plenaries. Since the details of sidebar meetings are not necessarily reported to higher-ups, such informal sessions provide both sides with opportunities for "thinking out loud."

In the initial stages of negotiations, informal sessions may be used to test the resolve of the negotiating counterparts and to explore and exploit differences in their positions. In the later stages, informal sessions or small formal sessions between lead negotiators may be used to make progress or explore possible compromises. In these sessions, the primary challenge is often to find a linguistic formulation for an agreement that is mutually acceptable and specific enough to close loopholes that might be exploited in later discussions. Even if there is a clear understanding about the context underlying an agreement, this does not mean that either the interpretation or the substance of any part of an agreement is immune to challenge at future stages of the negotiation and implementation process, and any concession agreed to informally might be retracted until everything has been agreed upon and the negotiation is finally concluded.

Informal Interactions and Hospitality

In the initial stages of U.S.–North Korean negotiations in June 1993, the negotiating teams had little in common and virtually no prior personal contacts that might have helped to facilitate communication. Moreover, little leeway was provided in negotiating instructions that had been dictated by the capitals. There were no means of informal communication outside the conference room that could be used to facilitate progress, and little progress was made in the first few days. Following a break in the negotiations, U.S. negotiators reviewed public statements issued by the North Korean government immediately following the announcement of its withdrawal from the NPT. The North Korean government's formulations suggested a greater amount of flexibility than was presented at the plenary negotiations. On the basis of these public statements, the North Korean side had a justification for compromise. The objective of the U.S. negotiators was "to play back positions in their own words" in order to reinforce communication at this make-or-break moment in which neither side was initially prepared to blink.[23] In order to make the initial joint statement palatable to Washington, negotiators used language from the UN Charter to provide sufficient room to issue an acceptable statement that allowed for the continuation of negotiations past the June 12 deadline by which North Korea had threatened to pull out of the NPT.[24]

During the second round of negotiations in Geneva, it became necessary to facilitate negotiations through telephone contacts between working-level members of the North Korean and U.S. negotiating teams outside the negotiating room as a means by which to make progress. The North Korean side tried its best to stage a welcoming and hospitable atmosphere when it hosted its first U.S.-DPRK meetings in Geneva, providing elaborate coffee-break settings.[25] Eventually, the prenegotiation process had grown sufficiently "ordinary" that the U.S. delegation was able to grease the wheels of informality by throwing a pizza party in Geneva for the North Korean side, an act of hospitality that facilitated the negotiating process through the normalization of informal contacts and the development of relationships between officials on the two sides.

Informal contacts over coffee or meals are effectively used by North Korean negotiators to test possible new negotiating positions and to probe for differences among negotiating counterparts. In the informal environment of conversation over a meal or some other break, North Korean negotiators "are dramatically more relaxed, available, or hospitable." They might reveal their "true" position or present possibilities for concessions or compromise and "may be extremely helpful in sharing negotiating positions" and explaining why they hold particular positions. However, they may revert to a more rigid position when full-scale formal talks subsequently resume, creating ambiguity regarding the "true" North Korean position on key issues, or whether an opportunity for compromise really exists on specific issues.[26]

North Korean negotiating team members have tended to pair up with counterparts on the other side of the table, engaging in informal discussions to flesh out areas of possible difference expressed by negotiating counterparts. If North Koreans can identify a weak point in the negotiating counterpart's position, rarely will they fail to press perceived weakness, contradictions, or divisions.

Middle Game: Determining Quid Pro Quos

After an often prolonged period of feeling out potential divisions or weaknesses in the position of the other side and consulting with the leadership in Pyongyang, North Korean negotiators may finally be prepared to cut a deal. However, the deal-making phase of a negotiation with North Korea usually comes only after it is apparent either that all possible alternatives that might expand North Korea's negotiating leverage have been exercised and exhausted or that the counterpart's bottom line has been reached and no additional concessions are available. Aware of the relative weaknesses of the North Korean position and of the structural difficulties within the North Korean system that inhibit compromise, North Korean negotiators resist concessions.

There is some difference of opinon among American negotiators on whether it is better to work with American or North Korean first drafts. On the one hand, some negotiators have argued that North Korean drafts include the core requirements that the North Korean government must have in order to conclude a negotiation successfully, even if such drafts also include items beyond the DPRK's bottom-line negotiating position. However, in the case of the Geneva Agreed Framework, the substance of the agreement was almost exclusively a product of American thinking, according to one negotiator. In this instance, American negotiators would "put the language settled on in front of the South Koreans,"[27] the ultimate litmus test for whether the language of agreement with North Korea was politically acceptable.

On the other hand, American-drafted documents may force North Korean counterparts to fight for their minimum position to successfully conclude an agreement. North Korean negotiators are reluctant to make counterproposals and are more prone to accept or reject a draft rather than to engage in technical negotiations to produce a compromise draft. In general, the pattern has been for North Korean negotiators to work with American first drafts, particularly when dealing with more technical issues.

American negotiators counsel the importance of taking a "package," or "basket," approach to the negotiation in order to make substantive progress. "A sequential approach limits one's ability to trade across issues," an essential ingredient in negotiating with a counterpart when there is a lack of trust. In the negotiations in Geneva over North Korea's nuclear program, "it took a long time to define the trade-offs" that would eventually form the basis of an agreement. These difficulties may have come about because the American "problem-solving mode" clashed with the North Korean style, which was more focused on defining the broad parameters of a fundamental "package solution." "Their commitment to a simple objective is not consistent with the American penchant for a complex solution," according to a senior diplomat involved with the talks.[28]

Given the nature of North Korea's leadership and its sensitivity to appearances of weakness, unavoidable concessions are masked by rhetorical toughness or remain unacknowledged. However, the middle-game phase of the negotiating process involves quiet expressions of flexibility, including the testing of trial balloons and bargaining in search of the best possible deal. Following the period of testing, or prenegotiation, changes in the North Korean negotiating position in the middle game may be quite dramatic as obstacles previously intended to create stalemate may be suddenly swept off the table or dropped as problem issues. However, apparent expressions of flexibility will disappear the closer one gets to an agreement. Such hardening of negotiating positions as one comes closer to cutting a deal is intended both to squeeze additional concessions out of the other side and to prove to higher-ups in Pyongyang that the terms of agreement are the best available.

Breaks and Pauses in the Negotiation

One characteristic of U.S. negotiations with North Korea has been a recess for a period of from one or two days to several weeks following a series of initial discussions. The purpose of a recess is to assess preliminary progress and consult with home governments. Depending on progress made in the initial discussions, this period of assessment may be used by both U.S. and North Korean negotiators to identify areas of potential flexibility in an opponent's position; to reverse flexibility that has previously been shown for tactical or strategic reasons; to reaffirm the progress, direction, thinking, and political mood of those in the home capital; or to mark incremental progress or backsliding in one's own position as well as that of the negotiating counterpart. It is not necessarily clear to U.S. negotiators which of these tasks are most important to their North Korean counterparts during a period of assessment, but such a break offers U.S. negotiators the opportunity to perform many of the same tasks.

Pauses may be particularly useful for providing the North Korean lead negotiator an opportunity to report on the direction of negotiations and, if necessary, to receive revised instructions. Although North Korean negotiators sometimes have been given flexibility to make certain concessions or adopt fallback positions, in other instances it has been clear that the North Korean negotiator is on a tight leash. In these cases, a break to report progress or to return to Pyongyang to evaluate negotiating progress might be useful to facilitate negotiations, but it could also be a stalling tactic. During the third round of U.S.-DPRK talks in Geneva in September and October 1994, a gradual softening in the tone of opening statements of Vice Minister Kang Sok Ju appeared to mark progress and to indicate a trend toward eventual compromise. On the other hand, recess periods in the Berlin negotiations (which were headed by Kim Jong U, chairman of the External Economic Affairs Commission, rather than by a foreign ministry deputy to Kang Sok Ju) in the spring of 1995 over the source of technology to be used in North Korean light-water reactors constituted a stalling tactic that failed to induce additional U.S. concessions. Kim Jong U's role in leading the Berlin negotiations also signified a North Korean attempt to use a second track to squeeze additional concessions from the United States, to test the possibility of negotiating a more favorable deal, and to demonstrate to North Korean decision makers in Pyongyang that no better deal was possible.

Sometimes breaks have been necessary not because of North Korea's need to revise its negotiating instructions, but rather to allow for consultations within the U.S. government or with counterparts in South Korea. Such a consultative process takes on more importance in the context of the need to coordinate with allies in Seoul, whose interests were involved with and represented in the U.S.-DPRK talks in Geneva and in the U.S.-DPRK negotiations over the statement of regret following the September 1996 submarine incident.

End Game and Implementation:
Cyclical Versus Linear Views of Negotiation

Once a formula for resolving a particular problem has been agreed upon and bargaining over the actions that each side must take as part of an agreement has been completed, the negotiation reaches the final stage. The end game involves a thorough review and testing of the weakest points in an agreement. After having shown flexibility in coming to terms as part of the negotiation process, the North Korean position hardens as provisions of agreement are tested. New questions are raised both to satisfy remaining doubts voiced by superiors in Pyongyang and to explore the possibility of gaining remaining concessions as the price of closing the deal. The result is often delay, in which the terms of the entire agreement are subject to question, with the possibility that all efforts invested in reaching agreement may prove to be wasted. Even after approval has been given from governments of both sides, North Koreans typically engage in last-ditch efforts to seek further concessions, resulting in last-minute delays and challenges on the most contentious points of the agreement.

According to American negotiators, the end game—when one thinks a deal is finally within reach—has been the most drawn-out, wearing, and frustrating part of a negotiation with the North Koreans. The negotiations on the type of reactor to be supplied under the Geneva Agreed Framework are one example of North Korean testing of an agreement even after it has been signed. As one senior American negotiator said, "Only after you have a deal does the actual negotiating begin. It is a grueling, exhausting process that revolves around every detail."[29]

The end game preceding the signing of the Geneva Agreed Framework represents one last test of wills intended to bluff—or shame—the negotiating counterpart into making concessions on key issues. Near the end of negotiations on the Agreed Framework, only a few sensitive points of disagreement remained. The U.S. team suddenly received a call from the North Koreans, who announced that the American delegation should hurry over to the North Korean mission in Geneva for a ceremony to sign the agreement. Upon arrival at the North Korean mission, the U.S. delegation found that the red carpet had been rolled out, the press had been called for a public announcement, and preparations had been made for an official announcement and signing ceremony.

The only catch was that Ambassador Gallucci had not been briefed on how the final settlement of the outstanding issues had been achieved. When Ambassador Gallucci asked his counterpart, Minister Kang, how these issues had been settled, Minister Kang responded that there had been no settlement of the remaining language, that the concessions proposed by the American side were unacceptable, and that therefore the North Korean language would be used. After realizing that the North Korean side had prematurely called a signing ceremony before the negotiations were finished, the U.S. negotiating team turned and walked out. As we will explore in the next chapter, the North Korean side used brinkmanship and bluffing as facilitating tactics—to force the U.S. side either to accept an incomplete agreement or to suffer inconvenience and the humiliation of failing to meet public expectations that an agreement had finally been achieved.[30]

Even after an agreement has been signed, North Korean negotiators may raise challenges on particularly contentious issues as part of the implementation process, whereas Americans expect both sides to honor the terms of an agreement without continuous challenge once it has been signed and ratified. American negotiators conceive of the negotiation process as linear, with a distinct beginning, middle, and end, marked by clear and measurable stages of progress. Korean conceptions of negotiation, however, may be more cyclical. The need to revisit and define ever more detailed levels of specificity as part of a negotiation process may be natural from a Korean perspective, despite the frustration for American negotiators of returning to the same issues, with relatively little sense of progress. This means that during the course of implementation, North Koreans will continue to challenge the interpretation and the letter of the most sensitive parts of an agreement, taking advantage of potential concessions in practice that could not be won at the negotiating table. It is necessary to maintain an attitude of firmness and a willingness to enforce the terms of implementation when the terms of an agreement are challenged. Perhaps most revealing, however, is that according to a cyclical conception of negotiations with North Korea, there really is no end game in a negotiation process. The next negotiation—this time over implementation—is just around the corner.

3

Patterns in North Korea's Negotiating Style and Tactics

"Koreans can be your best friends, or they can be your worst enemies," according to one unofficial Western interlocutor with extensive experience in dealing with North Korea.[1] But what determines North Korean perceptions of whether the negotiating counterpart is a potential friend or an intractable enemy? Is it possible to move from enemy to friend (or to identify and develop cooperation based on mutual interests)? How might perceptions of the negotiating counterpart as a friend or as an enemy affect tactical choices in a negotiation?

The rhythms of the negotiating process examined in the previous chapter are subject both to the external context of negotiations and to tactical manipulations as part of the negotiations themselves, and the use of certain kinds of tactics may also signal stages in the negotiating process. These tactics are determined by the legacy of North Korea's historical experience and by its institutional structure, which we explored in chapter 1. Following an examination of how the atmosphere surrounding a negotiation may critically influence the direction and nature of North Korean tactical approaches to negotiation, we will explore common North Korean negotiation tactics, including reliance on crisis diplomacy and brinkmanship and attempts to manufacture leverage despite North Korea's relatively weak position.

Crisis diplomacy is a manifestation of North Korea's partisan guerrilla legacy and an excellent means by which weak states can enhance leverage against powerful states in negotiations on specific issues. Brinkmanship is a unilateral strategy influenced by North Korea's historically isolated position and reinforced by the influence of communist negotiating style and tactics. It employs threats, bluff, and forms of blackmail to extract maximal concessions from a negotiating counterpart. North Korea has also demonstrated a unique ability to manufacture negotiating leverage for itself as a result of its own weakness by negating its own options and relying on the "good will" of the negotiating counterpart while simultaneously retaining the capacity to threaten the counterpart's interests. In negotiations with the United States, tactics that have reinforced perceptions of equivalency have been paramount, sometimes even at the expense of gaining substantive benefits. And North Korean facilitating tactics, including the use of trial balloons, emotional displays, and deadlines to induce agreement, also play a critical role in the negotiation process.

PUNUIGI, KIBUN, AND *KOJIP*: CONTEXT FOR EXAMINING NORTH KOREAN NEGOTIATING STYLES

North Korean interlocutors emphasize the concept of *punŭigi* (atmosphere) as a primary factor affecting the likelihood of progress in negotiations. *Punŭigi* might be defined as the favorability of the overall external environment to the pursuit of North Korea's negotiating agenda. If North Korean negotiators determine the *punŭigi* to be favorable, informal interlocutors who have regular contacts with North Korean officials argue that it will be possible to develop good *kibun*—a relationship or friendship interaction characterized by "good feeling" —with negotiating counterparts in a very cordial and "businesslike" atmosphere. If they determine *punŭigi* is unfavorable, North Korean negotiators will demonstrate *kojip*—an unyielding attitude, stubbornness, or perseverance—to show commitment to uncompromising positions and principles until such time as the *punŭigi* becomes favorable to give-and-take.

Many unofficial interlocutors with North Korea emphasize the importance of good *kibun,* attained through the development of positive personal relationships, as a basis for making progress in carrying out certain types of projects. In their view, good *kibun* with North Korean counterparts serves as the basis for mutual favors that might cut through structural or bureaucratic obstacles stemming from decades of mistrust. This informal relationship-building approach as a vehicle for creating a good *punŭigi* for negotiations reinforces North Korean and more broadly Asian concepts of relationship building as an essential component of the negotiation process.

Stephen Linton, who grew up in South Korea as part of a family with over a century of history as missionaries in Korea, assisted the Reverend Billy Graham in his successful visits to Pyongyang. Linton has been involved in many facets of unofficial interaction with North Korea and argues that "personal relationships are of paramount importance to people in the DPRK and must be cemented before anything concrete can be done . . . human relations should never be made conditional to something else."[2] Through establishing a relationship based on mutual understanding rather than mistrust, according to this view, one can achieve objectives at a much lower price than that required in a more cautious or distant relationship.

K. A. Namkung, another unofficial interlocutor who has taken a relationship-building approach with North Koreans, has suggested that North Koreans have trouble "talking to 'secular,' 'modern' Westerners," underscoring the gap in cultural understanding between Korean and Western perspectives on relationships.[3] This "cultural approach," the "'back door' which provides much easier access to a society than the ideological front door nations often present to outsiders,"[4] is commonly advocated by unofficial interlocutors with North Korea. However, it has not been easily applicable to an official context, in which mistrust can be overcome only through a gradually accumulated record of accomplishment.

The counterpoint to relationship building is the will to persevere in the midst of enormous difficulties or hardships through demonstration of *kojip* (stubbornness). Regardless of whether *kojip* is necessary to face down more powerful opponents or to protect core interests, demonstrations of resolve through stubbornness have long been employed by Koreans to wear down larger opponents to secure concessions. The major impression of Thomas Hubbard, deputy assistant secretary of state for East Asia and the Pacific, in his initial encounter with North Korean counterparts in June 1993, was "the stubbornness of the North Koreans."[5]

Kibun and *kojip* describe the fundamental choices that may shape North Korea's tactical responses in a negotiation. The direction of the choice will be shaped by assessments of the *punŭigi* surrounding the talks. North Korean views of the primary choices involved are demonstrated simply and clearly in numerous North Korean public statements that Pyongyang "would answer dialogue with dialogue and strength with strength," a common form of matching behavior in negotiations. On the one hand, negotiation involves identification of areas of potential cooperation and agreement, requiring trust building as part of a process of moving from an adversarial relationship to a more normalized relationship. On the other hand, the tactics of toughness, stubbornness, and confrontation—so familiar during the Cold War years—still manifest themselves and present obstacles to Western negotiators in their interactions with North Korean officials. The core of the dilemma for the U.S.-DPRK relationship lies in whether the United States and North Korea can change their long-standing relationship as enemies to one that allows for the development of good *kibun* by engaging in limited cooperation.

PATTERNS IN NORTH KOREA'S NEGOTIATING STYLE

American negotiators have routinely observed a variety of tactical patterns employed by North Korea to gain the attention of American counterparts, manipulate the atmosphere so as to maximize the possibility of concessions, and expand its own negotiating leverage vis-à-vis the negotiating counterpart. The most frequently observed patterns include the use of crisis diplomacy and brinkmanship and the creation of leverage by identifying and taking advantage of weakness, division, or irresolution on the part of negotiating counterparts. It is necessary to examine in greater depth each of these familiar tactics employed by North Korean negotiators.

Crisis Diplomacy

Crisis diplomacy, a highly effective characteristic of North Korea's negotiating style, is derived from North Korea's structural position as a nation that must force its way to the top of the negotiating agenda with the United States and from the historical legacy of the partisan guerrilla movement, in which unconventional tactics were a necessary component of North Korean strategy. In his 1988 book, *Power and Tactics in International Negotiation: How Weak Nations Negotiate with Strong Nations,* Mark Habeeb explains that weak states may increase their leverage in issue-specific negotiations relative to their aggregate power by preserving or expanding alternatives to a negotiated settlement, demonstrating commitment to achieving the identified negotiating goal, and maintaining control of the negotiating process. Throughout nuclear and other negotiations with the United States, North Korean negotiators have—whether instinctively, strategically, or unwittingly—used the tactics of crisis diplomacy to gain the attention of the United States.

North Korea has arguably used the tactic of crisis diplomacy for years in its attempts to gain the attention of the United States through the United Nations Command (UNC)/Military Armistice Commission (MAC) process with varying degrees of success.[6] Although it appeared that the Basic Agreement between North and South Korea and International Atomic Energy Agency (IAEA) inspections would lead to a relaxation of tension on the Korean Peninsula in early 1992, discrepancies in North Korea's reporting on its nuclear program came to light in the fall of that year. The distraction of political transitions in Washington and Seoul left the initiative to the IAEA to investigate North Korea's nuclear program. The IAEA—its effectiveness questioned by recent discoveries of a vast network of undeclared nuclear facilities in Iraq—requested unprecedented and intrusive special inspections in North Korea.

Pyongyang responded to the increased pressure by announcing on March 12, 1993, that it would withdraw from the NPT effective in ninety days—an action that clearly heightened tensions in both Washington and Seoul and framed the terms of debate to North Korea's advantage. North Korea had discerned the high priority placed on nuclear issues in Washington based on the message delivered by the United States in the January 1992 Kim-Kanter meeting. In addition, the United States was a leading supporter of indefinite renewal of the NPT at an international conference scheduled for early 1995, providing Pyongyang with potentially valuable negotiating leverage.

Until Pyongyang threatened to withdraw from the NPT, Washington had failed to take long-standing North Korean desires for dialogue seriously. As Michael Mazarr, a nuclear proliferation expert and senior fellow at the Center for Strategic and International Studies, argued at the time, North Korea's reasoning might be, "Why not provoke a crisis because we're not getting any economic or political benefits out of this?"[7] The instigation of a crisis over its nuclear program—and the automatic creation of a deadline for the resolution of the crisis—was an effective way to grab the attention of a new administration, making direct dialogue with the United States unavoidable.

North Korea had taken the initiative, defined the costs and benefits of alternatives to a negotiated settlement of the issue in terms of the survival of the global nonproliferation regime, and used a deadline of June 12, 1993, to gain control over the negotiations, effectively utilizing partisan guerrilla tactics. The remarkable benefits of crisis diplomacy to North Korea were demonstrated when the United Nations Security Council, rather than endorsing the idea of imposing international sanctions on North Korea, called for international negotiations with North Korea to resolve the issue. For North Korea, the crisis presented an opportunity not only to shape the agenda to focus on the future (rather than the past) of its nuclear program, but also to achieve Pyongyang's long-standing objective of establishing a direct relationship (unmediated by Seoul) with the United States.

The development of a self-induced crisis through the diplomatic maneuver of threatening withdrawal from the international nuclear nonproliferation regime proved to be an unparalleled opportunity for a weak government that had no other leverage than the potential threat of its nuclear program. It set the stage for negotiations with the

United States on North Korean terms. Without the instigation of a crisis that challenged a major global objective of the United States, North Korea would not have attained its goal of a direct bilateral dialogue with Washington. The United States had already inadvertently sent the signal that under normal circumstances, without fundamental (and possibly regime-threatening) policy change in North Korea, the best North Korea could hope for was a one-time, one-way discussion with the United States—not a dialogue through which mutual interests might be explored.

A second major instance of crisis diplomacy was the May 1994 decision by North Korea to unload fuel rods from its 5-megawatt reactor. This decision constituted a direct challenge to U.S. statements in negotiations with the North that such an action would constitute the crossing of a "red line" and would result in resumption of an international economic sanctions campaign at the United Nations. To better understand this use of crisis diplomacy by North Korea, it is necessary to briefly summarize the events that led up to the crisis.

Earlier attempts to restore deadlocked negotiations through working-level channels had already failed. In late November 1993, recently elected Presidents Kim Young Sam and Bill Clinton had agreed at their Washington summit to pursue a "broad and thorough" approach to North Korea in response to North Korean overtures. Almost five months of working-level contacts between North Korea and the United States in New York resulted in an Agreed Conclusion. This was a four-point plan to get U.S.–North Korean negotiations back on track through pledges to resume IAEA inspections and to hold working-level meetings to prepare for an exchange of special envoys between Seoul and Pyongyang. That deal fell through after a heated exchange over mechanisms for resuming inter-Korean dialogue at which the North Korean representative predicted that war would turn Seoul into a "sea of fire," torpedoing possibilities for resumption of U.S.–North Korean negotiations in Geneva.

Following the failure of this working-level attempt to restore the official dialogue, Pyongyang again instigated a crisis by flouting U.S. conditions for holding a political dialogue. The decision to unload the fuel rods from North Korea's 5-megawatt nuclear reactor held considerable risks, not because of the immediate danger from Pyong-yang, which had considerable experience in managing crises, but rather from the United States, where some in the nonproliferation community and other senior policymakers took this provocation as justification for considering preemptive military action against North Korea. Indeed, the risks of instigating crisis were illustrated by the U.S. military escalation in response to the DPRK's provocations. This response included the station-ing of Patriot missiles in South Korea, resumption of the push for inter-national economic sanctions at the United Nations, and Defense Secre-tary William Perry's consideration of an augmentation of the U.S. troop presence on the Korean Peninsula.[8]

The crisis atmosphere provided Pyongyang with an opportunity to return to the negotiating table on potentially more favorable terms. By instigating a crisis that could be defused only through communi-cation at the highest levels, Kim Il Sung had put himself in the driver's seat—if only he could find a channel through which to reestablish effective communication with the United States before the crisis esca-lated out of control. No more useful channel could have been used by Kim Il Sung than a dialogue with former President Jimmy Carter, who activated a long-standing invitation to visit North Korea for dis-cussions over the nuclear crisis.

Jimmy Carter's visit to Pyongyang in June 1994 was skillfully used by Kim Il Sung to defuse a growing military confrontation and to cre-ate conditions for a return to the negotiating table with the United States. First, Kim Il Sung was able to create conditions necessary to resume U.S.-DPRK negotiations. Following the failure of a bottom-up approach through working-level negotiations in New York, the insti-gation of a new crisis allowed Kim Il Sung to fix the attention of the Americans and induce a return to the negotiating table.

Second, crisis diplomacy effectively allowed North Korea to reshape the agenda. North Korea unilaterally raised the perceived costs to the international community of demanding a full accounting of the history of North Korea's nuclear program. Simultaneously, the North offered the prospect of future cooperation to cap and dismantle North Korean nuclear facilities in return for an end to the threat of a military crisis and for the provision of energy assistance through a long-term joint project that would enhance cooperation with the United States and gain exposure to new technology.

Third, crisis diplomacy allowed North Korea to send a signal regarding its ability as an independent actor outside the context of negotiations. This symbolic action reinforced carefully cultivated North Korean images of independence: North Korea had defied the only remaining superpower.

North Korea's escalation of crises has been tied to its larger objectives in the context of a negotiation: because North Korea is an apparently weak state with few alternatives, the instigation of crisis to seize the attention of a more powerful counterpart in an issue-specific negotiation is a necessary component of North Korea's negotiating strategy. It also happens to be precisely the sort of partisan guerrilla strategy most likely to have been favored by Kim Il Sung.

Crises have sometimes presented North Korea with unexpected opportunities to further its diplomatic objectives through negotiations, as was the case during the U.S. Army helicopter incident in December 17, 1994. CWO Bobby Hall and his colleague had misjudged the DMZ boundary on a snowy December day and inadvertently crossed into North Korean airspace, where their helicopter was shot down and the co-pilot killed. Efforts to negotiate Hall's release fell to Congressman Bill Richardson, who happened to be on his first congressional fact-finding trip to North Korea. In response to the incident, a series of UNC/MAC talks was also activated, including the first contacts since 1991 held at the level of military generals assigned to the MAC.[9] Progress was slow, as North Korea made political demands for the release of long-time North Korean political prisoners in Seoul and the initiation of regular military contacts between the United States and North Korea a prerequisite of Bobby Hall's release. Finally, after about ten days of talks through the MAC and following Richardson's return with the remains of the dead pilot, North Korea called for a special envoy to come from Washington to negotiate Hall's release.

Deputy Assistant Secretary of State Tom Hubbard became the highest-level State Department official to travel to Pyongyang for negotiations since the Korean War. Hubbard was again pressured by the North Koreans to agree to direct military talks between the United States and

North Korea. The eventual statement signed by Hubbard agreed to initiate military talks "through appropriate channels," which the United States defined as resumption of the MAC. North Korea used the Bobby Hall crisis to fulfill symbolic objectives, including the demand for an unprecedented visit to Pyongyang by an American official and the extraction of an ambiguous statement that allowed both sides to claim victory. Given that the Agreed Framework had been signed by North Korea and the United States only two months before the incident, there were limits to the political advantage that North Korea could extract from negotiations; however, this did not keep North Korea from probing for potential benefits by opening new negotiations during the Bobby Hall crisis.

North Korea commonly manipulates near-crises or lower-level tensions to create an atmosphere conducive to achieving its negotiating objectives. Other crisis inducement efforts have included the systematic dismantling of MAC-related institutional structures in 1994 and 1995.[10] Such actions appear to have been related to North Korean diplomatic proposals to initiate a direct military-to-military dialogue with the United States on North Korean proposals for a "new peace mechanism" that might replace the armistice.

North Korea's missile-testing maneuvers are another example of crisis instigation in order to build leverage in a negotiating context. In November 1996, a flurry of concern surrounded North Korean preparations for a possible missile test in the Sea of Japan, but the test was mysteriously canceled, perhaps in response to external diplomatic pressure. Following a first round of missile talks between U.S. and North Korean negotiators in April 1996, preparations for a missile test may have been intended to remind American counterparts that North Korea's missile program remained an issue for discussion. An August 1998 test of a multiple-stage rocket that came in the middle of U.S.-DPRK negotiations served to facilitate the resumption of U.S.-DPRK missile talks, following a June 1998 public statement by the DPRK expressing willingness to come to the table to test whether the United States would be willing to offer the right "price" for a settlement.

Aside from crises manipulated by North Korea as part of a strategy to influence negotiations with the United States, the possibility exists that an unexpected—as opposed to an induced—external crisis might cause North Korean leaders to seek breakthroughs in negotiations. This has happened on a number of occasions.

First, the Nixon opening to China and the signing of the Shanghai Communiqué in 1972 greatly shocked the entire region and changed the context of the confrontation on the Korean Peninsula. The initial North Korean response was to ask the United States privately in the fall of 1971—through a message from the North Korean leadership to U.S. leaders conveyed by PRC foreign minister Zhou Enlai—to initiate bilateral talks on the withdrawal of U.S. forces from the Korean Peninsula. Subsequently, Kim Il Sung sought a dialogue with South Korean counterpart Park Chung Hee that resulted in the negotiation of three principles for pursuing national reunification, signed on July 4, 1972. After a period of adjustment and reassessment by North Korea, further progress in inter-Korean negotiations stalled.

Second, the failed Soviet coup and subsequent breakup of the Soviet Union in 1991, which undoubtedly came as a serious shock to North Korea, appeared to create new potential for progress in prime minister–level North-South dialogue. The historic result was the signing of the Agreement on Reconciliation, Nonaggression, Exchanges and Cooperation between North and South Korea (widely known as the Basic Agreement) in December 1991. Again, following initial implementation of the agreement, North Korea indefinitely suspended implementation in 1992 as the nuclear crisis heated up.

On a smaller scale, the submarine incident of September 1996 appeared to catch the North Korean government by surprise. The accidental grounding of the submarine created a highly charged political standoff on the Korean Peninsula. To resolve the dispute, the North Koreans sought indirect negotiations with the South through a third party—the United States—issuing an unprecedented statement of regret for the provocation.

It remains to be seen whether North Korea's internal systemic failures, such as the food crisis and North Korea's economic decline, may bring North Korea to the table for substantive dialogue through the Four Party Talks or other tension-reduction negotiations on the

Korean Peninsula. However, it is likely that other major shocks or "crises"—intentional or accidental—will accompany renewed negotiations and induce progress in such talks.

Brinkmanship: The Advantages and the Risks of Crying Wolf

The most distinctive characteristic of North Korean diplomacy is brinkmanship, a negotiating tactic closely related to crisis diplomacy. Brinkmanship involves the mixing of aggressive and provocative tactics including issuing unconditional demands, blustering, bluffing, threatening, stalling, manufacturing deadlines, and even walking out of negotiations. Brinkmanship is a unilateral strategy in a negotiation and is most successful when the protagonist is able to demonstrate unconcern with its counterpart's reaction or with the negative situation created by such tactics. It is a strategy North Korean negotiators used effectively throughout the Cold War. The North Korean initial position before negotiations has been described by one negotiator as, "If you don't accept our proposal, we will walk out," or "We accept your proposal, but you do X first," a combination of a demand for a unilateral concession with a threat to break off a negotiation. Another American negotiator describes the difference between the U.S. and North Korean approaches this way: "We're criticized if we establish a goal and don't reach it; they are criticized for not asking for enough."[11]

Brinkmanship tactics were most effective in first encounters with American diplomats. "There were times when you would not know how serious they were," recounted one American official. "They often forced us into emotional highs and lows by putting everything at stake. It was all or nothing."[12] Examples include administration choices over whether to escalate and pursue economic sanctions in the face of North Korean rhetoric that such sanctions would be viewed as tantamount to war, suggesting that they would invite North Korean retaliation. According to one administration official, "Their intent was to make you believe that the decision for sanctions was a decision for war," a potentially dangerous self-fulfilling policy if crisis escalates to the brink, as it almost did during the nuclear crisis in June 1994.[13]

Brinkmanship in face-to-face negotiations was often easier to manage than "long-distance" brinkmanship, which was conducted through correspondence during periods when direct dialogue between officials was impractical or impossible. During times of crisis in which few direct channels existed for face-to-face negotiations, brinkmanship was more of an issue because North Korean positions were "brittle," and it was more difficult to take the hard edge out of a document that might be open to unintended interpretations but nevertheless had to be circulated to a wide variety of levels and departments within both governments. In long-distance brinkmanship, there was "no softening of words and no explanation" beyond the contents of the letter itself.

The success of brinkmanship depends partially on the ability of the party employing such a strategy to keep the opponent from discerning its own "bottom line," or willingness to compromise short of the maximal demand associated with the crisis. However, the repetition of the same threats or bluffing strategies has tended to lead negotiating counterparts to discount the seriousness of such actions as bluster or empty threats.[14] Such a tactic runs the danger of encountering the same response elicited by the boy who cried wolf. From their experience with a recurring pattern of North Korean brinkmanship, American negotiators have largely discounted such tactics as having no real significance, given North Korea's position of relative vulnerability— although it should be underlined that North Korean negotiators have not yet abandoned brinkmanship. After the effectiveness of an initial threat wears off, the negotiating counterpart becomes familiar with repeated brinkmanship tactics and ignores them.

In fact, brinkmanship tactics are often counterproductive once the utility of such tactics has been exhausted. "It's annoying to be yelled at all the time," says one American negotiator, noting that the hostility engendered by such actions may render them utterly ineffective, if not counterproductive, undermining the development of effective working relationships among negotiating counterparts. The risk is that real threats might be discounted as just so much more empty talk coming from Pyongyang. In addition, North Korean leaders may find it necessary to take greater and greater risks in order to grab the attention of negotiating counterparts in Washington.

The use of bluff or bluster at the negotiating table is a means by which to cover up one's own weakness, a tactic that actually serves to signal sensitivity to one's own inferior position. "When you have noth-ing else, pride becomes all important," one American observer notes. The inherent danger of a brinkmanship strategy is that outrageous threats may lead negotiators to discount the real sources of tension, resulting in the possibility of miscalculation and the risk of the potential escalation of conflict. "It is hard to tell if you've reached the core of their position," according to one American negotiator. Sometimes one may not discern one's counterpart's bottom line until after the counterpart has taken precipitous action, creating a new sense of crisis.[15] Among the primary components of a brinkmanship strategy are demands for unilateral concessions, bluffing and threats, manufacturing dead-lines, and threats to walk away from the negotiating table.

Demands for Unilateral Concessions

An initial component of North Korean brinkmanship has been de-mands for unilateral concessions in return for the opportunity to come to the negotiating table. Such unilateral concessions, if made in response to North Korean demands during the initial phases of a negotiation, have generally been pocketed rather than reciprocated.[16] Such behavior—in contrast to perceived American tendencies to "move the goal posts"—might be called "moving the starting blocks." Such attempts to extract benefits before negotiation are a sign that North Korea may have no interest in engaging in serious negotiations since failure to respond to a unilateral concession results in a loss of trust and damages the integrity of the interlocutor. On the other hand, a demand for a unilateral concession is a good way to signal a maxi-malist position, using an exaggerated demand far in excess of what is reasonable to influence a negotiating opponent psychologically. According to this logic, the higher the initial price for cooperation, the more favorable the terms of an eventual settlement.

The most visible example of North Korean pocketing of unilateral concessions has been the provision by South Korea and Japan, respec-tively, of 150,000 tons and 500,000 tons of rice to North Korea in the summer of 1995. Despite hopes that such donations might result in the resumption of political negotiations, North Korea made no reciprocal step.[17] The result was that the South Korean and Japanese governments were seen by the public as having been "taken" by North Korea, thereby making it more difficult for them to respond to subsequent North Korean demands for food assistance when the need became greater. In the case of the United States, North Korea demanded that light-water reactors to be supplied under the Geneva Agreed Framework be of non–South Korean origin, but the United States patiently resisted North Korean brinkmanship tactics. Likewise, North Korea demanded food in 1996 and 1997 as a prerequisite for participation in a joint briefing on the Clinton-Kim proposal for the Four Party Talks. Despite procuring only limited benefits as part of preparatory meetings, North Korea finally decided to come to the table for the Four Party Talks in December 1997.

Demands for unilateral concessions as the price for negotiation usually constitute an attempt to expose the counterpart's weakness or flexibility without offering anything in return. To give in during the initial stages is to encourage North Korea to make demands for additional unilateral concessions. Even compensation for joint activities, such as the first POW/MIA joint effort in North Korea in the summer of 1996, may be a target for unilateral concessions, particularly since there may be little conception of "market value" for particular services rendered. "They will ask you for as much as you are willing to give," according to one participant in such a negotiation, noting that North Korean interlocutors continually requested additional concessions—including financial remuneration—even after an issue appeared to be closed. Every person on a U.S. negotiating team is probed for signs that the United States has not yet reached its bottom line and may be prepared to yield further concessions. But in negotiations with North Korea, "our bottom line has dictated—their bottom line has always conceded to ours," another sign of North Korean vulnerability, according to one American official.[18]

North Korean unconditional demands are also a form of bluffing and are accompanied by a maximal and often unrealistic set of demands in exchange for North Korean cooperation. North Korean negotiating positions are unrealistically aggressive in the view of most American counterparts. North Korean negotiators "always push as far as they think they can go." Without the freedom to break off negotiations in a responsive show of brinkmanship to call North Korea's bluff—or at least to threaten to do so—the negotiating counterpart may be operating at a disadvantage.

Bluffing and Threats

Bluffing accompanied by unspecified threats has been a constant pattern in U.S.–North Korean negotiations. This tactic, often a component of North Korean propaganda that extends to opening plenary session statements, creates ambiguity about possible North Korean actions if negotiations break down, putting pressure on the negotiating partner to make concessions to avoid the "worst possible" outcome. It is also a tactic for concealing the "true" North Korean position in the initial stages of a negotiation. Such threats may be intended either to deter a proposed action by a negotiating counterpart or to coerce the counterpart into accepting North Korean demands. The threat of possible action by North Korea has raised the perceived costs for the United States of applying maximal pressure, leaving potential threats untested and possible bluffs unrevealed. As the United States has gained experience dealing with North Korea, more bluffs have been called, forcing North Korean negotiators to cave in, retreating—shamelessly—to meet the negotiating counterpart's demand.

North Korea effectively used threats when faced with the prospect of international economic sanctions in the spring of 1994 and routinely has used threats in propaganda attacking the South Korean government. The primary challenge in responding to these threats is that it is difficult to distinguish empty threats from real ones. A catalog of untested North Korean threats would include North Korea's threat in 1993 to withdraw from the NPT (forestalled by direct negotiations with the United States) and threats in 1993 and 1994 that an international drive for economic sanctions would be seen as an "act of war" (forestalled by Jimmy Carter's intervention and meetings with Kim Il Sung in June 1994).

Other threats in which bluffs were called include North Korea's original demands for over one million tons of South Korean rice in the summer of 1995. North Korea was shown to be bluffing when it failed to carry through on threats during the Geneva negotiations that it would reprocess spent fuel rods removed from the reactor.[19] North Korea's demand for a non–South Korean reactor in negotiations between Gary Samore and Kim Jong U in Berlin in September 1994 and subsequently in April 1995 was part of a six-month effort by the North Korean side to persuade the United States not to allow South Korea a central role in the reactor project. But the North Korean bluff was called when the United States did not make concessions on this issue following the April 21, 1995, "deadline" for settling this issue.

Brinkmanship is more effective if it is possible to retain credibility by showing that not all threats are bluffs. The North Koreans made good on their June 1998 threat to continue missile testing with the Taep'odong launch over Japanese territory on August 31, 1998. Likewise, the North did not bluff when it decided to remove fuel from its 5-megawatt reactor in the absence of IAEA supervisors in June 1994, an action that the United States had explicitly named as a "red line," the crossing of which would result in the termination of high-level talks and renewal of a drive for North Korea's economic isolation.[20] This sequence of events was clouded by the fact that IAEA inspectors, invited by North Korea to observe the defueling of the reactor, demanded additional inspections before agreeing to observe the removal of the fuel rods. North Korea also had something to hide, namely, the history of a nuclear effort that could be traced by the IAEA if the North Koreans were to allow IAEA inspectors to take samples from the fuel rods as they were removed from the reactor. In this case, North Korea had an explicit motivation for carrying through with its threat: to obscure evidence that might have quantified the status of North Korea's past efforts to develop a nuclear weapons program.

Manufacturing Deadlines

Another element of a brinkmanship strategy involves maintaining control of negotiations through the creation of perceived deadlines by which the counterpart should respond. The creation of a deadline is combined with demands for unilateral concessions and threats of negative consequences in the event of failure to respond. The sense of crisis produced might force a more generous response to North Korean demands than would be the case under normal circumstances.

North Korea's initial announcement to withdraw from the NPT included a deadline since the decision to withdraw would come into force within ninety days of its March 12, 1993, declaration. This deadline forced the international community and the United States to respond before the date North Korea's withdrawal would become effective. A major result of the defueling of North Korea's reactor in June 1994—beyond creating pressure that eventually led to an agreement to return to the negotiating table—was that the time limitations associated with the perceived need either to reprocess or to safely store spent fuel rods created a "deadline" by which the United States sought to ensure a perpetual continuation of North Korea's nuclear freeze through the Geneva Agreed Framework. North Korea's decision in late 1993 to deny IAEA inspectors' requests to carry out routine inspections (including changing film in cameras and checking seals in North Korea's declared nuclear facilities) threatened to erode the "continuity of safeguards"—that is, the ability of the IAEA to verify that North Korea was not engaged in nuclear weapons activities—thereby creating a sense of urgency and another effective deadline that limited U.S. and IAEA options for responding to North Korea's threats.

The United States effectively defied North Korean attempts to manufacture a deadline for resolving the question of which type of reactor would be supplied under the Geneva Agreed Framework. Framework provisions required the United States to begin work on the reactor project within six months of the signing of the agreement. But the issue of whether South Korea would be the central provider of the reactor remained unresolved. Negotiations between Gary Samore and Kim Jong U in Berlin broke down over this issue, and the six-month anniversary of the signing of the Agreed Framework passed without concessions on the part of the United States in response to North Korea's deadline pressure. North Korea's attempt to fix April 21, 1995, as a "deadline" instead of a "target date" was a failed North Korean attempt to create a sense of crisis in the negotiations.

Rather than abandoning the Agreed Framework, the DPRK government was forced to find a way back to the negotiating table for additional meetings in Kuala Lumpur between Tom Hubbard, deputy assistant secretary of state for East Asia and the Pacific, and Kim Kye

Gwan, North Korea's vice foreign minister. American patience in the face of North Korean attempts to manufacture a deadline in this case rendered brinkmanship ineffective, calling North Korea's bluff and seriously weakening North Korea's negotiating position.

North Korean negotiators have reacted to the external imposition of deadlines by waiting until the last possible minute before making a deal. According to one analyst of North Korean negotiating behavior, North Korean negotiators "never make compromises without a deadline. If the North Korean side doesn't take it as a deadline, it's not a deadline."[21]

Threats to Walk Away from the Negotiating Table

The most dramatic forms of brinkmanship have been North Korean threats to walk out of negotiations, an effective unilateral tactic if one can afford to abandon the potential benefits of a negotiated settlement. The threat to walk out is a means of creating pressure that might accompany a perceived deadline. Such a threat can be used as a stalling tactic or as a means by which to put psychological pressure on a negotiating counterpart to accept the North's negotiating position. And threats to walk out may not always be effective—or even possible. One example from the Geneva negotiations was Vice Foreign Minister Kang Sok Ju's decision—responding in outrage to an insistent American demand—to slam down his briefing book and stand up to leave the negotiating table. The only problem was that Kang had no place to go: this negotiating session was being held at North Korea's own mission!

A more surreal effect of the threat to walk out of negotiations was created in the Kuala Lumpur negotiations between Tom Hubbard and Kim Kye Gwan. As the negotiations progressed, members of the North Korean negotiating team were recalled to Pyongyang one by one; as the North Korean team dwindled, American counterparts began to wonder what would happen if only North Korean nameplates and empty seats remained on the other side.

At the same negotiations in Kuala Lumpur, the limits of brinkmanship were graphically illustrated when the North Korean negotiating team carried out its threat to walk out of the negotiations, only to call the American side later in the evening to explain that there was a need to "take a break." "The North Korean position became so weak that they could not credibly walk out," according to one American negotiator.[22] On another occasion, a session ended in apparent deadlock and the North Korean side threatened to terminate the negotiations; later that evening the North Korean side requested that negotiations be resumed the following day on the grounds that the North Korean negotiating team "did not have final instructions" from Pyongyang.

One response to North Korean brinkmanship might be to employ brinkmanship tactics in return. When Tom Hubbard expressed on an open telephone line his frustration with progress in negotiations to release airman Bobby Hall, his counterparts in Pyongyang responded more quickly, perhaps because they felt they had reached their counterpart's bottom line. At the first round of POW/MIA talks in Hawaii, Deputy Assistant Secretary of Defense for POW/MIA Operations James Wold (a retired U.S. Army colonel) called a recess to allow his North Korean counterparts to "develop a more realistic position," catching the North Koreans by surprise. "When they realize that you are willing to walk away," the North Korean delegates may show more flexibility because they feel that they have identified the maximum limit of possible gain to be expected on a specific issue for negotiation.[23]

The effectiveness of brinkmanship diminishes greatly once the United States and North Korea have reached an initial agreement that gives the North Korean government something to lose. Nonetheless, despite the seeming ineffectiveness resulting from repeated reliance on brinkmanship, such tactics have remained a part of North Korea's negotiating style. On issues such as North Korean missile development and sales to third countries, the continued danger of military confrontation near the DMZ, and management of North-South relations, North Korean brinkmanship tactics—particularly in the context of North Korea's apparent need to create a crisis atmosphere in order to negotiate—may remain a serious and potentially difficult challenge for American negotiators. Most serious is the effect of brinkmanship on a negotiating counterpart's ability to discover the North Korean bottom line, with the possible result—as in the case of North Korea's decision to defuel its nuclear reactor—that an apparently empty threat by North Korea may turn out not to be a bluff after all.

Creating Leverage out of Weakness

In addition to tactical uses of crisis diplomacy and brinkmanship, the third major identifiable characteristic of North Korea's negotiating behavior has been the ability to create negotiating leverage both by masking weakness and by using weakness in an attempt to gain additional concessions. North Korean negotiators assiduously study the weaknesses, divisions, and priorities of their negotiating counterpart and maneuver in the negotiation process to achieve maximal concessions while limiting cooperation on the priority issues of the negotiating counterpart. The identification of the nuclear issue as a priority for the United States and the international community provided North Korea with significant, otherwise unavailable leverage in U.S.-DPRK negotiations. By identifying the priorities and the weaknesses of the negotiating counterpart, North Korea can present aggressive, maximalist negotiating demands and show stubbornness in yielding to its counterpart's priorities in order to create issue-specific negotiating leverage to gain concessions far in excess of North Korea's aggregate national strength. Such a "guerrilla" negotiating style has relied on unconventional tactics that would not be available to North Korea if it were effectively integrated into the international system.

Employing a strategy of acquiescing only when pressured heavily on sensitive demands for North-South dialogue or North Korea's return to the IAEA, North Korea has increased its negotiating strength—but sometimes at a cost to its own interests. North Korea's strategy of creating leverage has been "tactically brilliant, but strategically stupid," according to American negotiators who believe that North Korea has passed up deals in its national interest for the sake of gaining leverage but has subsequently lost valuable potential benefits from employing a more flexible or cooperative stance at the negotiating table.[24]

Not only threats of strength (through threats of military conflict or the threat posed by North Korea's nuclear or missile development programs), but also threats accompanying weakness (for instance, the threat of chaos surrounding North Korea's collapse) have been

used by North Korean negotiators to extract concessions from negotiating counterparts. North Korean willingness to come to joint briefings on the Four Party Talks has been predicated on whether the West
responded to North Korean appeals for massive amounts of food aid,
a negotiation position that employs the threat of collapse or chaos as
leverage to gain needed economic benefits from the international
community. For instance, the North Koreans attempted to negotiate
with Congressman Bill Richardson on one of his trips to Pyongyang
the delivery of one million tons of U.S. and South Korean food aid in
return for DPRK cooperation on MIAs and the Four Party Talks. Before
Richardson left Pyongyang, however, this agreement broke down when
a Department of Defense representative in Pyongyang advised the
North Koreans that the deal had been reached without interagency
consultation and that U.S. law prohibits members of Congress from
negotiating on behalf of the U.S. government![25] Subsequently, North
Korean officials suggested that they would attend the proposed Four
Party Talks if they were guaranteed up to 500,000 tons of U.S. grain
on a grant or loan basis, rejecting offers to allow commercial deals.

Major tactical components of a North Korean strategy of expanding leverage to the maximum extent possible include the following:
blaming the other side for failure, showing *kosaeng* (suffering) in the
negotiation process, and manipulation of the concept of face saving
by playing the part of the innocent victim.

Blaming the Other Side for Failure

Along with crisis diplomacy and brinkmanship, it has been common
for North Korean negotiators to blame the other side for failure in the
event an agreement is not reached. If the negotiation process reaches
an impasse or breaks down, North Korean public propaganda will
routinely blame the other side's "unreasonable position" for causing
the breakdown. For instance, American negotiators found themselves
blamed for attempting to "dupe" or "hoodwink" their North Korean
counterparts by introducing the light-water reactor as a "Trojan horse."
This tactic may be useful as a means by which to put the negotiating
counterpart on the psychological defensive. As described in chapter 1,
it may also reflect the highly centralized, tightly politically controlled

environment of North Korea's socialist system, in which to admit mistakes may invite harsh punishment or humiliation.

"They seize the position of victim, and use it," states one American negotiator. For instance, the natural reaction of a negotiating counterpart to the North Korean assertion that "the United States is trying to strangle us" may be to demonstrate that the assertion is not true; by playing the part of the aggrieved or injured party and by limiting alternatives to their own position, North Korean negotiators manufacture leverage that may be used to induce opponents to make more concessions.[26]

An effect of aggressive North Korean assertions that "paint their enemies black and then blame them for being black" is to project blame onto the other side and create a defensive reaction in which the counterpart may be tempted to prove that the assertion is not true.[27] Blaming the other side for failing to make concessions or for failing to adopt one's own position is a classic psychological device to encourage concessions from the other side and is perceived to increase the likelihood that any final agreement will be closer to one's own position than that of the other side.

Criticism of the other side is routinely voiced through the North Korean public media organs and often echoed in plenary negotiation sessions, but such rhetoric serves to obscure rather than to shed light on the real North Korean position. For instance, the North Korean reaction to the submarine incident in the fall of 1996 is notable because the North Korean government was forced to admit a mistake, but it did so in an indirect and obscure manner, heaping portions of blame on the other side. The submarine was discovered in South Korea on September 18, 1996, and it took over a week for the North Korean Central News Agency (KCNA) to report the incident. The KCNA blamed South Korea for refusing to return the submarine and did not mention why the submarine and its crew had been stranded in South Korean waters. The KCNA simultaneously refuted South Korean media reports of a North Korean "spy boat" and "spies."[28] This public line was maintained throughout the incident.

Because of the distortions of North Korea's socialist system, mistakes in the North Korean position are never admitted; rather, North

Korean mistakes disappear into a resounding silence as unmentionable deeds that may be accompanied by newly aggressive positions designed to obscure or even deny the possibility that mistakes were made. Although North Korea was forced to issue an unusual statement of "deep regret" for the submarine incursion following eleven rounds of negotiations between North Korea and the United States in December 1996, North Korean negotiators successfully avoided apologizing directly to South Korea or admitting that the submarine had been sent to spy on South Korea. The sixty-six-word statement was issued on a station that broadcasts internationally and was not carried in domestic news reports. The statement was accompanied by a torrent of vituperative remarks toward South Korea and President Kim Young Sam, blaming South Korea for the incident and for the failure to return a submarine that was on "routine exercises." The day after the apology, the cremated bodies of the North Korean commandos were returned in a ceremony at Panmunjom that was also accompanied by a flood of vituperative propaganda over North Korean loudspeakers aimed at the South. Having been forced to make a public statement of responsibility for its own mistake, North Korean authorities doled out blame to the opposing side in amounts that effectively dwarfed the admission of the North's mistake.

Kosaeng: *Demonstrating Suffering in a Negotiation*

For North Korean negotiators, a prerequisite for reaching a negotiated agreement may be the need to show *kosaeng,* accompanied by perseverance or commitment, until the last possible moment to ensure that the negotiator has extracted as many concessions as possible from the negotiating counterpart. *Kosaeng* is an extension of *kojip* (stubbornness). For instance, it may be necessary for the lead negotiator to show that he has undergone pain or suffering before it is possible to move to a give-and-take negotiation process necessary to reach an agreement. The need to show *kosaeng* is twofold: to demonstrate perseverance to the negotiating counterpart in order to extract the most concessions possible, and to show to one's higher-ups back home that the potential deal is the best possible deal that can be achieved under the circumstances. The necessity of showing *kosaeng* often applies

most directly to circumstances in which it is necessary to offer difficult or controversial concessions if agreement is to be reached.

During the Geneva negotiations, the outlines of a deal appeared in
the August 1994 Agreed Conclusion, but further consultations were
necessary to settle the complex details that eventually became the
basis for the Geneva Agreed Framework. By early October, most of
those details had been settled, yet another two weeks of haggling
were necessary before it was possible to sign the Agreed Framework.
The review of these issues, the introduction of separate sessions between
Kim Jong U and Gary Samore in Berlin, and even last-minute attempts
by North Korean officials to renegotiate the most objectionable parts
of the Agreed Framework were all part of a need to demonstrate that
the North Korean team had "suffered" in their efforts to gain as
much as possible from the United States. Likewise, subsequent negotiations between the United States and North Korea in Kuala Lumpur
in the spring of 1995 dragged on as part of the same need to test what
in North Korea's view was the most objectionable part of the Agreed
Framework, the central role for South Korea in supplying light-water
reactors. Although the outline of an agreement was clear after about
ten days of negotiations in Kuala Lumpur, it took twenty-nine days
before the issue was finally settled. The intervening period was necessary for Tom Hubbard's counterpart, Kim Kye Gwan, to show that he
had the best deal possible (and for Hubbard to convince South Korean
counterparts that the American side had also "suffered" in resisting
North Korean entreaties for further concessions). Finally, the matter
was settled with simultaneous announcements from the United States
and North Korea in Kuala Lumpur and from the board of KEDO
(consisting of U.S., Japanese, and South Korean official representatives meeting in Seoul) on June 14, 1995.[29]

Saving Face

As with other Asian national styles, the North Korean approach to
negotiation attaches great importance to saving face *(ch'emyon)*—to
avoiding humiliation, especially (within the context of negotiations)
the humiliation of having to admit weaknesses or failures in one's
position. Congressman Gary Ackerman was told during a visit to

Pyongyang at the height of the North Korean nuclear crisis in October 1993, "For us, saving face is as important as life itself."[30]

For instance, face saving came to the fore as an element of negotiations as IAEA inspectors began to uncover evidence of North Korean cheating that contradicted North Korea's records and statements. The dilemma was whether the humiliating loss of face associated with public exposure and condemnation of North Korea's deception would wreck all prospects for a negotiated settlement, or whether the North Korean effort to conceal its earlier deceptions might be driven by an attempt to "save the face" of Kim Il Sung, whose statements denying the existence of a North Korean nuclear program would be proved as lies.[31]

Another example is the initial joint press statement issued in June 1993 following the first round of U.S.-DPRK discussions on nuclear issues. The DPRK was careful to make clear that it had not been pressured into suspending its withdrawal from the NPT; rather, the suspension was presented as a voluntary unilateral measure. The need to show independent action when coercive diplomacy has in essence forced concessions is an example of face saving invoked to remove the humiliation of having to back away from a previously held position. Another example is the insistence of North Korean negotiators on outlining concessions in a "confidential minute" negotiated along with the Geneva Agreed Framework, rather than having those concessions aired publicly as part of the agreement.

The issues of face saving and humiliation are also raised continually in the context of South-North dialogue; some South Korean conditions requiring North Korea to admit receiving assistance from Seoul seem to be aimed primarily at triggering a North Korean loss of face, or public humiliation. Likewise, North Korean refusal to acknowledge South Korean assistance has been interpreted by some South Koreans as a loss of face, a snub by a North Korean leadership that has resisted acknowledging the accomplishments and international prestige enjoyed in Seoul.[32]

North Korean negotiators have often required certain types of face-saving gestures when it becomes necessary to offer a concession or to back away from a previously held position. In these instances, face saving may be little more than a plea for help to get out of a difficult situation. On several occasions North Korean representatives have forced themselves into situations in which the only way out of deadlock relies on actions or concessions by the negotiating counterpart. "They paint themselves into a corner [by limiting their own freedom of maneuver to offer concessions of their own], then expect the other side to save them [by giving in to the North Korean position]," observes an American negotiator.[33] Taking action that humiliates a vulnerable negotiating counterpart may make the uncertain prospect of future cooperation even less likely. On the other hand, giving the North Korean side a respectable way out may involve making unnecessary concessions. The answer, according to one analyst, is that "the other side can't save their face. . . . [The North Koreans themselves] have to save their own face."[34]

Interestingly, face saving may also be used as a metaphor for confidence building, including the development of practical cooperation measures that are necessary to change the nature of U.S.-DPRK relations from a wholly adversarial relationship to one in which cooperation is possible. As one North Korean diplomat stated in a private conversation, "What we need is to find ways to save each other ['s face]"; only through the dramatic process of turning conflict into cooperation would the legacy of mistrust that characterizes U.S.-DPRK relations be fundamentally addressed.[35]

Other North Korean Negotiating Tactics: Reciprocity, Simultaneity, and Form Versus Substance

Other notable aspects of North Korean negotiating tactics include preoccupations with equivalency, simultaneity, and reciprocity in relations with the United States, including public expressions of equivalency in the negotiating relationship, even in cases where the underlying substance reveals significant North Korean concessions. For instance, North Korean negotiators have been highly attentive to the structure of joint agreements with the United States to ensure that the perception of equivalency is maintained, even where there are North Korean concessions on substantive issues. The Geneva Agreed Framework and other documents—such as the February 25, 1994, Agreed

Conclusion between the United States and North Korea and the initial June 11, 1993, joint press statement[36]—have been carefully crafted to underscore the appearance of equivalency and simultaneity of actions by the United States and North Korea. When substantive concessions have been made, North Korean negotiators have also requested that public statements reflect rough equivalency in terms of number of concessions made in order to save face, particularly if the North Korean side has been forced to yield substantive concessions. In some cases, the wording of a concession may be more important to North Korean negotiators than the substance itself.

For instance, North Korea accepted a light-water reactor of American origin, but not one specified as a "South Korean standard model" light-water reactor. North Korean negotiators would not agree to "special inspections" but did agree to come into compliance with IAEA standards to ensure "continuity of safeguards." In both cases, the external demands for North Korean concessions politicized certain terms and made them into "hot button" issues for the North Korean leadership. It became necessary to use alternative expressions to conceal North Korean concessions on these points. Emphasizing the concepts of equivalency and reciprocity, North Korean negotiators sought language that emphasized simultaneity of action consistent with their desire for a political agreement, rather than conditionality. Even Kim Il Sung emphasized the principle of reciprocity, saying, "The way to resolve the problem is for the United States to abide by its pledges. If the United States would simply agree to top-level talks with no preconditions, we could solve the problem."[37]

A corollary of the North Korean emphasis on equivalency with the United States in negotiations has been insistence on simultaneity rather than conditionality as the fundamental principle for carrying out negotiations and implementing agreements. The negotiations would falter each time the United States employed a conditional approach in which one side would have to take action in order to achieve progress without reciprocal measures by the other side.

An example of the North Korean resistance to conditionally structured agreements came following the second round of the Geneva negotiations in the fall of 1993, when North-South contacts and the resumption of IAEA inspections were presented as two conditions that the United States would require before resumption of negotiations. North Korean unwillingness to respond to the conditional approach stalled the talks for many months and almost led to the escalation of the crisis in late fall of 1993 as a result of the IAEA's inability to ensure the continuity of its inspection regime in North Korea. When American negotiators expressed future actions using conditionality, such usage brought heated objections from the North Korean side, which saw conditional statements as implying inequality or as an infringement on their sovereignty. "Hour after hour, I would be required to read, 'when you have done A, we will do B,'" reported one American negotiator whose North Korean counterpart would respond in effect by saying, "My instructions say if you mention preconditions, I am out of here."[38]

The modest Agreed Conclusion of February 25, 1994, negotiated between the United States and North Korea in months of contacts from September 1993 through February 1994, returned to the principle of simultaneity in the structure of the agreement that the United States would declare a cancellation of Team Spirit military exercises, a perennial focus of complaint by North Korean officials, and announce the third round of the Geneva negotiations in return for North Korea's willingness to allow IAEA inspections and establishing working-level contacts to prepare for the exchange of special envoys between the two Koreas. Although the Agreed Conclusion broke down over other issues, the principle of simultaneity of action leading to progress (reflected in the Geneva Agreed Framework and subsequent U.S.– North Korean agreements) versus conditional steps taken in sequence (for instance, demands that resumption of North-South dialogue be resumed before the fulfillment of actions desired by North Korea) was reinforced as an essential prerequisite for progress in negotiations with North Korea.

Facilitating Tactics: Time Pressure, Emotion, and Trial Balloons

Most of the negotiation tactics described thus far have been forms of pressure tactics or stalling tactics, but there are also instances in which North Korean negotiators seek to facilitate the progress or pace of negotiations with American counterparts. The most common forms of facilitating tactics have involved the use of time pressure; "building heat" for a negotiation through a show of emotion at the negotiating table; and the testing at informal sessions of "trial balloon" ideas for possible compromise that might facilitate progress in negotiations.

Although North Korean negotiators often use deadlines and other forms of time pressure to extract concessions from negotiating counterparts, on some occasions time deadlines may reflect the North Korean side's urgent need for agreement. In particular, North Korean negotiators may need to show progress on anniversary dates of key events. The North Korean push in negotiations with KEDO for a supply contract by the first anniversary of the Geneva Agreed Framework seemed to have been motivated by a need to demonstrate progress by a key date. The focus on the need to settle the type of reactor that would be delivered to North Korea by the six-month anniversary of the signing of the Agreed Framework may have had a dual motivation, to put pressure on American counterparts to compromise and to show progress by a "target date" that had been mentioned in the Geneva Agreed Framework itself. American negotiators reported surprising flexibility in August 1998 negotiations with North Korea, perhaps reflecting the DPRK foreign ministry's need for success in the run-up to fiftieth anniversary celebrations of the founding of the DPRK set for September 9, 1998.

A second means by which to move forward in case of deadlock in negotiations is "building heat" to resolve issues. An emotional display by one side or the other as a result of frustration when an impasse is reached may also be an opportunity for forward movement because it reveals a negotiator's bottom-line position on issues of significance in a negotiation. Emotional outbursts have occasionally been an important means by which to move past potential stumbling blocks in the negotiations. For instance, reports that the United States had positioned an aircraft carrier off the North Korean coast during the third round of the Geneva negotiations caused Vice Foreign Minister Kang Sok Ju to "explode" at the plenary session, an outburst that was signaled in advance to the U.S. side. Kang's visible anger and Robert

Gallucci's vigorous response were a means of dealing with external side issues without letting them become an obstacle to the substance of the negotiation.

During talks in Geneva, the question of whether North Korea would accept special inspections prompted a heated exchange between Gallucci and Kang. Despite strenuous objections by Kang in plenary sessions, at a private session between the two lead negotiators Kang made the key concession that allowed the negotiations to proceed. And Deputy Assistant Secretary Hubbard, after patiently negotiating in Kuala Lumpur over the type of reactor to be supplied under the Geneva Agreed Framework, finally pounded the table and asked his counterpart, "Are you going to select these [South Korean standard-model] reactors or not?" After it had become clear that this was the bottom-line American position, the North Koreans acquiesced, although they avoided making explicit concessions in the text of the joint announcement. In addition, displays of pique on the North Korean side of the negotiating table may be indicators of North Korea's bottom line.

Finally, North Korean negotiators are skilled at using informal conversations outside negotiations to launch trial balloons—possible compromises that might facilitate formal negotiations. American counterparts have heard a variety of ideas expressed informally that, if they have elicited a faborable response, have subsequently made their way into official North Korean negotiating positions. Trial balloons that have not been met with favor have simply disappeared. Given the extraordinary rigidity of North Korean public positions, the opportunity to launch informal trial balloons to facilitate negotiations is a welcome means by which to test new ideas without necessarily seeming to be formally committed to such approaches.

It is important to note that floating trial balloons or conducting other business in informal sessions does not necessarily represent progress in a negotiation; North Korean negotiators may come back to any issue on which agreement might apparently have been reached in prior discussions. It is a mistake to assume that a point has been finally agreed until all issues have been settled and laid out in a final, signed document. In the words of one American interlocutor, "If they don't write it down, it's never been said."[39] Although a commonly used tactic of North Korean negotiators in North-South dialogue has been to accept in principle generalized agreements that can later be interpreted in different ways, American negotiators in the MAC and in the U.S.–North Korean negotiations say that the DPRK has a record of abiding by explicit agreements that are a part of the formal record.

Having examined the process, structure, and tactical patterns of North Korean style in negotiations with the United States, let us turn to a comparison of North Korean tactics in U.S.-DPRK negotiations and North-South dialogue. Then we will examine whether North Korea's negotiating style changes in a multilateral negotiating context, as represented by the DPRK's negotiations with KEDO.

4

Comparing North-South and U.S.-DPRK Negotiating Patterns

When South Koreans ask Ambassador Robert Gallucci what it was like to sit across the negotiating table from North Koreans during a period of high tension in 1993 and 1994, the quick-witted quip from the ambassador is "Look in the mirror." This response reflects an underlying observation widespread among many American diplomats (among others) that there are numerous similarities in negotiating strategies and tactics employed on both sides of the DMZ. In this view, the common points among Korean negotiators may seem greater than the differences imposed by the experiences of division—through which Koreans in North and South have been socialized in opposing ideological and systemic environments.

Indeed, a close examination of South Korean patterns in bargaining and conflict resolution suggests that there are common characteristics in the respective North and South Korean approaches to negotiations. Nancy Abelmann's study of social conflicts over landownership in the late 1980s reveals patterns in the escalation and eventual resolution of social conflicts that roughly parallel aspects of North Korean negotiating style analyzed in the previous chapter. On the basis of that study and other work, three relevant lessons might be drawn from an analysis of South Korean patterns of managing and resolving conflict through negotiations: (1) the instigation of crisis is often necessary to create conditions under which it is possible to engage in negotiation—that is, escalation of tensions may be required to facilitate the pace and progress of negotiation; (2) in a society such as that of South Korea with a collective and hierarchical structure influenced by neo-Confucian tradition, negotiation takes on a "moral" significance because the negotiation itself involves a fundamental redefinition of the nature of the relationship between two parties; and (3) brinkmanship is not only a function of the need to create a crisis to force conditions for a negotiation; it may also be a manifestation of the need to maintain unity within the group so as to avoid fractionalization.[1] Such shared patterns in North and South Korean negotiating style underscore the likelihood that North-South negotiations will be characterized by matching, zero-sum, or crisis-inducing behavior designed in its initial stages to show toughness rather than to facilitate compromise.

This chapter will examine patterns in North-South negotiations, compare the North-South negotiating dynamic with the pattern of U.S.-DPRK dialogue, and analyze the implications of the differing North-South and U.S.-DPRK experiences for managing strategic consultations, a form of internal negotiation as part of the U.S.-ROK security alliance.

MATCHING BEHAVIOR IN NORTH-SOUTH DIALOGUE

The burdens of the history of confrontation between North and South Korea and the "Toughness Dilemma," in which uncompromising tactics are used so as to avoid the risks of being taken advantage of by one's negotiating counterpart, are two primary constraints that have encouraged matching behavior in inter-Korean dialogue. Such a dynamic of confrontation has all too often led to stalemate and breakdown at the negotiating table. The challenges of overcoming the burdens of history and adjusting tactics of toughness to facilitate compromise must be overcome before real progress in inter-Korean dialogue is likely to occur.

Given the extraordinary distrust engendered by almost five decades of competition for legitimacy between the two Koreas, it should not be surprising that the negotiating table might be an active venue for

inter-Korean competition. Negotiation has become a mutually acceptable venue for ritualizing inter-Korean competition since a battlefield
confrontation has long been recognized by both sides as too costly.
Although inter-Korean negotiations have made limited and sporadic
progress in some areas, they have often broken down as a result of the
dynamic of competition and one-upmanship inherent in the approach
of both sides at the negotiating table. Even under current circumstances, in which North Korea no longer has the luxury of treating the
negotiating table as simply another venue through which to act out
competition with the South, it has often been too difficult to abandon
the tactics of toughness in favor of compromise—even if compromise
might be in Pyongyang's national interest—if the price also required
a hint of symbolic surrender to Seoul.

The initiation of the 1972 North-South negotiation process itself
demonstrated the existence of an atmosphere in which negotiation
was primarily used as another form of competition, albeit one in which
restraint and negotiated cooperation were faint components of the
proceedings as a result of structural changes in the international environment. In the wake of the shock that accompanied Nixon's historic
visit to Beijing, both Kim Il Sung and Park Chung Hee were sufficiently
unsettled to be willing to take a chance on talks.

For his part, Kim Il Sung appears to have pursued the negotiation
of Three Principles for Korean Unification in 1972 as part of a long-
standing strategy to force the removal of U.S. troops from Korea in a
changing international environment that included the beginning of the
end of the war in Vietnam. According to DPRK ambassador to the German Democratic Republic Lee Chang Su, who briefed the East German
Politburo on North Korea's strategy in negotiating with the South,
"The purpose of the negotiation with South Korea was to concentrate
on forcing South Korean leaders into agreement, to free them from
U.S. and Japanese influence and to allow no U.S. intervention." For his
part ROK president Park Chung Hee found dialogue with the North
to be a useful self-defensive measure. "As long as you can touch an
opponent with at least one hand, you can tell whether he will attack,"
a close aide to Park Chung Hee reported him as saying at the time.
In the return visit of North Korean negotiators to Seoul later that

year, Park Chung Hee opted to negotiate an empty joint agreement emphasizing the "spirit of brotherly love" and "Red Cross humanitarianism," rather than allowing talks to fall apart in Seoul. Both Kim Il Sung and Park Chung Hee understood that North-South negotiations were primarily a venue for extending competition, rather than a process designed to achieve mutually satisfactory agreed outcomes. In this extraordinary atmosphere of distrust that existed even with the initiation of North-South dialogue, the negotiation of vague agreements in principle was a convenient pretext for concealing lack of seriousness in a negotiation while probing for potential weaknesses in the other side's negotiating position, a pattern that has characterized many aspects of the negotiating dynamic between North and South.[2]

The historical burdens that have halted progress in inter-Korean dialogue are perhaps seen most clearly in matching strategies and ritual one-upmanship over protocol issues. These sorts of disputes have consumed a great deal of time in inter-Korean negotiations. Perhaps the most famous and petty example of such haggling relates to positioning in the context of the Military Armistice Commission negotiations at Panmunjom, where meetings themselves became highly ritualized venues for propagandizing and where even the height of the respective symbolic national flagstands and the width of their bases on the table became surrogates for competition and pretexts for avoidance of negotiation over substantive issues. Such battles over protocol issues have extended consistently to the present, as demonstrated by another sort of "flag flap" between North and South Korea during the initial delivery of rice from Seoul to Pyongyang in July 1995. At that time, there was miscommunication over the ground rules for whether a South Korean ship should fly its colors in the harbor of the North Korean city of Chongjin, and the local harbormaster ordered the South Korean flag to be lowered and replaced by the North Korean flag, inciting public opinion in Seoul and demands for a North Korean apology over the incident. North Korean authorities quickly moved to rectify the incident by issuing an apology so as not to endanger the delivery of 150,000 tons of rice, but the initial apology by North Korea's head negotiator, Chun Geum Chol, was not deemed sufficient in Seoul because Chun's apology was issued in his capacity as the vice chairman of the Asia-Pacific Peace Committee, a nonofficial organization, rather than as a member of the External Economic Affairs Commission, his official position within the North Korean government. Partly out of pique at having been forced to apologize, North Korean officials subsequently attempted to extract a reciprocal apology from Seoul over alleged "spying" by a crew member of another South Korean ship who was apprehended taking photographs of Chongjin harbor.[3]

Even if the two Koreas desire to pursue dialogue and compromise in a negotiation, they may find themselves trapped by a fundamental dilemma in negotiation theory: the Toughness Dilemma, or the Negotiator's Dilemma, that is, whether a party in a negotiation should use toughness or softness as a strategy to induce the most favorable agreement possible. An elaboration of this dilemma appears in Harold Nicolson's description of two different "negotiation ethics," that of the Shopkeeper and that of the Warrior. The Shopkeeper always seeks to strike a deal through negotiation. The negotiating ethic of the Shopkeeper projects a process in which softness yields softness and reciprocal concessions lead to eventual agreement on a mutually satisfactory basis. The Warrior, on the other hand, seeks to settle conflicts with a winner-take-all approach, in which the only possible deal is on his own terms. The dilemma posed by Nicolson, an elaboration on the Toughness Dilemma, is "What happens when the Shopkeeper meets the Warrior?" A Shopkeeper who chooses to negotiate with a Warrior has no choice but to adopt a Warrior's tactics, but the Shopkeeper who chooses not to negotiate is also employing tactics of toughness that will likely lead to stalemate. A further wrinkle on the Toughness Dilemma for the Shopkeeper is that even in a negotiation in which both sides are willing to make concessions, toughness may enhance the terms of a deal but may also lead to deadlock if the negotiating counterpart responds with toughness instead of with softness.[4]

The nature of the competition and the level of distrust between North and South Korea as they engage in a multifaceted competition that extends to the negotiation table are such that toughness has been the preferred strategy, even in a bargaining situation where agreement may benefit both sides. Not surprisingly, such interaction has often ended in stalemate or in outcomes that a dispassionate observer might conclude as going against the interests of both parties. Any progress is hard-won, as can be discerned from the countless rounds of negotiation on a very broad range of subjects in a wide variety of forms, levels, and venues. In addition, it has been common for either party in North-South dialogue to pursue negotiations with ulterior motives often unrelated to the stated purpose of the negotiation process itself.[5] Kim Do Tae, in his historical examination of North-South negotiations, suggests that the difficulties of overcoming distrust were gradually reduced by occasional initiatives in which it served the interests of both sides to engage in negotiated cooperation; however, tactics of toughness usually prevailed over respective national interests even in these situations, occasionally leading to stalemate even when cooperation was manifestly in the interests of both parties to an agreement.[6]

In interviews, South Korean officials involved in crafting the Basic Agreement clearly expressed several aspects of the Toughness Dilemma faced by South Korean negotiators involved in dialogue with the North. First, the recognition of the North's own hard-line strategy limits the possibility or desirability of using softness as a tactical response. "If North Korea sees continuing concessions from our side, there are no incentives for compromise. [The North] will continue to take a strong position until they must accept the other side's demands," according to a senior defense official involved with North-South military talks.[7]

Second, there is widespread recognition among analysts in Seoul that North Korea's domestic political structure and external environment mean that "North Korea needs an enemy" and therefore must use tactics of toughness either to create enemies or to settle disputes without conceding to the positions of their negotiating counterparts. There is a lingering suspicion that North Korea's goal in participating in negotiations continues to be to score propaganda points rather than to sincerely engage in a negotiation process; there is also an implicit recognition of South Korea's own mixed motives in coming to the negotiating table.

Third, the frustrating dilemma of competing for legitimacy with the North in a "matching" competition characterized by one-upmanship shows itself in South Korean perceptions of how to respond to a counterpart that either appears never to be serious or is always trying to humiliate the other side. "Only force can correct North Korean behavior," according to one conservative South Korean strategist involved in defense planning. Another, more moderate, South Korean defense analyst similarly argues that the real question is "how to persuade or force the North Korean leadership to come to terms with peaceful unification—change will not come voluntarily."[8] North Korean tactics and one-upmanship force South Korean negotiators to match North Korean tactics, seeking to claim absolute victory in inter-Korean competition.

The role of incentives is limited in such a one-upmanship game. "Incentives must be linked to effecting change in North Korea on our terms," according to one South Korean analyst. Others are more skeptical, arguing that inducements "are no good because North Korea will pocket our concessions."[9] Another South Korean argument against softness, or inducements, is that North Korean negotiators will change their position only after it is clear that nothing can be gained unless they do; thus it is necessary to be tough in order to force change in the position of the other side. A factor that further complicates South Korean willingness to use softness or inducements as a negotiating tactic is bound up in North Korea's pariah status, a self-justifying reason for remaining unyielding at the negotiating table—and an implicit jealousy of North Korean freedom to pursue unrestrained guerrilla tactics. As one South Korean defense analyst noted, "South Korea is bound by international norms, but North Korea—as a rogue state—is not."[10]

FROM MATCHING TO FAILED COOPERATION: SOUTH KOREAN ASSESSMENTS OF THE BASIC AGREEMENT

Despite a series of cyclical ups and downs in inter-Korean dialogue, the most notable development in inter-Korean negotiations thus far has been the signing of the Agreement on Reconciliation, Nonaggression, Exchanges and Cooperation (also known as the Basic Agreement) in December 1991 between Pyongyang and Seoul. At the time of the signing, there was widespread euphoria and hope in Seoul that dialogue might bring about real progress toward cooperation and exchanges between North and South Korea, a potentially notable exception to an inter-Korean negotiating record littered from the very beginning in 1972 with a disheartening record of stalemate and frustration. Six high-level negotiating sessions had been conducted between prime ministers of North and South Korea, exchanges of soccer teams and dance troupes were held, and long-awaited family reunions—at least among the respective negotiating entourages—took place in 1990 and 1991. For the first time, it appeared that both North and South had abandoned tactics of toughness in favor of milder strategies, including positive-sum cooperation and exchanges.[11]

However, within a year the plans for joint committees to implement the Basic Agreement had broken down and the North was heading for a standoff not only with South Korea over implementation of mutual inspections of nuclear sites under the Joint Denuclearization Declaration, but also with the International Atomic Energy Agency, the United States, and the international community over discrepancies in reporting on North Korea's declared nuclear facilities, the details of which have been widely reported in other studies. From the perspective of the key South Korean players involved in negotiating the Basic Agreement, what went wrong? And what lessons are likely to be drawn for application to future negotiations with the North? Despite the structural changes in the atmosphere surrounding the Korean Peninsula, are the two Koreas destined to continue to apply matching tactics of toughness in a perpetual stalemate?

Despite the considerable hope that the signing of the Basic Agreement had engendered, the initial opinions of South Koreans involved in the negotiations have undergone revision following the breakdown of North-South dialogue and an increase in rhetorical competition between Pyongyang and Seoul. The assessments of South Koreans who negotiated with Pyongyang during this period fall into two categories. The first group believes that the North was sincere in negotiating the Basic Agreement, but that external factors undermined the prospect of developing mutual cooperation. This group, including Lim Dong Won, former assistant minister of unification and subsequently President Kim Dae Jung's national security adviser and minister of information, believes that North Korea really wanted the Basic Agreement to work, citing the lack of brinkmanship as a unique characteristic of the December 1991 negotiations that led to the signing of the agreement. "[North-South dialogue] in 1991 became a positive sum game; the nuclear negotiations were the exception to this rule."[12] A former unification ministry colleague involved with the negotiations echoes this view, noting that although the Basic Agreement was stalled as a result of the denuclearization effort,[13] the agreement itself is not time-bound, and both sides could return to implementation of the agreement at any time.

Lim believes the North showed evidence of its sincerity in implementing the agreement when Pyongyang moved forward to jump-start exchanges and cooperation in the summer of 1992 with the visit to Seoul of Kim Dal Hyun, chairman of the External Economic Affairs Commission, who was widely seen as a reformist figure in North Korea. Kim's itinerary included visits to plant sites of South Korea's leading industrial conglomerates (chaebol), including Hyundai and Daewoo. A subsequent return visit by South Korean industrialists scheduled for October never got off the ground as a result of growing pressures regarding results of IAEA inspections of North Korea's nuclear program combined with domestic political pressures in Seoul during the 1992 election campaign, which included the discovery of a prominent North Korean spy ring that had been operating in the South.

The second group has reluctantly concluded that the North Korean Warrior strategy has not changed following the end of the Cold War. The change in opinion is best represented by former Prime Minister Chung Won Shik, who led the South Korean delegation in high-level talks in 1991. Prime Minister Chung's assessment during the negotiations was "that the North Koreans were very serious about it. Now I think I was wrong; they were not sincere."[14] Other South Korean officials suggest that North Korea was trying to use North-South dialogue as the only available path to improved relations with Washington but was not really seriously interested in implementing the Basic Agreement itself. Such an attitude was expressed in a private conversation between the senior South Korean military representative to the talks, Major General Park Yong Ok, and his North Korean counterpart, Major General Kim Yong Chul, in a meeting shortly after the Basic Agreement was signed in record time and with surprisingly little change from the draft originally tabled by the South Korean side. When asked why the North accepted the agreement, Major General Kim responded to Major General Park, "It's your agreement, not our agreement."[15]

Underlying both optimistic and revisionist views of North Korean motives in negotiating the Basic Agreement is a recognition that North Korea negotiated the agreement from a position of weakness. A parallel conclusion has been that the South, recognizing Pyongyang's weakness, may have pushed too hard, resulting in an agreement that could not be fully implemented by the North because it contained provisions that may have been perceived as directly challenging powerful bureaucratic and institutional interests in Pyongyang, including the role of the military. One senior South Korean diplomat attributed the negotiation of the Basic Agreement to a North Korean fear of absorption by the South, reporting North Korean negotiators as saying, "If we let capitalistic germs into our country, we cannot survive."[16] Another noted that the North's fear of opening to the South and its psychologically inferior position compared with the South. "There is no way to reach an agreement with North Korea until they are ready," according to a former official of the Ministry of National Unification closely involved with the high-level talks in 1990 and 1991.

RECONCILING STRATEGIC AND TACTICAL APPROACHES BETWEEN ALLIES

A comparison of U.S. and South Korean approaches to negotiation with North Korea shows that there have been clear differences. To a certain extent, these differences are a product of the differing structural positions in which the United States and South Korea find themselves in dealing with North Korea.[17] With the Cold War over, North Korea has remained a threat to U.S. interests in stability on the Korean Peninsula but no longer has the ability to directly impinge on core American national interests. For South Korea, on the other hand, the threat from the North has remained as immediate and potentially devastating as ever. These differing structural positions are reflected in patterns of conflict management between North and South Korea at both strategic and tactical levels.

These differences in approaches to North Korea and the differing response strategies by North Korean officials in separate channels of negotiation with South Korea and the United States have created new challenges in managing the relationship between the United States and the ROK, two allies who share the same strategic objectives but may have radically different strategies for achieving a preferred outcome, particularly as the asymmetry in American and South Korean security threat perceptions began to emerge with the end of the Cold War. Those differences in approach between the United States and South Korea have been magnified by North Korea's dual strategy and response to each party as well as by differing culturally influenced preconceptions, interpretations, and misunderstandings between the United States and South Korea.

As a rogue state, unconstrained in its negotiating tactics and responses by international norms and yet constrained severely by its isolated international position, North Korea posed a Toughness Dilemma for the United States in formulating its approach to dealing with North Korea. In contrast to the standoff between North and South Korea, the negotiation between the United States and North Korea—once the North Korean nuclear threat was deemed a sufficiently high priority that it was necessary to negotiate—became a problem-solving exercise to find the right deal, rather than a competition for legitimacy between opposing sides.[18]

As a result of the establishment of a direct U.S.-DPRK bargaining channel in 1993, deeply rooted differences in strategy and tactics toward North Korea emerged as a new source of tension in U.S.–South Korean relations.[19] Despite intense policy coordination in response to the crisis, differences between Seoul and Washington over strategy and tactics on how to deal with North Korean brinkmanship heightened tensions between the United States and South Korea, with Seoul taking a tough response to American attempts at deal making. However, the South Korean strategy operated under the disadvantage of constraints imposed by the need to operate within international norms and within an alliance structure with the United States. The task of managing the U.S.-ROK alliance would prove to be almost as big a challenge as the management of a tough negotiation with the North Koreans.

By involving itself in a negotiating process with North Korea that also required the maintenance of its traditional security relationship with South Korean allies, the United States had "joined the life-and-death struggle for legitimacy between Seoul and Pyongyang."[20] Once direct U.S.-DPRK dialogue had been initiated, no concession or compromise in U.S.-DPRK negotiations proved too small to shock the South Korean public, to reinvigorate paranoid debate in some quarters over the possibility of a U.S. betrayal, or to remind South Korean officials of their own sense of helplessness at being sidelined from an issue that directly impinged on South Korean national interests but was beyond the control of the leadership in Seoul.

Despite the development of regular and reliable mechanisms for reporting on the progress of negotiating sessions between the United States and North Korea, there was abundant evidence of South Korean discomfort with the negotiating process between the United States and North Korea from the very beginning. Even the relatively empty —but unprecedented—joint statement issued following the first round of U.S.-DPRK negotiations in New York in June 1993 was greeted with disappointment in Seoul.[21] Its very existence marked a shift: Seoul no longer controlled channels of U.S. dialogue with Pyongyang.

The tensions between U.S. and South Korean officials over managing tactics toward North Korea showed themselves at key points in the negotiating process and in a variety of ways, even despite efforts to increase the frequency and the quality of diplomatic consultations. For instance, the process of preparing for the initial negotiations between North Korea and the United States held in New York in 1993 included review by the South Korean government of talking points drawn up for the American lead negotiator. South Korean desire to be included in the process of approving talking points for U.S. negotiators at initial stages of the Geneva negotiations in New York provided added pressure for an uncompromising stance, increasing the likelihood of a breakdown in negotiations. However, this process proved to be cumbersome and inefficient, as it put added pressure on an interagency approval process already facing severe time pressure, with the result that negotiators often did not receive final talking points until just before the opening of negotiations.

The decision by Seoul to send a high-ranking ambassador to Geneva to monitor U.S.–North Korean negotiations on the ground in the summer and fall of 1994 further demonstrated South Korean unease with the direct negotiation process. Such a channel—in parallel with regular reporting channels to South Korean counterparts—was deemed by U.S. negotiators as inefficient and an imposition, with the result that the high-level South Korean ambassador felt snubbed at the same time that American negotiators were showing hospitality to their North Korean counterparts: the "enemy." Despite a thorough reporting mechanism that included reporting channels directly to the Korean embassy in Washington and through the U.S. embassy in Seoul immediately following each negotiating session, South Korean discomfort at being outside the room could not be alleviated, and many U.S. negotiators came to the conclusion that no consultative mechanism could serve to wholly reassure South Koreans that their interests were being represented fully in the U.S.–North Korean negotiations. "There was a sense of feeling left out," said National Assemblyman Yang Sung Chul of the negotiating process. According to former ambassador Hyun Hong Choo, "We think that as Koreans, we can read their minds a little better" than Americans, who bring an incomplete set of mismatching cultural baggage to negotiations with the North.[22]

South Korean insistence on restoration of North-South dialogue before the Geneva negotiations could proceed underscored South Korean frustrations with being cut out of the process, despite top-level assurances that if faced with a choice between improved relations with North Korea and its obligations under the U.S.-ROK security alliance, the United States would without question side with South Korea. "The South kept saying the primary North Korean objective was to drive a wedge between us and the worst thing you can do is to meet with them at a higher level. We internalized that," observed Tom Hubbard, deputy assistant secretary of state for East Asia and the Pacific, underscoring the tensions stemming from the differing tactical responses of the United States and South Korea to North Korea's dual strategy.[23] The problem was that any deal the United States might propose, no matter how advantageous, would involve concessions that South Korea could not support. On the other hand, if tactics of toughness were applied, the North Korean side would respond in kind, leading to a stalemate and possible deterioration of the situation.

Perhaps the most dramatic example of U.S.-ROK differences in dealing with North Korea developed in the run-up to the Kim Young Sam–Clinton summit in Washington in November 1993. Word of internal U.S. government deliberations on possible responses to North Korea's public and private proposals for a "package solution" to the nuclear issue filtered back to Kim Young Sam during the meeting of the Asia-Pacific Economic Cooperation Group (APEC) in Seattle. These internal consultations were in their initial stages and the South Korean government had not been briefed on them, heightening Kim Young Sam's suspicions that the United States might try to cut a secret deal with North Korea and underscoring the fact that up to that point, South Korea had been kept on the sidelines of the negotiating process.

The response of Kim Young Sam—typical of a South Korean approach designed to protect its own interests even in consultations with its closest ally—was to insist on inclusion by demanding resumption of North-South talks through the exchange of special envoys as an essential element of the package approach to Pyongyang (termed the "broad-and-thorough" approach, rather than the "comprehensive" approach originally envisioned by American officials). Kim's performance on this occasion validated for American officials the observation made, in a different context, by a *Korea Times* reporter that "the real master of brinkmanship is President Kim [Young Sam], not Kim Il Sung or Kim Jong Il."[24] Rather than the reciprocity inherent in a deal-making approach that the United States had in mind, Kim Young Sam's approach emphasized conditionality: prospects for progress in negotiations with the North were conditioned on the North's willingness to meet South Korean demands for official North-South dialogue.

The details of how such an approach would be implemented were worked out by American negotiators in three months of working-level talks with North Korean counterparts in New York that resulted in a four-point document, the February 18, 1994, Agreed Conclusion between the United States and North Korea.[25] However, the implementation of the Agreed Conclusion with North Korea that came as a result of this effort, known among U.S. officials as "Super Tuesday," failed because of a clash between Seoul and Pyongyang at a meeting in Panmunjom. In response to a South Korean threat to seek sanctions, the North Korean negotiator remarked, "We are ready to respond with an eye for an eye and a war for a war. Seoul is not very far from here. If a war breaks out, Seoul will turn into a sea of fire." The American deal-making approach was again sunk by the familiar reflexive tactics of toughness, or matching behavior between North and South.[26]

American and South Korean differences in relationship to North Korea again showed themselves in the immediate response to the surprising and untimely death of North Korea's founder and only president, Kim Il Sung, on July 8, 1994. President Bill Clinton, recognizing that the United States had just initiated a sensitive negotiating process with Pyongyang in Geneva that could potentially lead to a nuclear deal with North Korea, offered condolences to the North Korean people on the loss of their leader, and Ambassador-at-Large Robert Gallucci visited the DPRK mission in Geneva and signed a book of condolences to Kim Il Sung. The gestures received criticism at home from Senate Majority Leader Robert Dole but otherwise proved to be a relatively minor political issue in Washington. However, the U.S. statement of condolence was played up in the North Korean media, emphasizing the gestures as an expression of American goodwill.

Kim Young Sam found himself in a very different position as a result of the intense South Korean domestic political reaction to Kim Il Sung as the archenemy who had invaded Seoul over four decades earlier. Despite the opening provided by Jimmy Carter for a historic North-South summit between Kim Young Sam and Kim Il Sung—originally scheduled for later that same July—Kim Young Sam followed majority public opinion, refusing to offer condolences and hunting down those South Koreans who tried to make public gestures of condolence for Kim Il Sung. In addition, the South Korean government released documents received from Soviet archives as part of the Soviet–South Korean rapprochement that clearly identified and labeled Kim Il Sung as the instigator of the Korean War, a further insult to a reeling North Korean regime. Perhaps the instinct of vituperation was simply the legacy of zero-sum competition; the North Korean opponent finally seemed to be on his knees, and the policy of the Kim Young Sam administration during subsequent months appeared to be based on assessments that Kim Il Sung's designated replacement, his son Kim Jong Il, would fail to consolidate his rule or extend control over North Korean society, leading to a political break-down for Kim Jong Il and a historic opportunity for Kim Young Sam to preside over the process of reunification. Regardless of Kim Young Sam's motive, the result was that North Korea forswore substantive dialogue with official South Korean counterparts—with the exception of quasi-official Red Cross talks to gain food assistance from the South—throughout the rest of Kim Young Sam's presidency.

The differing responses of the United States and South Korea to Kim Il Sung's death were shaped strongly by psychological, structural, and cultural responses to North Korea. The United States, as a poten-tial deal maker, took an expedient approach designed to facilitate substantive bargaining by providing North Korea with the symbolism of respect, while the core emotions that had accompanied the inter-Korean competition for decades welled up in Seoul, and the politics of revenge trumped a nascent policy supporting dialogue and possible reconciliation.

Perhaps the most dramatic expression of Seoul's fundamental dis-satisfaction with the process and approach inherent in U.S.–North Korean deal making was represented by Kim Young Sam's public dis-avowal of the deal that he and his government were supporting in con-sultations with U.S. government counterparts, including President Bill Clinton. In an extraordinary and revealing interview with the *New York Times* on October 7—as the final phase of negotiations on the Agreed Framework were beginning—Kim Young Sam expressed his concerns that the United States had shown "a lack of knowledge and an over-eagerness to compromise." "The problem is we think we know North Korea better than anyone," Kim argued. "We have spoken with North Korea more than 400 times. It didn't get us anywhere. They are not sincere. The important thing is that the United States should not be led on by the manipulations of North Korea." Emphasizing his dif-ferences with the U.S. negotiating team in Geneva, Kim argued, "If the United States wants to settle with a half-baked compromise and the media wants to describe it as a good agreement, they can. But I think it would bring more danger and peril"—an ominous and subdued hint of brinkmanship from an ally who had no choice but to accept the inevitably unsatisfactory results of a deal-making approach.[27] These comments came even as U.S. negotiators insisted on including a clause requiring North-South dialogue—the very issue that had effectively cut off prior attempts to come to a negotiated solution—as part of the Geneva Agreed Framework. Kim's outburst necessitated a redoubling of U.S. diplomatic efforts to gain reassurances that Kim and the South Korean government would back the Agreed Framework and its implementation.

The process of parallel negotiations between the United States and the two Koreas took its toll on U.S.–South Korean relations, the psychology of which suffered seriously despite the fact that de facto efforts at coordination remained more active than ever. Even if the initiation of a regular high-level dialogue on policy toward North Korea and the regular exchange of high-level visitors every six weeks to two months between Seoul and Washington provided an institutional mechanism for maintaining policy, the political fallout from differing approaches to dealing with North Korea would continue to reverberate as a source of low-level tension between Washington and Seoul over issues related to North Korea's food crisis, implementation of KEDO, and the pace of U.S.-DPRK relations in the absence of concrete steps toward North-South official dialogue, with periods of crisis requiring extraordinary consultation and negotiation between the two allies.

Even while U.S. leadership suffered the body blows of South Korean public criticism, coordination was strengthened through negotiations over implementation of the Geneva Agreed Framework, including determining how to designate the South Korean light-water reactor that would be provided to North Korea in the spring of 1995. American officials tried for months to get South Korea to take the lead in constructive public initiatives toward North Korea, including supporting Kim Young Sam's abortive proposal for Two-Plus-Two negotiations floated during President Kim's visit to Washington to dedicate the Korean War Memorial in the summer of 1995, a proposal that resurfaced in April 1996 as the joint U.S.-ROK proposal for the Four Party Talks. But when the South was in the lead, tactics of toughness predictably led to stalemate, which ultimately could be broken only through reluctant American involvement.

The submarine incident during the fall of 1996 provided the next serious test of U.S.–South Korean relations. Kim Young Sam reacted with vitriol to the North Korean submarine incursion, while the U.S. reaction was noticeably more measured. In addition to the development of a U.S. role in buffering the reactions of the two Koreas and mediating the eventual resolution of the crisis between North and South Korea, the submarine crisis and Kim Young Sam's reaction to it required a full-scale high-level diplomatic mobilization effort—culminating in a Kim-Clinton bilateral meeting at an APEC gathering in Manila in November. The purpose of this effort was to gain top-level assurances that South Korea would not overreact to the incursion through military confrontation or do anything to risk the Geneva Agreed Framework. The Framework was vulnerable to failure if South Korea failed to cooperate with obligations being carried out through KEDO.

Although the United States was able to hold together the Agreed Framework by brokering negotiations over a North Korean statement of regret, and even was able to pave the way for North Korean participation in the Four Party Talks first proposed by Presidents Clinton and Kim Young Sam in April 1995, the fallout from the tense atmosphere surrounding consultations between the United States and South Korea was clear. The mood was characterized by anonymous statements to the *New York Times* by State Department officials in the midst of the submarine crisis that dealing with South Korea was a "headache," followed by innumerable vituperations and countercharges in Seoul. Although the official mechanisms of coordination had never been more integrated, the psychological and cultural differences in strategy and tactics on how to deal with North Korea were clearly a sore point in U.S.-ROK relations. These differences stemmed from deep psychological and cultural factors and set a tone of tension and reluctant cooperation in which the institutional machinery of the alliance relationship continued to function. South Korean tactics wore down U.S. counterparts on many issues and probably served to put a brake on the pace of U.S. diplomacy toward North Korea, but at the cost of irritation and a surprising loss of goodwill among many of those officials who were responsible for working most closely with South Korean allies on a day-to-day basis.

Even in the context of an extraordinary close alliance relationship in which key security interests were put to the test, the fallout from the respective tactics and approach of American Shopkeepers and South Korean Warriors in dealing with the problem of North Korea is clear. One mechanism that grew out of this collaboration was the creation of an international organization including U.S., South Korean, and Japanese staff members that was responsible for implementing the provisions of the Geneva Agreed Framework and for carrying out an unprecedented light-water reactor construction project that would test traditional political and ideological bounds for cooperation—both between North and South Korea and between North Korea and the international community. We now turn to an assessment of negotiations between North Korea and the Korean Peninsula Energy Development Organization.

5

The U.S. Negotiating Experience Compared with KEDO

The Geneva Agreed Framework laid the basis for an eventual resolution of concerns about North Korea's nuclear program and provided a path for North Korea to rejoin the Nuclear Non-Proliferation Treaty. It also mandated the creation of a new type of international organization, called the Korean Peninsula Energy Development Organization (KEDO), to implement the terms of the Geneva Agreed Framework, including provision of heavy fuel oil to, and construction of light-water reactors in, North Korea. The foremost task of KEDO was to engage in additional negotiations with North Korea to determine the terms by which two 1,000-megawatt light-water reactors would be constructed in North Korea. The outstanding question as negotiations opened in the fall of 1995 was whether the DPRK government would accept an international organization such as KEDO, whose staff included South Korean and Japanese employees. The primary concern was whether North Korea might attempt to go "over the head" of KEDO and return to a strictly bilateral negotiating framework with the United States, excluding South Korean and Japanese participation in the negotiating process.

KEDO's board of directors is composed of representatives from the governments of the United States, South Korea, and Japan.[1] The first American executive director, Stephen Bosworth, and South Korean and Japanese deputies, Choi Young Jin and Itaru Umezu, assembled an organization consisting of about thirty American, Japanese, and South Korean staff to implement the arduous parallel processes of negotiating a supply contract with the DPRK while simultaneously negotiating arrangements for the construction of a South Korean–style light-water reactor (LWR) with the Korean Electrical Power Company (KEPCO). KEDO was also responsible for delivering 500,000 tons of heavy fuel oil (HFO) per year as stipulated in the Geneva Agreed Framework. The decision-making process of KEDO is consensual, requiring the assent of each of the governments represented on the board of directors before action is taken on specific issues.

The KEDO experience with North Korea provides an excellent comparative example for testing patterns in North Korea's negotiating behavior in bilateral negotiations with the United States, explored in chapters 2 and 3, and in examining the differences in North Korean negotiating style between bilateral and multilateral negotiating contexts, particularly in situations where South Korean negotiators are involved. The composition of KEDO and the nature of its organizational mission provide a comparative context for analyzing North Korean negotiating patterns, revealing notable similarities and differences in North Korea's negotiating approach and presenting useful lessons based on North Korea's dealings with American, Japanese, and South Korean representatives of KEDO.

THE GENEVA AGREED FRAMEWORK: CONTEXT FOR KEDO-DPRK NEGOTIATIONS

The Geneva Agreed Framework spelled out a series of simultaneous reciprocal steps by each side to resolve the North Korean nuclear issue, but it was simply a road map (or framework) projecting the sequence and timing of agreed-upon future actions, not a binding set of contractual commitments or treaty responsibilities. The success of the Agreed Framework depends on two critical elements: (1) the willingness of the DPRK to honor its agreements in principle through implementation of a project requiring South Korea's involvement as the central actor, and (2) the cooperation of South Korea, Japan, and the United States and other countries to support the establishment and operation of KEDO in fulfilling the terms of the Agreed Framework.

The nature of South Korea's central role in the supply of a light-water reactor to North Korea immediately became a key stumbling block following the signing of the Agreed Framework, requiring eight months of subsequent on-again, off-again negotiations between the United States and North Korea in Berlin and Kuala Lumpur. The simultaneous achievement of the June 14, 1995, agreement in Kuala Lumpur and the formal establishment of KEDO in Seoul among the United States, Korea, and Japan were major turning points that allowed implementation of the Agreed Framework to proceed.

For North and South Korea, KEDO became a bridge for achieving compromise on the technical issues of the LWR project while allowing direct interaction between two parties with a historical and psychological legacy of extreme reluctance to compromise (a zero-sum negotiating approach). KEDO also became the only active and regular vehicle for North-South contact following the vitriolic North Korean reaction to President Kim Young Sam's refusal to offer condolences upon the 1994 death of Kim Il Sung. Although KEDO was never intended as a viable channel for political dialogue between North and South Korea, it did represent the single area of sustained technical cooperation and contact between North and South Korea throughout the second half of the Kim Young Sam administration. The accomplishments of KEDO in this regard led South Korean KEDO deputy director Choi Young Jin to propose that the KEDO model of "camouflaged inter-Korean dialogue" should be applied to other venues, including the April 1996 joint proposal for the Four Party Talks issued by President Kim Young Sam and President Bill Clinton.[2]

In addition, the compromise crafted in Kuala Lumpur and Seoul on June 14 marked the inauguration of several parallel negotiating processes: internally among the South Korean, U.S., and Japanese governments and between KEDO and its various contractors including KEPCO; and externally between KEDO (the officially designated channel for LWR negotiations) and North Korea.[3]

SUPPLY CONTRACT NEGOTIATIONS:
NORTH KOREAN TESTS OF KEDO'S VIABILITY

As KEDO assumed responsibility for negotiating with North Korean representatives to implement the Agreed Framework, there was no assurance that the North Koreans would accept their new negotiating counterparts at KEDO, which no longer consisted only of American diplomats but also included South Korean and Japanese representatives. Although the DPRK had explicitly recognized KEDO in the Kuala Lumpur agreement, it was not clear until the conclusion of supply contract negotiations in December 1995 whether the North would honor KEDO as an independent negotiating counterpart or attempt to renew direct negotiations with the United States. Tactics of delay intended to avoid commitments already made in the U.S.-DPRK negotiations were, frankly, precisely the worst-case behavior that the new KEDO negotiating team expected from North Korean counterparts as they girded themselves for "North Korean obstinacy," about which American officials involved in the Geneva negotiations had warned.

The DPRK's initial probing of KEDO's organizational allegiances did not bode well for a smooth negotiation with Pyongyang. A month after the conclusion of the Kuala Lumpur agreement and the formal establishment of KEDO, newly appointed KEDO executive director Stephen Bosworth made known his desire to visit Pyongyang with his deputies for discussions on the LWR project. North Korean authorities responded with an invitation only to Bosworth, excluding his Japanese and South Korean deputies. If Bosworth had visited Pyongyang unaccompanied by his two deputies, the visit would have been perceived as a return to the old U.S.-DPRK negotiating pattern of going around South Korean and Japanese counterparts, the principal element of South Korean criticism regarding the Geneva negotiations. Bosworth refused the invitation. Subsequent North Korean testing of KEDO involved the venue for negotiations, the composition of delegations, and who would pay the travel costs for North Korean negotiators to the meeting. Bosworth resisted these initial North Korean prenegotiation demands, no doubt designed to probe for potential weaknesses or opportunities for unilateral concessions.

The first meeting was scheduled for September 1995 in Kuala Lumpur.

Ambassador Bosworth began his first round of negotiations with an organizational structure in formation, with no permanent office space, and keenly aware of the potential challenges of harmonizing the differing perspectives and interests of the United States, Japan, and South Korea toward the North Korean nuclear issue. The United States emphasized maintenance of regional stability and the importance of halting nuclear proliferation. Japan was concerned with regional security, but a consensus did not exist with regard to the extent to which Japanese financial support might be called upon to help stop North Korea's nuclear capability. Policymakers in Seoul remained inexorably divided over whether to "squeeze" or "please" North Korea.[4]

With an organization composed of staff with a mix of international experience—including Japanese and Korean staff on loan from career government service who had their own past reporting relationships to their respective governments—KEDO faced the major challenge of building a united organizational culture. Bosworth emphasized that officials who joined KEDO were no longer working directly for their respective governments but had now joined an organization that had its own independent purposes separate from the political objectives of the respective governments on the board of directors. He emphasized to representatives of the South Korean and Japanese governments during his initial visit to Seoul and Tokyo that as a KEDO official, he did not represent U.S. views. He went out of his way to negotiate certain concessions of particular symbolic significance in Seoul early in supply contract negotiations with the DPRK. He even subtly emphasized his independence from the United States linguistically, calling his new organization *kay-do*, in contrast to *kee-do*, the pronunciation of choice among representatives of the U.S. government. By setting an example of independence from Washington, Bosworth implicitly encouraged other KEDO staff to think and act consistently with the interests of their new organization instead of simply representing views of their home government. To further emphasize the point, baseball caps with the KEDO logo were presented to new KEDO staff, a tangible manifestation of the fact that coming to work in New York,

American, Japanese, and South Korean officials were now part of "the KEDO team."

Following an exchange of initial positions in Kuala Lumpur during the initial week of negotiations, the KEDO-DPRK negotiations reconvened in earnest in New York in early October. It quickly became clear that the supply contract negotiations would not be completed by the Agreed Framework first-anniversary target date for completion (October 21, 1995) originally set by the North Korean side. Throughout the initial stages of the negotiations, it was not clear to the KEDO negotiating team whether the North Korean negotiating team had come to negotiate or to stall, as the North Koreans initially presented a very rigid negotiating stance in the talks. Then, Ambassador Ho Jong suddenly withdrew four intractable issues that had stymied initial stages of the negotiations, showing a softer approach that signaled the DPRK's willingness to pursue a successful negotiation. According to one senior KEDO official, "he swept them off the table," and it became clear that the North Korean side would make a deal.[5] However, until the moment those issues disappeared, it was difficult for KEDO officials to discern the "true position," or bottom line, of the North Korean team.

One notable aspect of the KEDO negotiations is that while initial North Korean predispositions toward the use of brinkmanship, crisis diplomacy, and use of time deadlines remained quite strong, some of North Korea's strongest and most vitriolic threats were muted compared with the decibel level U.S. officials had been accustomed to in previous negotiations. For instance, threats to refuel the 5-megawatt experimental reactor at the center of the 1994 crisis dissipated as KEDO negotiations progressed, perhaps because the ineffectiveness of such threats grew increasingly apparent and perhaps because as benefits began to accrue from the project and HFO deliveries began to arrive in North Korea, Pyongyang for the first time had something concrete to lose in negotiations, namely, critically needed energy supplies. As a result, use of brinkmanship became a less effective and riskier strategy.

The most difficult issue in the supply contract negotiations was whether KEDO would make concessions on the issue of who would be responsible for connecting the LWRs to North Korea's domestic power grid. The South Korean press initially focused on this issue, forecasting that the North Korean negotiators would demand an upgraded power grid and other add-ons that might increase estimated project costs by as much as $1 billion. These reports pressured KEDO negotiators not to make undue concessions and raised their concern about the possibility of a breakdown in negotiations; however, North Korean brinkmanship during the supply contract negotiations was muted in comparison with the high-volume vitriol of public pronouncements accompanying the Geneva negotiations. In fact, the DPRK starting position in the KEDO negotiations was actually considerably less than the $1 billion projected in the South Korean press. The question of how the grid might be connected to the power plant remained unsettled (and a matter unrelated to KEDO's mandate, according to KEDO staff); this issue was effectively "kicked down the road" in order to avoid a stalemate in the negotiation and implementation process. In the initial stages, KEDO held the line on concessions to North Korea, agreeing only to give in on incidental expenditures such as those directly related to LWR plant site preparation (amounting to less than $100 million).

The other major issue in supply contract negotiations was the question of terms of repayment, which the North Korean side insisted be included as part of the contract to underscore that the LWRs were not a "gift" but rather were built as part of a commercial transaction between North Korea and KEDO. This position emphasized the principle of reciprocity and underscored North Korea's ideological principle of self-reliance. This negotiation was also necessary because Japanese legal regulations required that the LWR supply arrangement be in the form of a loan to ensure that the government of Japan would be able to contribute to the project. According to KEDO officials, the repayment issue was a good example of a situation in which North Korean negotiators appeared to knowingly sacrifice the possibility of additional substantive concessions on financing to cut a deal that would avoid symbolic concessions to Seoul unacceptable to the Pyongyang leadership. The terms of repayment—in which North Korea is obligated to repay LWR construction costs over twenty years following the completion of the reactors—delay payment sufficiently that even if the terms of repayment are fully honored, the amount paid will represent only one-quarter of the real cost of constructing the reactors, initially estimated to be about $4 billion.[6]

To head off North Korean stalling and to avoid brinkmanship on every single issue, Ambassador Bosworth and the KEDO staff decided early in the negotiating process that the supply agreement would be as comprehensive as possible and would lay the foundation for subsequent negotiations on specific components of the project. By initially taking a comprehensive approach designed to eliminate issue-by-issue haggling, Ambassador Bosworth followed the "package solution" approach of the Agreed Framework. This approach had the effect of building on commitments already made by the North Koreans in the Agreed Framework, but at a more specific level of detail. The supply agreement became an elaborate framework for a much more intensive and prolonged process of protocol negotiations on a wide range of technical issues, including site and services for the project, privileges and immunities for KEDO personnel, methods and types of transportation to and from the project site, and protocols on training and safety, among others.

In fact, as the supply contract negotiations became more difficult, it became apparent that the minimum gesture by KEDO required to keep the North Korean team at the negotiating table was the continuation of the flow of HFO, an obligation of the United States under the Agreed Framework. The provision of HFO has taken on a political significance beyond its utility as a resource to meet North Korean energy needs. After all, the form of HFO supplied to North Korea was useful only in selected power plants and could contribute to only a small portion of North Korea's overall energy sector. Other supplies besides HFO would have been much more cost-efficient in providing energy to meet North Korea's national requirements.[7] HFO deliveries became the critical symbol of KEDO's bona fides and, by extension, of the sincerity of the United States in honoring commitments made in the Geneva Agreed Framework. By July 1996 it was necessary to expand deliveries to Nam'po for delivery to a second HFO-consuming plant near Pyongyang.[8] The North Koreans also dug a giant hole in the ground near Sonbong in order to take deliveries of the HFO that had been promised under the Agreed Framework.[9]

Agreement in supply contract negotiations was finally reached in mid-December. The delays from the late October target date set by the North Koreans for conclusion of negotiations were attributable in part to the technical complexities of the negotiations, in which the North Korean delegates had little if any prior experience or understanding to guide them.[10] In essence, KEDO negotiating teams had to walk the North Korean delegation through most of the technical details and explain why various mechanisms were necessary before a negotiation process could proceed. A second factor in the delay was that management of internal consultations between KEDO and the South Korean, Japanese, and U.S. governments took longer than anticipated. Finally, the "extreme sensitivity" of the North Korean side on issues involving North-South relations would repeatedly prove to be a stumbling block in managing the KEDO negotiation process.

CHARACTERISTICS OF PROTOCOL NEGOTIATIONS

Initiation of protocol negotiations pursuant to the supply contract started a process between KEDO and North Korea with a similar dynamic in each phase: an initial education phase in which KEDO officials explained the technical basis and reasons for the protocol under negotiation; evaluation by DPRK officials to understand and present the specific issues involved to the leadership in Pyongyang; stalling, waiting, and lack of progress while DPRK negotiators sought additional concessions (and proved to the leadership in Pyongyang that they had reached the KEDO bottom line); and eventual capitulation to KEDO positions.

The technical nature of the supply contract and protocols and the nature of KEDO as an international organization that had to develop an internal consensus were the two major new factors in the negotiating process. The changed dynamic of the negotiation process—now in essence an exercise with a strong multilateral component—diminished cultural influences as an independent variable, although muted expressions of now familiar North Korean tactics were still predictable components of the negotiating process.

The internal negotiation process in which the South Korean, Japanese, and U.S. governments signed off on negotiating positions formed within KEDO yielded a lowest-common-denominator position since consensus was necessary before KEDO could go forward with any substantive initiative. While one government might exert a veto power over the others by stalling or preventing compromise on particular initiatives, the practical constraint of needing the support of others to keep the process moving forward encouraged cooperation and lessened intransigence.

If a single government made demands that the other governments found too rigid, the whole process would grind to a halt until the inflexible position was changed or other governments agreed to accept the more extreme negotiating position. In some cases, the extreme negotiating position might be adopted but then revised after it became clear that such a strategy would be rejected out of hand by the North. KEDO staff report that such differences have been over tactical approaches, with the United States generally driving for a more flexible process and South Korea arguing for a more rigid tactical one to deny undue concessions to the North. Japanese members of KEDO argue that they have often found themselves in a mediating position, able to subtly smooth rough edges from American or South Korean positions and tilt the scales of compromise to shape a consensus. On occasion, for instance, American staff members of KEDO have felt that the ROK was simply "using KEDO in order to stick its finger in the eye" of the North Koreans by cloaking a South Korean position on a particular issue for negotiation in a KEDO context. Another KEDO staff member, explaining the challenge of the KEDO-DPRK protocol negotiations, notes that "multilateral talks take into account the national interests of four countries that are all mixed up—all of these must be satisfied (not completely but to a certain extent)" for the negotiations to go forward.[11]

KEDO staff describe the internal negotiation of consensus as "difficult," "painstaking," and "requiring patience, time, and good negotiating skills." On the other hand, one KEDO member pointed to the combined strengths melded within KEDO by its mixed international composition: "The United States brings creativity, the ROK brings insight of North Korea's soul, and Japan brings a precise examination of each issue, or meticulousness" to the negotiation and implementation process.[12] In many respects, the process of achieving compromise within KEDO was at least as difficult as negotiating with North Korean counterparts. One result is that KEDO positions, once formulated, have been difficult to change, inhibiting the possibility of concessions and severely limiting the negotiating flexibility of KEDO representatives.

On the North Korean side, the major change in the supply contract and protocol negotiations was the need to field mixed-composition delegations drawing from different ministries and specialized units within the North Korean bureaucracy. While foreign ministry officials remained involved and retained overall control of the process at almost every stage of the protocol negotiation, there were clearly discernible differences in perspective among representatives of different North Korean ministries.[13] As protocol negotiations proceeded, it also became clear that there was a limited pool of officials and technical specialists on the North Korean side with the requisite understanding and experience to engage in technical negotiations, with the result that education became a necessary part of the protocol negotiation process.[14]

Two additional developments probably influenced North Korean strategy and tactics during the protocol negotiations in 1996 and 1997. First, severe flooding in the summer of 1995 had revealed clearly North Korea's structural inability to feed its own people, transforming the image of North Korea as a dangerous and potentially lethal country during the Geneva negotiations to that of a country in inexorable economic decline. There was increasing speculation that North Korean political control might not be sustained and that North Korea could become a failed state. Such images served to undermine the credibility of North Korean attempts to employ brinkmanship in the KEDO negotiations. Second, with the signing of the Geneva Agreed Framework and the delivery of HFO, North Korea for the first time had something to lose in the event that negotiations did not succeed. The specter of failure at the negotiation table finally weighed more heavily on the North Korean side than it did on the West.

Even so, KEDO negotiators discovered that their counterparts were remarkably resistant to the realities of the relative power relationships between KEDO and North Korea and showed "total insensitivity" to changed power relationships stemming from their own vulnerability. Although North Korean negotiators could no longer credibly wield the threat of an active nuclear program, they were not noticeably more flexible despite their relatively weak negotiating position. When it became clear, however, that the only deal possible on many issues in protocol negotiations was the one presented by KEDO, North Korean negotiators accepted the terms of the protocols rather than walking away or returning home empty-handed. The political decisions in Pyongyang to support the Agreed Framework had already been made. Absent a wholesale reversal at the highest levels, it seemed that while North Korean negotiating teams had to stay in New York long enough to demonstrate their toughness as negotiators, no North Korean negotiator was free to return home without claiming to have removed obstacles to improved U.S.-DPRK relations by making progress on the LWR project.

Indeed, during some protocol negotiations North Korea made remarkable concessions that went far beyond what KEDO staff themselves expected, including on sensitive issues related to North Korea's sovereignty. For instance, the KEDO negotiating team got more than expected in negotiating rights of limited extraterritoriality for KEDO staff and subcontractors in North Korea and was able to negotiate unprecedented levels of access in negotiations over telecommunications and transportation access to the KEDO work site. Now that these precedents have been established, they might be a starting point for negotiation of future arrangements by multinational companies willing to take the risk of mounting infrastructure and other project investments in North Korea.

The multilateral composition of KEDO appears to have made the negotiating process more difficult for the North Korean negotiating team, which was less able to take advantage of internal differences within KEDO among the U.S., Japanese, and South Korean governments on particular issues. "The North Koreans do not understand how hard it is for us to put something on the table" and have "no clue about the massive internal battles" that must be settled before KEDO even gets to the negotiating table, according to one KEDO staff member.[15] North Korean officials have often angrily attributed KEDO's inflexible positions—accurately or not—to the "problems" or "position of a concerned government," a not-so-veiled reference to the South Korean government being the major stumbling block to the resolution of agreements on more favorable terms. On the other hand, the political imperative to show progress has possibly induced some North Korean negotiators to make concessions on issues that might normally have taken longer to settle.

A variety of approaches have been taken within KEDO regarding the use of sidebar discussions between the American head of delegation and his North Korean counterpart. One advantage of meetings between the senior American and North Korean officials is that they may facilitate early agreement because the North Korean side may interpret what is conveyed in such meetings as the bottom-line position of the KEDO side. In supply contract negotiations, Ambassador Bosworth used private meetings with his counterpart, Ambassador Ho Jong, to develop a "relationship of confidence" and to signal in advance various KEDO positions that might be introduced into the formal negotiations. As the relationship developed, Ambassador Ho reciprocated.

The disadvantage of having such discussions in a KEDO context is that they fall back into the pattern of bilateral exchange between the United States and North Korea and may raise suspicions regarding whether the American negotiator may naively concede prematurely to North Korean demands. If an American head of a delegation has developed a close relationship with senior South Korean colleagues in KEDO, such questions may be overcome by careful precoordination and assurance that there are no "surprises" following one-on-one consultations with North Korean counterparts. In the absence of such a relationship, avoidance of sidebar conversations unless absolutely necessary has assisted in preserving transparency and maintaining harmony on the KEDO side of the negotiating table, even if it means that negotiations have taken longer to conclude.

Another benefit of protocol negotiations is that the volume and the level of technical detail in the negotiations have required direct interaction between North and South Korean members of KEDO, including as direct counterparts leading certain negotiations. At certain working-level negotiating sessions, explanatory phases of negotiations were conducted in Korean as a matter of efficiency, facilitating direct interaction between North and South Korean representatives. Subsequently, limited American manpower on the KEDO staff made it impossible for negotiations to proceed at certain points with an American as head delegate present at every moment of the protocol negotiation process. This situation was initially resisted strongly by North Korean negotiators, who emphasized that the LWR project was agreed to by the United States and North Korea. After initial protests, the North Korean side accepted subgroup negotiations on certain issues with South Korean counterparts as a practical necessity. Most notably, Deputy Director Choi Young Jin effectively led negotiations in North Korea on transportation protocols with his North Korean counterpart, Chang Chong U.

The multilateral structure of the KEDO negotiation and new constraints on North Korean brinkmanship created by North Korea's own recognition of the necessity of compromise have, according to KEDO negotiators, made cultural patterns less of a variable than personality, environment, and institutional structure in protocol negotiations. Deputy Director Choi Young Jin and Chang Chong U were able to develop a positive working relationship despite the structural impediments of North-South relations, thanks to cultural similarities and the personalities and skills of the two individuals.

According to South Koreans on the KEDO negotiating team, it was possible for South Korean staff of KEDO to build friendly relationships with their counterparts as part of a process of trust building through KEDO, although considerable mistrust remained in the context of formal negotiations. In some cases, personality clashes and bureaucratic politics have been the primary obstacles to progress; that is, the negotiator—or the staff in respective countries responsible for managing the KEDO issue—felt that a show of toughness would enhance one's position within the bureaucracy. Perhaps the most interesting new variable in the KEDO experience has been that a series of negotiations was conducted with North Koreans in North Korea, where by most accounts the North Korean negotiating team appeared to feel more relaxed and self-confident. However, many concessions made in initial negotiating sessions in Pyongyang were taken back and renegotiated during subsequent rounds of negotiations in New York.

THE SUBMARINE INCIDENT: TEST OF KEDO'S SURVIVABILITY

The Achilles heel of KEDO and, by extension, of the Geneva Agreed Framework has been the possibility that external political conditions might not allow the intensive cooperation necessary to build two light-water reactors in North Korea. This is why one initial argument in support of the Agreed Framework was that implementation would facilitate real interaction between North and South Korea and thus could be used as an instrument for cooperation, exchange, and reconciliation between North and South Korea.[16] In other words, political dialogue between North and South Korea would be an inevitable component of implementation of the Agreed Framework.

On September 18, 1996, KEDO's survivability in the face of increased confrontation between North and South Korea was tested when a taxi driver discovered a North Korean submarine that had been grounded on a failed spying mission to the South. The bodies of eleven of the crew members among the twenty-six North Korean intruders were found on the scene. They had been executed on the spot by trained commandos onboard. One intruder, Yi Kwang Su, was apprehended and interrogated; he broke down, confessing details of the mission after having drunk four bottles of *soju,* a Korean liquor. Fourteen commandos remained at large, presumably on their way back to North Korea by foot.

The submarine incident became a major political trauma in Seoul, as tens of thousands of South Korean troops were mobilized to search the region near the beached submarine for escaped North Korean commandos, who had been trained for survival in the face of hostile conditions. A dragnet consisting of over 60,000 South Korean soldiers was mobilized to search for the missing commandos. The incident was magnified by South Korean president Kim Young Sam's political rhetoric, which stressed the need for retribution against the North. North Korea attempted to defuse the incident through a combination of vague public admissions of submarine activity (but not of guilt for conducting espionage) and quiet diplomacy with the United States through discussions between America desk director Ri Hyong Chol and counterparts at the U.S. State Department during an October visit to Washington.[17]

As frustration built in Seoul during a nearly monthlong manhunt for a handful of missing North Korean commandos, Kim Young Sam's calls for retaliation included a freeze on KEDO activities. Although KEDO never suspended its own engagement process with the DPRK and HFO deliveries continued throughout the incident, a freeze of KEDO activities was among the various reprisal methods at the disposal of the South Korean government. In fact, the submarine incident occurred at the same time that a DPRK negotiating team was in New York for site-and-services protocol negotiations. Initially, the incident had little effect on the negotiations themselves, which proceeded without interruption. The North Korean side even appeared to have hastened the conclusion of negotiations following the submarine incident, and the site-and-services protocol was initialed about a week after the submarine incident occurred, but before the escalation of tensions and public threats between the two Koreas.

KEDO officials tried to prevent erosion of progress in implementing the project in a very difficult and tense environment. President Kim Young Sam threatened to halt KEDO operations and Assistant Secretary of State for East Asia and the Pacific Winston Lord, on a visit to Seoul, declared a "pause" in the implementation of the KEDO project. It was decided that the last of the site survey teams, whose job was to determine the site of the LWR, could not travel north in such a tense atmosphere for fear of possible reprisals, even if these individuals (most of whom were ROK citizens) were visiting North Korea under KEDO auspices. The atmosphere of tension in Seoul demonstrated clearly KEDO's dependence on a stable and cooperative environment between North and South Korea. As confrontation escalated, it was increasingly difficult for KEDO to carry out activities with North Korea.

In response, the level of North Korean propaganda escalated, with public threats to unfreeze its nuclear activities and a decision to halt progress in the canning of spent fuel at Yongbyŏn under the supervision of contractors working for the Department of Energy. This action represented a first step toward undermining the Agreed Framework and was viewed with concern among officials in Washington, who worried that the nuclear agreement with North Korea might unravel.

A major focus of the United States during the period of the submarine incident was to isolate the Geneva Agreed Framework—and by extension KEDO—from the worsening cycle of political confrontation between North and South Korea. The APEC meeting in Manila in November 1996 provided an opportunity for President Clinton to underscore directly with President Kim Young Sam the importance of keeping the Agreed Framework in place while managing political tensions between North and South Korea. Specifically, U.S. officials worried that the ROK might even consider military action against the North in retaliation for the submarine incursion without prior consultations, possibly drawing the United States unwillingly into the conflict. In view of Kim Young Sam's increasingly belligerent political statements before the Manila summit, the South Korean press noted that the press release following the bilateral meeting between Kim and Clinton emphasized U.S. priorities, taking a half-step back from Kim's hard-line demands for an unequivocal apology from North Korea— demands that were widely viewed as unachievable given North Korean pride and obstinacy. Following the APEC summit meeting between Clinton and Kim, U.S. briefers including Assistant Secretary Lord emphasized the importance of a North Korean "gesture" of regret for the incident, suggesting that the bar was lower than what Kim Young Sam's earlier political rhetoric had implied.

Immediately following the Clinton-Kim summit, Congressman Bill Richardson visited Pyongyang for the purpose of retrieving Evan Hunziger, a young American who had been captured by North Korea as a spy after swimming across the Yalu River as part of his own personal missionary effort to save North Korea. Hunziger had been held in North Korean custody since August, and Richardson's visit to procure his release provided a pretext for removing this issue as an obstacle in U.S.–North Korean relations. It was also an opportunity to informally reaffirm the U.S. desire to continue a negotiation process initiated during Ri Hyong Chol's October visit to New York for meetings with U.S. officials. During the October meetings, Ri had hinted at the possibility of a North Korean statement of regret for the submarine incursion, offering a potential exit from the atmosphere of tension. The problem then became deciding on the form of statement that would be politically acceptable to Seoul.

During the first three weeks of December, U.S. negotiators met with North Korean counterparts in a proxy negotiation designed to pacify South Korean outrage at the incursion. During almost a dozen sessions, American and North Korean officials determined the strength of the statement of regret, to whom it would be directed, and how it would be disseminated. Throughout the negotiation, the critical decisions regarding what would constitute a satisfactory statement were made in Seoul. In the end, the begrudging public admission of regret —issued through KCNA's foreign broadcast and sandwiched on either side by a torrent of slander against Kim Young Sam—was touted as unexpectedly forthcoming. It was compared with Kim Il Sung's personal statements of regret following the 1976 axe murder incident at Panmunjom. The North Korean statement effectively broke the Gordian knot of tension between North and South and paved the way for North Korea's acceptance of a joint briefing with the United States and South Korea regarding the Four Party Talks proposal. It also removed political obstacles to a response to North Korea's food crisis by both South Korea and the United States. Shortly after the North Korean statement was issued, Ambassador Ho Jong traveled to New York to sign the site-and-services protocol, and the normal pace of KEDO operations and interaction with North Korea was immediately resumed.

The submarine incident demonstrated the vulnerability of the KEDO operation during periods of high political tensions between the two Koreas. One result of the crisis was that it provided a clear rationale for pursuing contacts on the fundamental issue of replacing the armistice with a more permanent peace mechanism. This was the primary objective of the Four Party Talks that had been proposed by Presidents Kim and Clinton in April 1996. A powerful political motivation thus lay behind U.S. diplomacy on the Korean Peninsula throughout 1997, the focus of which was to entice North Korea into accepting the Four Party Talks proposal. Without progress in a political dialogue on tension reduction such as that promised through the Four

Party process, the Geneva Agreed Framework and KEDO would not be sustained.

GROUNDBREAKING: A SHIFT TO INTERNAL
NEGOTIATIONS WITHIN KEDO

The August 1997 groundbreaking for the LWR project in Sinp'o, North Korea, attended by official representatives from Pyongyang and KEDO member countries and by KEDO's senior staff, marked a major turning point in KEDO's implementation of the LWR project. After two years of negotiation over a supply contract and protocols, KEDO had finally reached the construction phase of the reactor project. This phase would include visits to the North by hundreds of South Korean contractors to work on the project and the initiation of a significant level of economic exchange through the LWR construction effort. And North Korean officials had tangible evidence that KEDO really did intend to build a light-water reactor as promised in the Agreed Framework.

In statements at the groundbreaking ceremony, representatives from KEDO and the DPRK marked the progress that had already been made through the negotiation process, even before the initiation of the "physical implementation phase" of the project. Ambassador Ho Jong emphasized that the project can progress "only when it is free from being misused for unjust political purposes in any case"—a reference to the political tensions caused by the submarine incident —and "particularly when the principle of simultaneous actions agreed between the DPRK and the U.S. is strictly adhered to."[18] Likewise, Ambassador Bosworth emphasized the establishment of a "business-like and professional relationship based on principles of mutual respect and reciprocity."[19] The senior representative of the ROK government, Chang Sun Sop, declared that the project was "a kind of test or touchstone to know if the two divided Koreas can work together."[20]

Groundbreaking for the LWR represented a shift in KEDO's work in two fundamental aspects. The negotiations had finally moved from the negotiation of promises in principle to real implementation of contractual obligations consistent with supply contract and protocol agreements. The negotiation of a formula for delivery of the LWR was over, and the on-the-ground implementation of contractual obligations—accompanied of course by additional bargaining—had begun. Second, with the implementation stage of the KEDO project the focus of KEDO shifted from developing a negotiation strategy to deal with North Korea to the imperative of managing internal negotiations on how to divide a fixed pie—the shares of financial burdens that would be assigned to the respective governments and contractual opportunities that would be assigned to the companies involved. Management of these parallel processes has been the primary challenge facing KEDO in the post-groundbreaking stage of its existence.

Groundbreaking also marked a subtle shift in views of time as they affected the KEDO project. Until groundbreaking had actually occurred, the view of some South Korean representatives of KEDO was that "time is on KEDO's side. Seoul's approach is that if we can't have what we want, OK."[21] However, after site work had begun, cost and wage pressures, compensation for missed schedules, and delays imposed concrete burdens on KEDO, fostering the perception that KEDO would lose leverage in negotiations. South Korean efforts to settle all possible protocol issues in KEDO before actually engaging in the groundbreaking process were an attempt to bolster KEDO in a strategy of negotiating from a position of strength.

Initial implementation of the KEDO project also demonstrates North Korean sensitivity to time pressures. In particular, North Korean authorities moved quickly and cooperatively to settle an incident early in the LWR construction process in which South Korean construction workers threw away a newspaper with a picture of Kim Jong Il, a criminal act under the political system in the DPRK. Local North Korean public security officials halted all work at the project site and demanded an apology from South Korean workers following the discovery of the incident, taking it as an affront to the North Korean political system and its top leadership. However, KEDO officials were quickly able to work out this problem with negotiating counterparts from the foreign ministry in charge of managing relations with KEDO, suggesting that the North Korean political leadership was also sensitive to the costs of prolonged delays in the implementation of the project. The incident also demonstrated the cultural differences between the South Kore-ans, who felt that the issue had been blown severely out of proportion, and the North Koreans, who are quick to respond to even an unin-tended affront to the Dear Leader.

KEDO has been beset by a number of drawbacks that have limited its performance as a negotiating counterpart to North Korea. The primary drawback has been that KEDO remains subject to political influences from the consultative process and relationships that exist between Pyongyang and Seoul, Tokyo, and Washington, respectively. The clearest evidence that KEDO is not immune from politics is the submarine incident, which threatened to derail the entire process of implementing the Geneva Agreed Framework and effectively halted most KEDO implementation activities. However, other bureaucratic issues under the surface have also threatened to interfere with KEDO's implementation process.

Another source of frustration in KEDO's negotiating process has been the unequal emphasis on priority of decisions and level of atten-tion paid by the respective governments in Seoul, Tokyo, and Wash-ington. The bureaucratic process of coordinating policy positions among the governments (now including the European Union) has been inordinately slow. On occasion, the KEDO decision-making process has been stalled by bureaucratic inattention or wrangling during consultations with governments in Seoul, Tokyo, and Wash-ington. In Tokyo, KEDO decisions may suffer from a bloated bureau-cratic process requiring too many approvals from disparate agencies within the government. In Seoul, overattention to KEDO tactics on a day-to-day level has slowed responses on various issues. In Washing-ton, the problem is bureaucratic inattention by high-level officials with the power to push forward the process, manage heavy fund-raising burdens, and defend KEDO funding from rear-guard attacks by a skeptical Congress.

A third challenge to KEDO is the need to maintain internal cohe-sion and solidarity while determining the financial obligations of its founding members. Along with that process, competition for sub-contracting responsibilities among firms from the respective countries is also likely to be fierce. Organizationally, KEDO must manage and resolve frictions among its members while keeping the implementation process on track.

SIMILARITIES AND DIFFERENCES BETWEEN KEDO-DPRK AND U.S.-DPRK NEGOTIATIONS

The preceding description of patterns in negotiations between KEDO and the DPRK reveals certain contextual changes that influenced patterns in North Korean negotiating behavior. Changes in North Korean negotiating tactics were influenced primarily by the fact that KEDO is a multilateral organization, and secondarily by the constraints imposed on North Korea both by its new vulnerability and by its need to cooperate to gain tangible benefits. North Korean negotiators were less able to take advantage of internal differences within KEDO because its internal consultation process requires reaching consensus before presenting negotiating positions to North Korea. North Korean tactics of crisis diplomacy, brinkmanship, and creation of leverage continued but were much more ineffective in multilateral negotiations on technical issues. The relative inflexibility of KEDO's internal coordination process has meant that fewer concessions are available to North Korea without reaching a negotiating stalemate. Drawing on these lessons, there are several significant differences between the U.S.-DPRK and KEDO-DPRK negotiations that deserve further consideration.

First, with the establishment of KEDO, the nature of the negotiation process with North Korea changed from political to technical, focused on implementation of a prior agreement. The KEDO negotiations with North Korea have been substantively different from political negotiations between the United States and the DPRK over nuclear issues. Agreement in principle on the parameters of action by either side was broadly defined by the Geneva Agreed Framework, while the task of KEDO was to negotiate the technical details of implementation within the parameters of the Geneva Agreed Framework. Even if issues arose that may have had political implications, concessions on technical issues were easier to justify in the KEDO process because the commitment of the top leadership to a political agreement had already been made. The commitment to follow through is simply a matter of implementing a prior decision by North Korea's top leadership.

Thus, contrary to initial expectations on the part of KEDO staff and others, the KEDO-DPRK negotiation channel proved to be less difficult than the U.S.-DPRK channel once KEDO was able to prove its own bona fides as a legitimate negotiating counterpart. Although the negotiating tactics of North Korean negotiators with KEDO counterparts have been roughly similar to tactics used with U.S. counterparts, tendencies toward brinkmanship have been muted. North Korea has found itself with no choice but to make certain concessions in order to lay the basis for moving forward with implementation. Unlike previous agreements in principle in the North-South context, the Geneva Agreed Framework was structured in such a way that North Korea has a vested interest in pushing toward implementation to begin seeing concrete results. Further tests of North Korean cooperation may occur depending on the pace of progress in the construction of the LWR.

Second, the coordination process in determining KEDO positions is internal and based on consensus, compared with the relative difficulty of coordinating negotiating positions with the ROK or other allies when the ROK and Japan are outside the negotiating process, as was the case during the bilateral negotiations between the United States and the DPRK in Geneva. Agreements are no longer subject to second-guessing by regional partners such as the ROK or Japan because those parties are themselves participants in the negotiations and governments must approve and agree in advance on any concessions before they can be presented formally to the DPRK. The existence of an indivisible international coalition embodied by KEDO prevented North Korean negotiators from exploiting differences in orientation among the parties, thereby limiting North Korean alternatives to cooperation.

Third, the technical subject matter of the negotiations conducted by KEDO has put North Korean counterparts into a relatively weaker position. However, unlike in previous North-South negotiations in which talks may have been broken off to avoid revealing North Korean ignorance on specific issues,[22] the KEDO structure has been effective as a tool for educating North Korean counterparts on the necessity of instituting technical measures as part of the project, even if lack of technical expertise has been a source of frustration that has slowed the negotiating process. Despite its limited technical understanding of the light-water reactor project, the North Korean negotiating team could not afford to walk away from the table given the political investment made by Pyongyang in support of the project.

Fourth, KEDO as an institution has no historical baggage with North Korean counterparts, unlike the United States, South Korea, or even the United Nations. The history and structure of confrontation between North Korea and the United States or South Korea are quite clear; even the United Nations suffers in its credibility from a North Korean perspective because it took sides in the "police action" against North Korea during the Korean War. Instead, KEDO is an international organization with no historical precedent, created specifically to provide light-water reactors to North Korea. Arguably, the absence of a negative historical legacy has been a significant factor in allowing KEDO to be accepted as a legitimate negotiating partner with North Korea.

As actual construction has begun on the project, North Korean cooperation in resolving difficult issues has been surprisingly forthcoming in the initial phases. Does this mean that North Korean brinkmanship tactics have ended as practical cooperation has begun, or does stepped-up North Korean cooperation represent a turning point in which an adversarial negotiating process is gradually being replaced by exercises in trust building through joint cooperation? It is likely that further snags will occur and that political tensions will once again intervene to halt progress on the KEDO project; however, the process and the benefits accruing to North Korea from the project itself now outweigh the potential gains resulting from noncooperation as a tactic designed to increase leverage. One result may be that North Korean tactics may shift from a focus on extracting benefits connected with the threat of noncooperation to the promise of additional cooperation as an inducement to expand benefits to North Korea.

If this observation regarding changes in North Korea's strategic orientation proves true, it will be a clear demonstration that North Korean tactics are evolving as a result of the experience of negotiating with the United States. Some negotiators on the U.S. side—now familiar with the repeated drama and rhythm of North Korean tactics —may be more pessimistic about the ability of North Korean negotiating counterparts to adopt new negotiating strategies and tactics. Others draw a more negative example of North Korean learning by citing frequent North Korean references to military hard-liners back home in Pyongyang as an adaptation of familiar "good cop–bad cop" tactics often employed by U.S. negotiators—who must recognize the limitations imposed on their negotiating power by Congress and public opinion.

Nonetheless, it seems likely that as a result of practical cooperation on a day-to-day basis, both sides may begin to shed their instinctive mutual distrust and to look more favorably in general on other projects requiring sustained negotiated cooperation. To the extent that KEDO implementation creates a basis for such cooperation, it may drive future adaptations in North Korea's negotiating style.

Conclusion

North Korea on the Edge

Contrary to conventional wisdom among U.S. policymakers, North Korea's negotiating style and objectives have conformed to a consistent and all-too-predictable pattern. Those elements of the U.S.-DPRK negotiating equation that might fairly be termed "irrational" have less to do with North Korean negotiating behavior and more to do with the inconsistencies and the lack of coordination between American and South Korean negotiating approaches and the sporadic attention to North Korea as a policy priority despite the stakes and the size of the U.S. defense commitment on the Korean Peninsula.[1]

The DPRK used brinkmanship strategies to good effect during the Cold War to gain concessions as side benefits of participating in negotiations without paying a price in return. During the negotiation of the Armistice Agreement and subsequent MAC negotiations, the North used intimidation where possible and made rare concessions in pursuit of its own uncompromising, unilateral objectives. Even the quarter century of North-South dialogue held since 1972 has served primarily as an extension of zero-sum competition for legitimacy rather than as a forum in which counterparts have sought to achieve "win-win" agreements, despite sporadic, limited progress on issues where agendas happen to coincide.

However, the diminished structural position of an isolated North Korea in the post–Cold War era has created a new situation. Under current circumstances, North Korea has no choice but to pursue negotiations to gain the resources necessary to perpetuate regime survival. Although North Korean negotiators no longer have the luxury of pursuing a unilateral approach to negotiations by walking away from the table, they have not abandoned deeply ingrained tactics of brinkmanship, crisis diplomacy, and attempts to maximize leverage by identifying and withholding the highest-priority demands of the negotiating counterpart. Such tactics often cause stalemates and fail to serve North Korea's strategic objectives, despite Pyongyang's interest in gaining the benefits resulting from negotiated cooperation. The difficulty of adapting to these new circumstances is reinforced by North Korea's own sensitivity to issues involving sovereignty (a legacy of the Japanese colonial period), the long-standing influence of *juche* (self-reliance) ideology, and the inefficiencies of North Korea's own vertically oriented socialist bureaucratic structure. A major challenge North Korean negotiators face under these circumstances is the need to adopt negotiating tactics that take into account the limitations imposed by North Korea's socialist structure without risking the loss of critical benefits that may be gained as a result of a negotiated agreement.

The failure of North Korean negotiators to adopt new tactics more suited to their current circumstances of isolation and relative weakness is evidence of the influence historical legacies and long-standing Korean practices have had on North Korean officials at the negotiation table. The influence of Kim Il Sung's own guerrilla partisan experiences provided North Korean negotiators with a ready model for how a relatively weak, rogue state might maximize its negotiating advantages by pursuing unconventional tactics. The guerrilla partisan experience, through which leaders feel unconstrained by norms that might limit the options of full-fledged members of the international community, has had direct application to and influence on North Korean preferences for crisis diplomacy and brinkmanship to gain the attention and respect of negotiating counterparts.

The searing experience of having lost national sovereignty to Japanese colonial rulers has also influenced North Korean negotiators to defend national sovereignty at almost any cost. The sensitivity of North Korean negotiators on sovereignty-related issues and the defiant measures taken in defense of national sovereignty during international negotiations are expressions of North Korea's perceived vulnerability stemming directly from the colonial experience.

The rigidity of the DPRK's Stalinist institutional structure has inhibited flexibility at the negotiation table and has tied the hands of North Korea's negotiating representatives, who have relatively little authority to make concessions without the direct approval of North Korea's top leadership. The vertically oriented structure of North Korea's system may limit the ability of the negotiator to report fully to his superiors. In fact, the negotiator himself may have authority over and knowledge of only a limited set of issues owing to the stovepipe nature of North Korea's bureaucratic structure and the control of information as an instrument of power within North Korean society, legacies from North Korea's adaptation of Soviet-style institutions and structures.

The influence of traditional Confucian norms has sharpened sensitivity to issues of hierarchy and relationship to one's negotiating counterpart, adding to the sense of competition and importance of symbolic protocol issues in sensitive negotiations between North and South Korea, while necessitating a focus on equivalency and reciprocity in negotiations with the United States. In addition, the North's ideology of self-reliance requires that substantive concessions be concealed behind the veneer of equivalency. The emphasis on self-reliance ensures that North Korean concessions or changes in a negotiation position will neither be acknowledged nor revealed openly. Kim Il Sung's cult of personality requires an immediate defense by North Korean negotiators in the case of any perceived slight toward the ruling first family.

Perhaps because of the rigid structure of North Korean institutions or the extent of political control within North Korean society, the process of negotiating with North Korea has a distinct and predictable rhythm. Plenary sessions are used primarily for rhetorical purposes and to pursue psychological advantage; informal sessions are used to probe for weaknesses, float trial balloons, and identify the outlines of a negotiated settlement. Only after carefully reviewing alternatives and seeking the most advantageous atmosphere for arriving at a

negotiated settlement will North Korean negotiators respond positively to the negotiating counterpart. Only if the atmosphere is determined to be right will North Korean negotiators engage in bargaining,
and their position will harden to maximize concessions by the other
side as one approaches the end game of a negotiation.

Punŭigi (atmosphere) is critical to determining whether North
Korean negotiators will respond with good *kibun* (feeling) to facilitate
negotiations or will demonstrate *kojip* (stubbornness) as a delaying or
stalling tactic. North Korean negotiators have found that crisis diplomacy is a powerful tool for enhancing alternatives, demonstrating
commitment, and maintaining control of an issue-specific negotiating process to diminish the strength of a more powerful negotiating
counterpart such as the United States. It also serves to shape the agenda
by fixing the attention of the negotiating counterpart on favorable
terms and throws the negotiating counterpart off balance by forcing
a response to North Korea's own negotiating agenda and priorities.
Although the effectiveness of brinkmanship tactics through stalling,
bluffing, using time pressure, and threatening to walk away from negotiations may be on the wane, the ability of North Korean negotiators
to identify points of leverage to gain concessions in negotiation has
been impressive.

By seeking equivalency and reciprocity in its negotiations with the
United States while engaging in zero-sum, one-upmanship tactics
with South Korea, North Korea has manipulated differences between
the United States and South Korea to gain advantage. South Korea's
Toughness Dilemma and tendency to respond to North Korea with
its own brand of one-upmanship is likely to create stalemate. As a
result, substantive progress in North-South dialogue may be hard to
come by, even if it is in the interests of both North and South Korea
to come to a negotiated settlement. Differing North Korean approaches
in dealing with the United States and South Korea and differing tactical and strategic considerations between the United States and South
Korea following the end of the Cold War have made the policy coordination task between Washington and Seoul more difficult as both
capitals have attempted to calibrate their respective policies toward
North Korea.

Finally, multilateral negotiations conducted through KEDO have focused on technical issues. These negotiations have limited the capacity of North Korean negotiators to effectively use brinkmanship or crisis diplomacy tactics, particularly in cases where Pyongyang has something to lose if prior agreements are jeopardized. KEDO has provided an effective venue for direct interaction between North and South Korean counterparts to carry out a concrete joint project requiring mutual cooperation. The inclusion of South Korean counterparts as part of KEDO negotiations has reduced frictions between the United States and the ROK that had existed during U.S.-DPRK negotiations. Other factors that have facilitated the success of KEDO's negotiations with North Korea are that the agenda is composed of technical issues rather than political issues and that KEDO as an institution carries with it no historical baggage and is designed specifically to provide the benefits to North Korea that accrue from participation in the Geneva Agreed Framework.

COUNTERSTRATEGIES FOR MANAGING A NEGOTIATION WITH THE DPRK

The initial U.S. experience of negotiating with North Korea was one of negotiating with "opaque" counterparts in the midst of crisis "while rolling down the runway" toward potential conflict. Today, however, there is a growing database of information and accumulated experience regarding North Korea's negotiating style. In fact, this book could not have been written without drawing extensively on that database. Past U.S. negotiations with North Korea offer a number of lessons about how best to respond to North Korean negotiating strategies and tactics.

Be aware of the stages in the "drama," or ritual, of negotiation and the importance of "atmosphere" in determining North Korean negotiating moves. It is unrealistic to expect dramatic progress in negotiations with the DPRK until the leadership in Pyongyang has decided it is ready to make a deal. Such a determination will not occur until after North Korean negotiators have methodically explored alternatives and attempted to exploit divisions among negotiating counterparts through informal contacts and prenegotiation. Such a process will of necessity require the cultivation of personal relationships on both sides through which an effective exploration of possible alternatives may occur; otherwise, the margin of error by both sides in understanding the specifics of the counterpart's position will be increased. Expect the North Korean official position to remain uncompromising throughout this phase and until after trial balloons have been launched and available solutions have been explored. During this "period of testing," it is necessary to show firmness to reduce North Korean efforts to exploit weakness or division and to limit perceived alternatives to negotiation that might possibly be considered by leaders in Pyongyang.

After it is clear to the leadership in Pyongyang that negotiation is the only possible avenue by which to meet its objectives, the North Korean side will signal clearly that it is ready to pursue a negotiated solution— for instance, by announcing the desire to pursue a "package solution." At this stage, the North Korean side will show flexibility in its position, but such flexibility will decrease considerably in an attempt to draw out concessions as part of the end game of the negotiation. The components of any package solution may involve certain North Korean concessions, but North Korean negotiators will attempt to mask concessions to the extent possible through the rhetoric of equivalency or through insistence on confidentiality regarding the details of those concessions.

Don't confuse North Korea's rhetoric with its reality. Some rhetoric designed to show toughness may include an invitation to come to the negotiating table—for instance, the DPRK announced that it would continue missile exports unless the United States was willing to provide compensation for not doing so. Despite the high-volume bluster of certain North Korean press statements, the substance of which is often repeated by North Korean negotiators in initial plenary sessions, the reality of North Korea's position may be communicated clearly both through highly directed media messages and through informal or unofficial channels. Such channels allow North Korean negotiators to retain the right to deny certain statements publicly as well as to conceal weaknesses in their own negotiating position. Careful and comprehensive analysis of informal or deniable signals may be the best available way of discerning North Korea's own bottom line.

Expect North Korea to use exaggerated rhetoric to conceal its dependency. Be prepared for the mismatch between North Korea's public self-assurance, bluster, and maximalist demands and the relatively limited price of agreement that North Korea may find itself willing to accept in the end. Recognize the North Korean pattern of "caving in" and giving up maximum rhetorical demands in the face of the reality of what the market will bear.

Resist North Korean attempts to search for weaknesses within a negotiating team or to exploit divisions among negotiating counterparts. The best antidote to North Korean exploitation of weaknesses or divisions during the "period of testing" is the development of a clear strategy based on an interagency consensus or agreement among allies. For instance, North Korean attempts to exploit U.S.-ROK tactical differences may be countered by more closely coordinating U.S.-ROK bilateral relations. South Korean officials could profitably use indirect or U.S.-led negotiations as a vehicle for gaining North Korean concessions based on reciprocity rather than the one-upmanship dynamic of North-South dialogue; for its part, the United States should be more sensitive to opportunities for facilitating progress in North-South dialogue.

Before an agreement is reached, North Korean negotiators will repeatedly probe for weaknesses and will return over and over again to issues on which divisions among negotiating counterparts may develop. Even following apparent agreement on some issues, it is important to recall that nothing is agreed to until everything is agreed to. Following the signing of a negotiated agreement, the implementation phase will include additional testing of provisions of the agreement in practice. The habitual return by North Korean negotiators to issues considered by American counterparts to have already been resolved may reflect a cyclical rather than a linear view of the negotiation process. The only effective response to such tactics is to rebuff them firmly and consistently.

Expect crisis-oriented tactics; avoid allowing the DPRK to maintain the initiative; limit North Korean alternatives; and control the negotiating agenda. One of the biggest failures of U.S. diplomacy toward the DPRK thus far has been the U.S. inability to maintain the initiative, allowing the DPRK to effectively employ crisis diplomacy to force the United States into a defensive position. The joint Four Party Talks proposal was a rare occasion on which the United States and South Korea took the initiative, limiting North Korean alternatives and blunting the potential for crisis diplomacy. However, the dynamic of negotiations as part of the Geneva Agreed Framework was driven primarily by the DPRK's crisis diplomacy. It may be necessary to respond to some of the DPRK's legitimate demands to "give them something to lose" and to contain dissatisfaction that might lead to the revival of crisis-oriented tactics. Neglect is not an effective strategy for dealing with the DPRK, since North Korea's level of tolerance for a crisis atmosphere is higher than that of the United States.

Identification of the framework and circumstances under which certain issues might be taken up is one way of taking the initiative in negotiations with North Korea; however, such approaches must also recognize the legitimacy of elements of the North Korean negotiating agenda if they are to have any real prospect of success. Such a process may require simultaneously limiting North Korean alternatives to negotiation and offering political or economic inducements sufficient to overcome North Korean resistance to coming to the negotiation table. The structure and the timing of such inducements, however, may be controversial if they appear to be the result of North Korean blackmail or if they appear to reward North Korea for using crisis-oriented tactics. At the same time, it is necessary to impose clear penalties on North Korea that effectively limit attempts to pursue crisis-oriented alternatives to negotiated cooperation.

Signal negotiating objectives, but don't overinvest in them, or the price for North Korean cooperation may be inflated. The higher priority an item appears to be on the U.S. agenda, the higher the price likely to be demanded by North Korean negotiators for reaching agreement on that item. For instance, the extraordinary public focus and attention given to

North Korea's nuclear weapons program provided Pyongyang with an opportunity to expand its leverage in negotiations with the United States; even the prospect and implications of the DPRK's own collapse have been used as negotiating leverage by Pyongyang. Downplaying priorities while continuing to seek quiet progress may be a more effective strategy for gaining cooperation. Examples include DPRK cooperation on POW/MIA issues and DPRK cooperation with the Department of Energy on storage of nuclear fuel rods.

By the same token, the content of agreements and expectations for implementation must be precisely defined since ambiguities will be subject to challenge. Although American negotiators have noted that North Korean counterparts will keep agreements, it is often the case that obligations are interpreted by the North Korean side as narrowly as possible, particularly in the absence of a "friendship" relationship. North Koreans have adhered to the letter of specific agreements but at the same time have challenged both the spirit and the terms of implementation of those agreements, seeking to discover how determined the other side is to enforce implementation.

Multilateral negotiations and/or negotiations on technical issues (versus bilateral negotiations on political issues) may blunt the effects of North Korean brinkmanship and crisis-oriented tactics. KEDO negotiations with the DPRK over technical implementation have proved to be relatively more effective in making progress with North Korea than bilateral U.S.-DPRK negotiations over political matters. KEDO has effectively incorporated a consensus-oriented process of formulating negotiating positions based on the specific requirements necessary to move forward in implementing a project that will eventually yield tangible benefits to North Korea, giving North Korean negotiators a powerful economic incentive for facilitating cooperation rather than inducing crisis.

To the extent that issues can be depoliticized and/or multilateralized, such conditions appear to be less advantageous to North Korean negotiating tactics. For instance, negotiations between the DPRK and the UN World Food Programme have effectively depoliticized certain aspects of highly sensitive and intrusive demands for foreign monitoring and have certainly made more progress than bilateral inter-Korean

Red Cross negotiations, which have political overtones. The Four Party Talks may be an effective vehicle for blunting certain North Korean brinkmanship tactics; however, the sensitive political/security component of those talks may also be a factor that will inhibit progress. Negotiations in a depoliticized, or technical, channel often will contain the greatest prospect of substantive progress, whereas political negotiations will receive greater scrutiny by the top DPRK leadership.

Present a detailed strategy based on common interests, but leave North Korean negotiating counterparts with a face-saving way out of any corner. Because North Korean negotiators are reluctant to put forward concrete initiatives for fear of revealing their own bottom line, expect to take the lead in presenting constructive initiatives for consideration. A combination of firmness—to eliminate North Korean consideration of alternatives to a negotiated settlement—and generosity—to ensure that the DPRK is not boxed into the corner of resorting to high-stakes, crisis-oriented tactics—should characterize the presentation of a concrete series of steps to resolve issues based on a consideration of mutual interests.

Recognize that application of pressure that limits North Korean alternatives without providing an escape route may have the practical result of forcing North Korea to consider undesirable alternatives to negotiation or to take unorthodox steps to regain the upper hand in determining an agenda for negotiations. It is necessary not only to raise the costs to North Korea of pursuing alternatives to negotiation, but also to identify North Korean interests and offer concessions sufficient to convince North Korean counterparts that the escape route is worth taking.

Use crisis escalation tactics—such as time deadlines and threats to walk away —judiciously. North Korean negotiators may prefer to use time deadlines or crisis diplomacy because they themselves may be susceptible to such pressures. However, the danger of bluffing is that it damages one's own credibility if the bluff is called. Don't hesitate to show emotion as a means of defining the importance of key issues and signifying one's own bottom line. Be prepared to follow through with crisis escalation tactics, but only if you are prepared to defuse the crisis or contain North Korea's alternatives in responding to such tactics.

To a certain extent, the preferred tactics of North Korean officials in inducing concessions by their negotiating counterparts may also be precisely the tools by which it is possible to "motivate" North Korean officials themselves. North Korean threats to walk away may, ironically, convey the need for a satisfactory negotiated settlement; likewise, the willingness of the negotiating counterpart to walk away, or by the same token, to set a deadline by which negotiations must reach a conclusion, may demonstrate new eagerness by North Korean negotiators to make progress in negotiations under the right circumstances. However, the application of such pressure must be accompanied by a careful analysis of North Korea's perceived alternatives and a willingness to risk and to resist the potential ratcheting up of crisis-oriented tactics.

Have patience, patience, and more patience. After having presented a concrete formula for arriving at a negotiated settlement, expect the DPRK to test all the alternatives. It is necessary to firmly respond to North Korea's exploration of alternatives to the settlement under consideration to convince North Korean counterparts that brinkmanship and crisis escalation tactics will not lay the groundwork for a more advantageous deal. The best way to demonstrate that internal weaknesses or divisions among allies cannot be exploited is to show consistency in one's policy positions, even when those positions are being tested by North Korean attempts to instigate a crisis.

PROSPECTS FOR FUTURE NEGOTIATIONS WITH NORTH KOREA

To sum up the two major lessons of this study for future negotiations with North Korea: The good news is that it is possible to negotiate with North Korean counterparts, although the process may be painstaking and the path may be circuitous and full of setbacks and apparent detours. The bad news is that major progress in negotiations with North Korea will likely be accompanied by real or apparent crisis, either instigated from within or externally imposed. Periods of crisis may mark a major turning point in negotiations, or they may mark the beginning of a downward spiral of failure and instability.

Two issues have the greatest potential to influence the direction and context of future negotiations with North Korea. First, it remains to be seen whether North and South Korea may be able to finally abandon their zero-sum policies toward each other. With the inauguration of Kim Dae Jung as president of the ROK and the adoption of his Sunshine Policy, it has become possible to make a preliminary test of this thesis. Kim Dae Jung's policy toward North Korea emphasizes an improved relationship with Pyongyang, declaring that economic exchanges are considered separate from political issues in North-South relations. Does such a change in policy transform the future dynamic of North-South negotiations, or will such an effort to reverse the zero-sum dynamic of North-South competition be resisted or undermined in either Pyongyang or Seoul?

Second, although the DPRK continues to utilize outmoded tactics of toughness through brinkmanship and crisis diplomacy, the political leadership in Pyongyang continues to weaken and the perceived threat from North Korea has steadily diminished. At the same time, the North Korean leadership itself has recognized its own relative weakness vis-à-vis South Korea and the rest of the world by pursuing alternative threats, including the development of weapons of mass destruction such as missiles, nuclear weapons, and chemical and biological warfare capabilities. Doubts about North Korea's survivability have both diminished its leverage and forced it to explore unconventional alternatives in view of the imbalance in relative economic strength and power projection capabilities between North and South Korea. The effect has been that political and financial support among negotiating counterparts for a flexible approach to North Korea has diminished at the same time that North Korea is seeking unconventional means by which to maintain negotiating leverage. If Pyongyang's core security needs were addressed, would the leadership in Pyongyang be able to adjust its tactics to better fit its needs in a situation where it has something to lose—namely, the benefits that may accrue from a successful negotiation?

The initiation by Kim Dae Jung of the Sunshine Policy, a more accom-modative policy of reconciliation with the DPRK, at first glance might be expected to have potentially major effects on the North-South nego-tiating dynamic. With the adoption of this policy, one of the two parties on the Korean Peninsula has finally declared its intention to abandon zero-sum tactics of confrontation in favor of a strategy in which gains for one side will not be automatically interpreted as losses for the other. Thus, it is a test of whether it is possible to transform the structure and dynamic of the North-South relationship from a zero-sum rela-tionship among competitors to one of peaceful coexistence. However, the practical application of such a policy change faces two key obstacles: (1) the traditional, habitually ingrained pattern of each side viewing the other as the enemy, and (2) the frustration that is likely to mount if the other side responds in its own traditional zero-sum manner, unwill-ing to acknowledge or respond to such reconciliation measures.

Both of these obstacles are illustrated in the results of the first inter-Korean dialogue held under President Kim Dae Jung's administra-tion in Beijing in April 1998. The resumption of inter-Korean dialogue in Beijing provided North Korea with a perfect opportunity to test whether and how the forward-leaning rhetoric of the Kim Dae Jung administration might be translated into reality. Despite the changes in South Korea's declaratory policy, however, South Korea was constrained by its divided domestic politics and, perhaps most important, the legacy of past tactics in inter-Korean dialogue. The Kim Dae Jung adminis-tration, already perceived as progressive, could not be perceived as giving the North something for nothing, a deadly mistake that Kim Young Sam had made in his initial rice negotiations with North Korea in June 1995.

The focus of the South Korean authorities was on exchanges of divided families as an issue on which progress would pay rich domestic political dividends and also further inter-Korean relations. As a prin-ciple for moving forward on both divided family issues and fertilizer assistance, reciprocity—that is, the need for North Korea to respond in kind to South Korean generosity—has been an essential domestic political requirement for public support of North-South dialogue in

South Korea. However, the two sides were unable to "resolve in parallel" fertilizer and separated family issues.

The negotiating table was once again the venue for ritual competition between North and South Korea, and Seoul had no choice politically but to follow the same tactics of toughness that had led to familiar breakdowns in prior negotiations. Despite the development of parallel agenda items on which quid pro quos might be struck, the legacy of past inter-Korean negotiations made it difficult to forge a new pattern of agreement. Predictably, the session ended in breakdown but served to shape the terms of subsequent official dialogue between North and South Korean authorities.

Second, the DPRK's tactics of toughness—reflecting a unilateral strategy of brinkmanship and crisis diplomacy—have become less and less effective as perceptions of the threat from North Korea have steadily diminished. As the North Korean state has weakened as a result of its economic and political decline, doubts about its survivability have raised questions among counterparts about the desirability of offering generous concessions to a negotiating counterpart who may offer little in return.

At the same time, the leaders in Pyongyang have also recognized that current trends are strongly against them and have relied more heavily on unconventional measures, including continued development of a ballistic missile program and possibly even covert development of a nuclear weapons capacity, even while abiding by the letter of the Agreed Framework. Once again, North Korea has used guerrilla tactics and unconventional means necessary for a weaker party to attempt to level the playing field against an overwhelmingly stronger opponent, recognizing that such tactics offer the only possibility of survival. As long as leaders in Pyongyang perceive that they have something to lose—that is, the benefits resulting from keeping commitments made in prior negotiations—brinkmanship and crisis-oriented tactics will be less pronounced. At the same time, the search for alternatives or tests of the counterpart's resolve to enforce the terms of an agreement are inevitable and should be expected. If the leadership in Pyongyang stands so close to the brink of failure that it perceives itself as having nothing to lose, the specter of collapse itself will be used as a last-ditch tactic to gain leverage against neighbors who fear the spillover effects of chaos in North Korea.

The central dilemma is that according to a brinkmanship strategy based on toughness, North Korea's greatest leverage is its potential threat, yet as it trades away the threat to gain the benefits of negotiation necessary to ensure its survival, leverage is diminished as negotiating counterparts can again afford to ignore North Korea's concerns and take for granted the absence of confrontation. Under such circumstances, there is little rationale for North Korea's counterparts to offer concessions or even to come to the negotiation table, reinforcing North Korean reliance on the old strategy of inducing crisis and stirring up trouble to avoid being taken for granted or ignored.

This dilemma is graphically illustrated in the implementation of the Geneva Agreed Framework. As the process of implementation has gone forward and as North Korea's economic problems have grown more severe and more obvious, the perceived costs of the project have risen as North Korea appears to be getting benefits far greater than are justified by the actual level of its threat. The perception of North Korea's growing weakness has made political support for the project in South Korea, Japan, and the United States more difficult to secure, raising questions about whether the United States and the international community, rather than the DPRK, will be able to meet their commitments under the Agreed Framework. Likewise, to the extent that negotiating counterparts view the North Korean regime as likely to collapse, the rationale is diminished for giving additional concessions or even coming to the negotiating table with the DPRK at the Four Party Talks or in other negotiating venues.

In such a situation, the only viable strategy for North Korean negotiators is to return to the threat that North Korea will abandon the old agreement, reinforcing reliance on old tactics that themselves may jeopardize the critical material benefits derived from the agreement itself. The negotiating stalemate resulting from the growing imbalance between perceptions of the DPRK's diminishing strength and the need to provide the DPRK with concessions sufficient to ensure that it has something to lose from breaking agreements is likely to reinforce the old negotiating dynamic of threat, crisis, and brinkmanship.

For instance, North Korea's test of a multiple-stage rocket in August 1998 was a clear demonstration that the DPRK could mobilize a revitalized threat. Whether the test was designed as a negotiating tool, an attempt to showcase technology for potential sale to third countries, or an effort to develop an offensive capacity that could be used against its enemies, Pyongyang's action served in part to counter perceptions that the North may go away quietly or is no longer a negotiating partner able to extract concessions. Unable to mobilize attention to its own agenda with the United States in the absence of crisis, North Korea predictably returned to crisis-oriented tactics to regain attention, although such tactics ran counter to North Korea's strategic objective of gaining an improved relationship with the United States. Until North Korea can identify a way of moving fully from a relationship with the United States, South Korea, and other members of the international community based on confrontation to one based on compromise and the search for common interests, North Korean negotiators will continue to be constrained by their own structural and organizational inefficiencies and are not likely to easily escape the self-reinforcing historical legacy, tradition, and tactics of negotiating on the edge.

Appendix I

Interviewees

The author wishes to thank the following individuals, who gave generously of their time and thoughts regarding the process of negotiating with North Korea based on their firsthand experiences. Without their generosity, it would have been impossible to complete this study.

UNITED STATES

Guy Arrigoni, Department of Defense

Robert Carlin, Department of State

Richard Christenson, Department of State

Major Steve Cohen, Department of Defense

Nicholas Eberstadt, American Enterprise Institute

Gordon Flake, Mansfield Center for Pacific Affairs

Edward K. H. Fong, Department of State

Lt. Col. Robert Flury, UNC/MAC

Robert L. Gallucci, Georgetown University

Jeff Goldstein, Department of State

Todd Harvey, Department of Defense

Thomas Hubbard, Department of State

Charles Kartman, Department of State

Jimmy Lee, UN Command Military Armistice Commission (ret.)

James Lilley, American Enterprise Institute

Stephen Linton, Eugene Bell Foundation

Alan Liotta, Department of Defense

Lt. Col. Greg Mann, Department of Defense

Chris Miller, Department of State

Mark Minton, Department of State

Douglas A. Morris, Department of State

K. A. Namkung, Atlantic Council of the United States

William Pendley, Air War College

C. Kenneth Quinones, Department of State

Dennis Reynolds, Department of State

Spence Richardson, Department of State

Gary Samore, National Security Council

Daniel Russell, Department of State

Shinn Rinn-sup, Congressional Research Service

Col. Mark Shoemaker, U.S. Forces Korea

Lt. Col. Martin Wisda, Department of Defense

Joel Wit, Department of State

Col. James T. Young (ret.)

Philip Yun, Department of State

JAPAN

Arata Fujii, Ministry of Foreign Affairs

Hajime Izumi, Shizuoka University

Noboru Nakahira, Ministry of Foreign Affairs

Masao Okonogi, Keio University

Shuji Shimokoji, Ministry of Foreign Affairs

SOUTH KOREA

Ahn Chung Shi, Seoul National University

Cha Young Koo, Ministry of National Defense

H. E. Chung Won Shik, former prime minister

H. E. Han Sung Joo, Korea University

Han Yong Sup, National Defense University

Kim Do Tae, Research Institute of National Unification (now Korea
  Institute of National Unification)

Kim Yong Ho, Institute of Foreign Affairs and National Security

Koo BonTae, assistant minister of unification

Lim Dong Won, Kim Dae Jung Peace Foundation (currently minister
  of unification)

Gen. Park Yong Ok, Ministry of National Defense

Song Jong Whan, Embassy of Korea

KEDO

Desaix Anderson, executive director

Stephen Bosworth, executive director

Choi Young Jin, deputy executive director

Masaaki Ono, deputy executive director

Eunsoo Kim, director, Policy and DPRK Affairs Division

Hitoshi Murata, assistant director, Policy and DPRK Affairs Division

Lucy Reed, general counsel

Mitchell Reiss, assistant executive director

Jason Shaplen, assistant director, Policy and DPRK Affairs Division

Itaru Umezu, deputy executive director

Appendix II

Chronology of U.S.-DPRK
Negotiations, 1990–97

This chronology of major negotiations conducted with North Korea in the 1990s is selective, not exhaustive, and is chiefly intended to help readers put the negotiations referred to in this book into context.

1989–91	Counselor-level U.S.-DPRK talks are held in Beijing.
1990–91	Six rounds of high-level North-South talks are held in Seoul and Pyongyang.
December 13, 1991	North-South Basic Agreement (Agreement on Reconciliation, Nonaggression, Exchanges and Cooperation) is signed.
December 31, 1991	Joint Agreement on the Denuclearization of the Korean Peninsula between North and South Korea is announced.
January 7, 1992	DPRK announces that it will join IAEA and accept monitoring of North Korea's declared nuclear facilities.

January 20, 1992	Arnold Kanter, under secretary of state for political affairs, and Kim Yong Sum, Korean Worker's Party secretary for political affairs, meet in New York. This is the highest-level U.S.-DPRK political meeting to occur since the end of the Korean War.
July 1992	Kim Dal Hyon, chairman of the DPRK's External Economic Affairs Committee, visits Seoul.
September–December 1992	North-South Subcommittee for Nuclear Matters breaks down; IAEA discovers discrepancies in North Korean records and pushes for unprecedented "special inspections"; South Korea announces discovery of North Korean spy ring; presidential campaigns in the United States and South Korea lead to the election of Bill Clinton and Kim Young Sam, respectively.
March 12, 1993	North Korea announces that it will withdraw from the Nuclear Non-Proliferation Treaty (NPT).
June 5–11, 1993	First round of U.S.-DPRK negotiations held in New York, led by Robert L. Gallucci, assistant secretary of state for political/military affairs, and Kang Sok Ju, vice foreign minister; DPRK agrees to suspend its withdrawal from the NPT.
July 11–18, 1993	Second round of U.S.-DPRK negotiations is held in Geneva. Idea of light-water reactors is officially raised by North Korean delegation.
November 24, 1993	Clinton–Kim Young Sam summit meeting in Washington, D.C., announces "broad-and-thorough" approach to dealing with North Korea and initiates working-level negotiations with DPRK.

February 18, 1994	The United States and DPRK announce "Agreed Conclusion," four points designed to bring both sides back to the negotiating table and to ensure continuity of IAEA monitoring and inspections of DPRK nuclear facilities.
May–June 1994	DPRK unloads fuel rods, leading to break off of negotiations.
June 1994	Carter visit to Pyongyang yields agreement with Kim Il Sung to maintain spent fuel rods in storage and to resume U.S.-DPRK negotiations.
July 8, 1994	Third round of U.S.-DPRK negotiations opens in Geneva. Kim Il Sung dies; negotiations are suspended.
August 5–13, 1994	Third round of suspended U.S.-DPRK negotiations resumes.
August 15, 1994	President Kim Young Sam publicly pledges ROK willingness to provide DPRK with South Korean light-water reactors during Liberation Day speech.
September 16–20, 1994	U.S.-DPRK negotiations continue in Berlin, led by Gary Samore, deputy assistant secretary of state for political/military affairs, and Kim Jong U, chairman of the External Economy Commission.
September 23–October 1994	U.S.-DPRK negotiations continue intermittently in Geneva.
October 21, 1994	U.S.-DPRK Geneva Agreed Framework is announced.

November–December 1994	U.S. sanctions on magnesite trade are lifted; South Korea announces lifting of certain restrictions on North-South business contacts; expert-level talks on safe storage of North Korea's spent nuclear fuel open in Pyongyang; DPRK delegation visits Washington for first round of negotiations over liaison offices.
December 17, 1994	CWO Bobby Hall's helicopter is shot down after crossing to Northern side of DMZ. UNC/MAC negotiations and efforts by Congressman Bill Richardson, visiting North Korea for the first time, fail to secure Hall's release. Deputy Assistant Secretary Thomas Hubbard flies to Pyongyang to negotiate Hall's release on December 30, in a major test of the Geneva Agreed Framework.
March–April 1995	Berlin negotiations between Gary Samore and Kim Jong U break down over the type of reactor to be provided to the DPRK under the Agreed Framework.
May–June 1995	Negotiations over the type of reactor to be provided to the DPRK resume in Kuala Lumpur between Thomas Hubbard and Kim Gye Gwan, vice minister of foreign affairs.
June 14, 1995	Kuala Lumpur agreement on type of light-water reactors to be provided to North Korea is announced. KEDO board, including U.S., ROK, and Japanese official representatives, meets in Seoul and designates the Korean Electric Power Company (KEPCO) as the prime contractor for the LWR project.

September 11–12, 1995   KEDO-DPRK negotiations over supply contract begin in Kuala Lumpur, led by KEDO executive director Stephen Bosworth and DPRK ambassador-at-large Ho Jong.

October 1–December 1995   Supply contract negotiations continue in New York and are concluded on December 15, 1995.

January 1996   Kim Byong Hong, DPRK foreign ministry bureau chief, leads delegation to first round of talks on the MIA issue held in Hawaii.

May 26–29, 1996   Congressman Bill Richardson visits Pyongyang for talks on pending issues between Pyongyang and Washington, including the issue of POW/MIA remains.

April 1996   First round of bilateral talks, held in Berlin, between DPRK and the United States on North Korea's development and export of missiles.

April 16, 1996   Presidents Bill Clinton and Kim Young Sam announce the Four Party Talks proposal during bilateral summit held on Cheju Island.

May 1996   Second round of MIA talks is held in New York.

September 18, 1996   North Korean submarine incursion discovered on east coast of South Korea. Kim Young Sam mobilizes thousands of troops for a monthlong manhunt for DPRK operatives, only one of whom is captured alive.

October–December 1996   United States holds twelve rounds of working-level negotiations with DPRK in New York on a North Korean statement of regret necessary to reactivate normalized KEDO operations.

November 25–27, 1996	Congressman Bill Richardson visits Pyongyang for negotiations with Vice Foreign Minister Kang Sok Ju over the submarine incident and to secure release of Carl Hunziger, an American held in the DPRK for over two months on spying charges.
December 29, 1996	DPRK issues a public statement of "deep regret" for the submarine incursion.
January 1997	First round of U.S.-ROK "joint briefing" of DPRK on the background behind the Four Party Talks proposal.
May 1997	Second round is held.
September 1997	Third round is held.
December 1997	First round of the Four Party Talks is formally inaugurated in Geneva.

Notes

INTRODUCTION

1. C. Kenneth Quinones, interview by author, February 1998.

2. See Denny Roy, "The Myth of North Korean 'Irrationality,'" *Korean Journal of International Studies* 25, no. 2 (summer 1994).

3. In this shocking incident, North Korean soldiers brutally attacked a South Korean work detail that was trimming trees inside the DMZ, killing two American officers accompanying the work detail. See Don Oberdorfer, *The Two Koreas: A Contemporary History* (Reading, Mass.: Addison-Wesley, 1997), 79.

4. See Lee Sigal, *Disarming Strangers: Nuclear Diplomacy with North Korea* (Princeton, N.J.: Princeton University Press, 1998), 35.

5. Robert L. Gallucci was a holdover from the Bush administration and a specialist on nonproliferation whose previous dealings had included proliferation issues in the former Soviet Union and Iraq. He had been chosen to lead the negotiations over other officials such as the newly confirmed assistant secretary of state for East Asia and the Pacific, Winston Lord, because the Clinton administration wanted to send the signal that this negotiation was seen as a nonproliferation problem and that the scope of negotiations would not be expanded to include other issues in U.S.-DPRK relations.

6. Robert L. Gallucci, interview by author, December 1996.

7. State Department official, interview by author, April 1995.

8. See Jerrold L. Schecter, *Russian Negotiating Behavior* (Washington, D.C.: United States Institute of Peace Press, 1998); see also Richard H. Solomon,

Chinese Negotiating Behavior: Pursuing Interests through "Old Friends" (Washington, D.C.: United States Institute of Peace Press, 1999). To expand available case studies analyzing national negotiating styles, the United States Institute of Peace has also commissioned studies on German and Japanese negotiating styles.

9. Hans Binnendijk, ed., *How Nations Negotiate* (Washington, D.C.: National Defense University Press, 1987).

10. Alexander L. George, *Bridging the Gap: Theory and Practice in Foreign Policy* (Washington, D.C.: United States Institute of Peace Press, 1993).

11. See Raymond Cohen, *Negotiating across Cultures,* rev. ed. (Washington, D.C.: United States Institute of Peace Press, 1997), 11. Cohen also contributed a chapter entitled "An Advocate's View" to Guy Olivier Faure and Jeffrey Z. Rubin, eds., *Culture and Negotiation* (Newbury Park, Calif.: Sage, 1993). In addition, Harry Triandis, an anthropologist who has written much on cross-cultural interactions among different groups, defines a cultural group as consisting of "people who have in the past, and who are now, communicating among themselves, and thus have arrived at shared understandings of how to perceive their social environment, and how to solve the key problems of existence." See Christopher Rob McCusker, "Individual-Collectivism and Relationships in Distributive Negotiation: An Experimental Analysis" (Ph.D. diss., University of Illinois at Urbana-Champaign, 1994), 44.

12. In chapter 1 of *Negotiating across Cultures,* Cohen cites the work of Lorand Szalay to illustrate the necessary components of communication that are central to the process of negotiation; not just the message itself must be transmitted correctly, but also the intentions of the sender must correspond with the meaning attributed by the receiver for successful communication to occur. For instance, cultural, linguistic, and temporal differences may characterize the respective styles of collective and individual societies: individualistic societies prize individual action, self-expression, or personal achievement and prefer direct talks or "getting down to business." A society in which governments face periodic elections is more likely to feel the stress of deadlines and to seek to achieve specific goals within a clear schedule. Collectivist societies attach significance to "face" within a group and are concerned about maintaining loyalty to and upholding the honor of the group, use language indirectly and subtly in order to avoid upsetting the harmony or consensus of the group, and might put less emphasis on time as a constraining factor in measuring process, achievement, or accomplishment.

As one considers the relative location of U.S. culture on an individualist-collectivist scale, the United States clearly should be categorized as an

individual-oriented society. North Korea, with its relative isolation and cultivation of a unique national identity, top-down political structure, and emphasis
on self-reliance and "single-hearted unity," might be considered the ultimate
example of a collectivist society. Therefore, many patterns explored in academic research on individualist-collectivist negotiations may apply to the
U.S.–North Korean case study. Other issues likely to affect the process and
outcome of negotiations will also be taken into account, including the character of the issues being dealt with, the institutional framework within which negotiations are managed, and the personalities of the negotiators involved.

One way of looking at the relationship between structural and cultural
factors in negotiation might be to think of structural factors as the "hardware"
of a negotiation and culture as the "software" of a negotiation. See Scott Snyder, "Negotiating with North Korea: Patterns from the American Experience"
(paper presented at American Anthropology Association annual meeting,
Washington, D.C., November 19, 1997).

13. Among those sources are C. Turner Joy, *How Communists Negotiate*
(New York: Macmillan, 1955); Herbert Goldhammer, *The 1951 Korean Armistice
Conference: A Personal Memoir* (Santa Monica, Calif.: RAND, 1995); William
Stueck, *The Korean War: An International History* (Princeton, N.J.: Princeton
University Press, 1995); Rosemary Foot, *The Wrong War: American Policy and
the Dimensions of the Korean Conflict, 1950–1953* (Ithaca, N.Y.: Cornell Univer-
sity Press, 1985); Cold War International History Project, *The Cold War in
Asia*, nos. 6–7 (winter 1995–96, Woodrow Wilson Center for International
Scholars, Washington, D.C.); and Al Wilhelm, Jr., *The Chinese at the Negotiat-
ing Table* (Washington, D.C.: National Defense University, 1995).

14. The three principles declare that reunification should be achieved
through "independent Korean efforts without being subject to external
imposition or interference; through peaceful means, not through use of
force against each other; and through pursuit of great national unity, tran-
scending differences in ideas, ideologies, and systems."

15. Studies of inter-Korean negotiating behavior include Song Jong
Hwan, "How the North Korean Communists Negotiate: A Case Study of the
South-North Korean Dialogue of the Early 1970s," *Korea and World Affairs* 8,
no. 3 (fall 1984): 610–664; Kim Do Tae and Ch'a Jae Hoon, *Pukhan-ui Hyop-
sang Chon-sul Tuksong Yŏngu: Nam-buk Taehwa Salyedul Chungsimulo* (Seoul:
Minjok Tongil Yonguso, December 1995); Kim Do Tae, "North Korea's Con-
sistent Negotiating Style," *Vantage Point* (Seoul), April 1995, 31–40; Kim Do
Tae, "Change and Continuity in North Korea's Negotiating Behavior in the

Post–Cold War Era," *Social Science and Policy Research* 17, no. 2 (1995): 10; and Dong Bok Lee, "Negotiating with North Korea: Strategy and Tactics" (text of a presentation at the seminar "Negotiating with the North after Kim Il Sung," American Enterprise Institute, Washington, D.C., August 15, 1994).

16. Turner Joy, *How Communists Negotiate* (New York: Fidelis, 1971), 61. "Because of our American tendency to feel that a deadlocked issue should be solved by mutual concessions, the Communists are on favorable ground in applying their delaying tactics. By proposing that 2 plus 2 equal 6, and by then delaying an agreement interminably, the Communists hope to lead us to agree that 2 plus 2 equal 5."

17. Ibid., 130.

18. See Chuck Downs, *Over the Line: Dealing with North Korea under the Armistice* (Washington, D.C.: American Enterprise Institute, 1999).

19. The most comprehensive version of these studies is Kim Do Tae and Ch'a Jae Hoon, *Pukhan-ui Hyop-sang Chon-sul Tuksong Yongu.* Quotation from Kim Do Tae, "North Korea's Consistent Negotiating Style," 32.

20. For instance, Turner Joy's book opens with the following statement: "Communists neither blunder into conferences nor rush pell-mell to engage in negotiation. *First, they carefully set the stage.* Their concern for maintaining 'face,' as well as their regard for practical advantages arising from favorable negotiating conditions, causes the Communists to consider carefully the physical circumstances in which a parley is to occur." Concern with maintaining "face" is more properly a concept that stems from Asian cultural influences than from ideology, yet Turner Joy treats the concept as part of communist negotiating behavior. See Turner Joy, *How Communists Negotiate,* 1.

21. Alfred Wilhelm, Jr., *The Chinese at the Negotiating Table* (Washington, D.C.: National Defense University, 1995).

22. Kathryn Weathersby, "New Russian Documents on the Korean War," in Cold War International History Project, *The Cold War in Asia,* nos. 6–7 (winter 1995–96): 30–35.

1. THE NORTH KOREAN CONTEXT

1. This observation is developed more fully in Charles King Armstrong, "State and Social Transformation in North Korea, 1945–1950" (Ph.D. diss., University of Chicago, 1994).

2. See Edward Wagner, Carter Eckert, Michael Robinson, et al., *A New History of Korea* (Cambridge, Mass.: Harvard University Press, 1990); and

Bruce Cumings, *Korea's Place under the Sun: A Modern History* (New York: W. W. Norton, 1997).

3. See Michael Robinson, *Cultural Nationalism in Colonial Korea, 1920–1925* (Seattle: University of Washington Press, 1988); and Carter J. Eckert, *Offspring of Empire: The Koch'ang Kims and the Origins of Korean Capitalism* (Seattle: University of Washington Press, 1991).

4. See Koh Byung Chul, *The Foreign Policy Systems of North and South Korea* (Berkeley: University of California Press, 1984). From the 1980s, similarities between the structures and philosophies of government in North and South Korea have been diminished with the influence of democratization in South Korea and the resultant leveling of traditional structural and social hierarchies.

5. Suh Dae Sook, the foremost biographer of Kim Il Sung in English, notes that "it is [Kim's] partisan activities to which the North Koreans trace their revolutionary tradition. They maintain that other revolutionary activities, Nationalist and Communist alike, are unimportant." With the consolidation of partisans at the heart of North Korea's leadership in the early 1960s, exaggerated accounts of heroic guerrilla exploits spread, and the study of guerrilla activities was "no longer recommended, but ordered." See Suh Dae Sook, *Kim Il Sung: The North Korean Leader* (New York: Columbia University Press, 1987), 174. The real story of Kim Il Sung's resistance is more ambiguous regarding his role in the anti-Japanese resistance. An assessment written by Kim Il Sung himself in the early 1940s after a decade of sporadic guerrilla resistance against Japanese invaders, forthrightly acknowledges the failure of the guerrilla movement, which had been scattered and pushed back into Soviet territory by 1941. See Armstrong, "State and Social Transformation."

6. The critical dialogue reported by Kim Il Sung from his negotiation with Commander Wu Yi Cheng is as follows:

"Won't you join *jiajiali*? [*Jiajiali* was a Chinese brotherhood in which new members bowed down to existing members as sons might bow to show allegiance to their fathers.] It is better than the communist party, I think," [Wu] said casually.

Now I had received an embarrassing invitation to join such an organization. If I declined, the negotiations which had gone smoothly so far might be deadlocked; but if I accepted, he would take me to a Buddha and make me bow there and then, which would mean making myself subordinate to Wu Yi-cheng. When preparing for the negotiations, we had not anticipated this kind of situation. Anyway, I had to resolve the dilemma.

"It would be a fine thing for you and I to enter a *jiajiali*, but before we join another organization we are obliged to obtain permission from the party organization. If it is not granted, I can do nothing. Let us leave the matter until I obtain permission from our organization."

"Ha, ha! Then, it seems you are a half-baked commander, not a fully fledged one."

Commander Wu looked at me with a slightly dissatisfied expression on his face and all of a sudden asked me, "Do you drink, Commander Kim?"

"I can drink, but don't even if I want to, lest it hamper me in fighting against the Japanese."

"Your communist party is agreeable to me. I wish to cooperate with you but I am afraid I would have to imbibe Marxism. Spreading communism among our people is not good."

"Don't worry about it, Commander. We have no intention of propagating communism. We will only carry out anti-Japanese propaganda."

"Your party is very gentlemanly for a communist party. But it was wrong of the communists in Wangqing to disarm Commander Guan's battalion. What is your opinion of that incident?"

"What more is there to say about it? It was the most serious mistake of all possible mistakes. So we severely reprimanded the Wangqing special detachment last year."

"Commander Kim, you are a fair-minded soldier. By the way, some people say that the communist party is right in everything it does. How could that be?"

"A communist is also a man. So how could he make no mistakes? I, too, make mistakes now and then, for I am not a machine, but a man. When one tries to do a great deal of work, one is bound to make mistakes sometimes. So we study hard and improve ourselves so that we shall commit fewer errors."

"You are right. Lazy men who do nothing will make no mistakes. The communists do many things and this we appreciate. In general, it is amusing to talk to you, Commander Kim. You are candid, so we do understand each other." (Kim Il Sung, *With the Century* [Pyongyang: Pyongyang Publishing House, 1991–95], 3:172–174.

7. See Bruce Cumings, "The Corporate State in North Korea" in *State and Society in Contemporary Korea*, ed. Hagen Koo (Ithaca, N.Y.: Cornell University Press, 1993). As Kim Il Sung proceeded to establish his leadership in North Korea, he relied on fellow guerrilla partisans to support him. The loyalty of Kim's partisan supporters allowed him to overcome rival factions competing for power in the late 1940s, successively eliminating nationalists who had remained in Korea under Japanese occupation and members of the Russian and Chinese factions in North Korea during the 1950s and 1960s. During the period of consolidation, guerrilla partisans with whom Kim fought against the Japanese were rewarded with "core" leadership positions at the top of the party, military, and state structures of the DPRK, which they held for half a century.

8. See the testimony of Oleg Rakhmanin in Don Oberdorfer, *The Two Koreas: A Contemporary History* (Reading, Mass.: Addison-Wesley, 1997), 19. Kim

Il Sung is described as "careful and prudent, weighing his every word. He was afraid the Chinese would learn what he said to us . . . [Kim was] a calculating character—a chess player who calculates his every move."

9. Suh Dae Sook, *Kim Il Sung: The North Korean Leader* (New York: Columbia University Press, 1987), 176–208.

10. See Chuck Downs, *Over the Line: Dealing with North Korea under the Armistice* (Washington, D.C.: American Enterprise Institute, 1999).

11. See Yang Sung Chul, *The North and South Korean Political Systems: A Comparative Analysis* (Boulder, Colo.: Westview Press, 1994), 219–265.

12. See Armstrong, "State and Social Transformation," 113.

13. See Suh Dae Sook, *Kim Il Sung*, 68–69.

14. See Adrian Buzo, "Stalinism and Traditionalism in the DPRK," *Korea Observer* (autumn 1995): 345–377.

15. See Armstrong, "State and Social Transformation," 258–263.

16. See Yang Sung Chul, *North and South Korean Political Systems*, 219–265.

17. See Kim Il Sung, *With the Century*, 3:257.

18. See Suh Dae Sook, *Kim Il Sung*, 90–91. Kim Il Sung also used charges of collaboration with former Japanese colonial overlords to discredit those at the top of social and governing structures in the South, which remained virtually unchanged following the end of Japanese rule.

19. Kim Il Sung recounts this "vivid" lesson from his father, having witnessed the failure of the March First Movement: "It is unlikely that robbers who have intruded into your house and are wielding knives will let you live simply because you make a fuss begging them for mercy. If the man outside is also a robber, he will not come to your aid when he hears your cry. If you want to save your life you must fight the robbers. You can prevail over those who are around with knives only when you fight them with a knife." Kim Il Sung, *With the Century*, 1:50.

20. Ibid., 293–294, 341. Kim rejected factionalism but insisted on following the socialist path of violent revolution, portraying himself favorably and distinguishing himself starkly as a "true" patriot in "reminiscences" of encounters with almost every major nationalist figure of the time, including An Chang Ho, Cho Man Sik, Kim Ku, Syngman Rhee, and others.

21. See Armstrong, "State and Social Transformation," 203, 224.

22. Ibid., 200.

23. See Kim Il Sung, *With the Century*, 3:248–249.

24. See Richard H. Solomon, *Chinese Negotiating Behavior: Pursuing Interests through "Old Friends"* (Washington, D.C.: United States Institute of Peace Press, 1999).

25. See Wagner, Eckert, Robinson, et al., *A New History of Korea.*

26. See Kim Il Sung, *With the Century,* 2:422.

27. Alexandre Y. Mansourov, "In Search of a New Identity: Revival of Traditional Politics and Modernization in Post–Kim Il Sung North Korea" (paper presented at faculty research seminar, East Asian Institute, Columbia University, New York, January 23, 1995), 6–13. Mansourov also compares the trauma of this period of North Korea's history, in the context of the collapse of socialism, with the extreme insecurity that the Yi dynasty rulers felt following the replacement of the Ming dynasty with the "barbarian" Chi'ing leaders.

28. Like factional struggles that arose over the proper length of the mourning period following the death of Yi dynasty King Hyojong in 1659 (following the fall of the Ming dynasty and its replacement by Manchu Qing dynasty rulers), there was a factional struggle within the North Korean leadership over the length of the mourning period to be observed by Kim Jong Il. See ibid., 6–13.

29. See Jhe Seong Ho, "North Korean Human Rights: A Premise of Unification," *Korea Focus,* 3, no. 1 (1995): 64.

30. See Lee Ki Baik, *A New History of Korea,* trans. Edward W. Wagner with Edward J. Shultz (Cambridge, Mass.: Harvard University Press, 1984), 33, 39–40. During the Unified Shilla dynasty from the seventh to the tenth centuries, the aristocracy was ranked according to a strict hierarchy, the "bone rank" order, in which relative place in the hierarchy was assigned according to the purity of one's lineage. The system was structured according to Confucian and Buddhist influences. See Edward Wagner, Carter J. Eckert, Michael Robinson, et al., *Korea Old and New: A History* (Cambridge, Mass.: Harvard University Press, 1990), 42–53.

31. This observation is based on a variety of sources, including comments by Korean-Americans who have met family members remaining in North Korea.

32. I owe this observation to Nicholas Eberstadt, panel presentation at the University of Maryland, "The Food Situation in North Korea," February 1997.

33. See Henry H. Em, "The Nationalist Discourse in Modern Korea: Minjok as a Democratic Imaginary" (Ph.D. diss., University of Chicago, 1995), 15–47.

34. See Andre Schmid, "Rediscovering Manchuria: Sin Ch'aeho and the Politics of Territorial History in Korea," *Journal of Asian Studies* 56, no. 1 (1997): 26–46.

35. See Lee Woo Young, "Northern Defectors in South Korea," *Korea Focus* 5, no. 3 (May–June 1997): 36; originally published in *Shindonga*, May 1997.

36. See Kim Il Sung, *With the Century*, 2:40.

37. See Oberdorfer, *Two Koreas*, 19.

38. See British Broadcasting Corporation, "Commentary Says Sovereignty More Important than Agreement with USA," Central Broadcasting Station, Pyongyang, May 8, 1995 (from Lexis-Nexis news service).

39. See Koh Byung Chul, *Foreign Policy Systems*, 74–77. The Yusin period is named for the new Korean constitution introduced and approved through intimidation of the Korean public in 1972. Borrowing from the same word used in Japan to describe the Meiji "Restoration," the constitution arrogated to Park sweeping dictatorial powers. See Wagner, Eckert, Robinson, et al., *Korea Old and New*, 365.

40. See Oberdorfer, *Two Koreas*, 23.

41. See "Kim the father, Kim the son . . ." *Economist,* June 3, 1995, 6.

42. See Oberdorfer, *Two Koreas,* 22.

43. See Armstrong, "State and Social Transformation," 268.

44. See Oberdorfer, *Two Koreas,* 21.

45. For instance, see Yue Daiyun with Carolyn Wakeman, *To the Storm* (Berkeley: University of California Press, 1985).

46. See "Kim the father, Kim the son . . ."

47. See Armstrong, "State and Social Transformation," 277.

48. "Foreign Minister Kim Yong Nam Makes Speech at Memorial Service," Korea Central News Agency, July 20, 1994 (from Lexis-Nexis news service).

49. See Armstrong, "State and Social Transformation," 280.

50. K. A. Namkung, quoted in Lee Sigal, *Disarming Strangers: Nuclear Diplomacy with North Korea* (Princeton, N. J.: Princeton University Press, 1998), 149. This is also a primary conclusion supported by Armstrong, "State and Transformation."

2. THE PROCESS OF NEGOTIATING WITH NORTH KOREA

1. Perhaps the major exception may be seen in the context of zero-sum North-South negotiations during periods when the benefits of agreement are forgone in order to prevent the counterpart from also accruing benefits.

2. Steve Linton, "Approach and Style in Negotiating with the DPRK" (paper presented at Columbia University Center for Korean Research, New York, April 6, 1995), 6.

3. See Don Oberdorfer, *The Two Koreas: A Contemporary History* (Reading, Mass.: Addison-Wesley, 1997), 144–148, 222.

4. Toshimitsu Shigemura has made this argument on several occasions. See Toshimitsu Shigemura, "North Korea–Japan Relations: Struggles between Pendulum and Following" (paper presented at the conference "North Korea in Transition and Policy Choice: Domestic Structure and External Relations," Seoul, May 28–29, 1998).

5. Pyongyang and Washington have also been venues for certain types of negotiations or consultations, although the preference has been for high-level political negotiations to take place in other venues.

6. This point has been made by John Merrill and Bob Carlin on numerous occasions. See John Merrill, "Reading and Misreading North Korea," Center for War, Peace, and the News Media briefing, October 26, 1996, and Dallas conference, March 21, 1997.

7. Ibid.

8. Japanese analyst, interview by author, June 1995.

9. Indeed, South Koreans involved with the prime minister–level talks in 1990–92 agree that the North perceived dialogue with South Korea during this period as a necessary—if unpalatable—route to its ultimate goal of engaging in improved relations with the United States.

10. Most of these contacts with representative institutions and delegations were arranged by Ambassador Ho Jong, then deputy permanent ambassador of the DPRK Observer Mission to the United Nations. The Institute of Disarmament and Peace hosted a wide range of delegations, including meetings with General Stilwell and the International Security Council and two delegations arranged by the Asia Society in May 1991 and October 1992, led by Professor Robert A. Scalapino, among others. See *Divided Korea* (1992) and *Divided Korea II* (1993), reports of Asia Society study missions to the Korean Peninsula.

11. Ambassador Ho Jong actively sought an upgrading of political talks about the U.S.-DPRK relationship and "pursued the dickens out of" Deputy Assistant Secretary of State for East Asian and Pacific Affairs Desaix Anderson at every opportunity to lobby for a higher-level dialogue between Pyongyang and Washington.

12. In fact, the activities of the Institute of Disarmament and Peace were curtailed drastically by Pyongyang once an official dialogue between the United States and North Korea was established.

13. Following a second round of negotiations in New York in May 1996, joint U.S.–North Korean military teams were formed to search for and recover remains in North Korea.

14. W. Jeffrey Smith, "Korean Talks Jeopardized by New Tensions: U.S. Opening to North Strains Relations with South," *Washington Post*, February 17, 1997.

15. The meeting was hosted by the Asia Society on September 30, 1992.

16. Don Oberdorfer reports that "some of his [Quinones's] colleagues were amazed that he had spoken on the telephone to North Koreans, but he pointed out that the North Koreans had placed the call." *Two Koreas,* 283–294.

17. It is notable that Kim Jong U, a vice minister, felt slighted by having to deal with a much lower ranking official, but he did engage in talks despite his personal discomfort.

18. Likewise, American presentations at plenaries are usually official policy formulations designed to present a strong initial negotiating position.

19. For instance, Eduard Shevardnadze's experience when he informed the DPRK that the Soviet Union intended to recognize South Korea was consistent with observations of American officials regarding private and public behavior of North Koreans in negotiating sessions, as well as the nature of the relationship of negotiators with top-level leadership. During the negotiating session in Pyongyang, "Soviet officials noticed that the Korean foreign minister spoke into his microphone as if he were addressing an unseen audience of greater importance than the delegation in front of him. At first he said he was not ready to reply to Shevardnadze's presentation but would do so later. Then, after being handed a note by an aide who entered the room from outside, he pulled out a prepared document and launched into a lengthy and bitter response." Oberdorfer, *Two Koreas,* 215.

20. State Department official, interview by author, June 1995.

21. Japanese officials, interviews by author, June 1996.

22. This is a pattern that is familiar in the context of the MAC (UNC/ MAC personnel, interviews by author, June 1995) and inter-Korean negotiations, for instance, over the Basic Agreement (see Oberdorfer, *Two Koreas,* 263–264).

23. State Department official, interview by author, June 1995.

24. For additional information on the first round of nuclear negotiations with North Korea in New York, see Oberdorfer, *Two Koreas,* 285–286.

25. Ibid., 89.

26. State Department official, interviews by author, June 1995, 1996.

27. Former State Department official, interview by author, December 1997.

28. Ibid.

29. Ibid.

30. Ibid.

3. PATTERNS IN NORTH KOREA'S NEGOTIATING STYLE AND TACTICS

1. Interview by author, August 1996.

2. Steve Linton, "Approach and Style in Negotiating with the DPRK" (paper presented at Columbia University Center for Korean Research, New York, April 6, 1995), 3, 4.

3. See Lee Sigal, *Disarming Strangers: Nuclear Diplomacy with North Korea* (Princeton, N.J.: Princeton University Press, 1998), 149.

4. Linton, "Approach and Style," 2.

5. Sigal, *Disarming Strangers,* 63. Sigal argues (p. 8) that North Korean "tit-for-tat" negotiating behavior should really be seen as a reaction to the U.S. approach, which has consisted of hostility, intransigence, and brinkmanship in dealing with North Korea.

6. See Chuck Downs, *Over the Line: Dealing with North Korea under the Armistice* (Washington, D.C.: American Enterprise Institute, 1999).

7. As quoted in Sigal, *Disarming Strangers,* 61.

8. This recommendation, under consideration at the very moment President Carter called to announce he had cut a deal with Kim Il Sung, was set aside as a direct result of the Carter intervention.

9. North Korea had suspended contact at that level in response to the naming of a South Korean general as head of the MAC.

10. North Korea effectively dismantled the Neutral Nations Supervisory Commission (NNSC) by withholding electricity, water, and communications support to Polish monitors who were forced to leave the country and by requesting that the Chinese withdraw their representation at Panmunjom.

11. Interviews by author, June 1996.

12. Ibid.

13. Sigal, *Disarming Strangers,* 122.

14. As Don Oberdorfer notes, the numbing effects of brinkmanship have a down side because they blur one's sense of how close to a crisis point one might be: "North Korea had become skilled at brinkmanship, increasing its leverage by playing close to the edge of the precipice; the problem was that it wasn't always clear just where the edge was." Oberdorfer, *Two Koreas,* 305.

15. Interviews by author, June 1996.

16. One exception to the North Korean pattern of pocketing of unilateral concessions was Pyongyang's response to the U.S. announcement to withdraw land- and air-based nuclear weapons from the Korean Peninsula in September 1991. According to Ambassador Richard H. Solomon, assistant secretary of state for East Asia and the Pacific during the Bush administration, "Normally, you would expect [the U.S. nuclear initiative] to be pocketed since we had not negotiated this with them. Instead it led to reciprocal acts by them." (As quoted in Sigal, *Disarming Strangers,* 32; interview with Richard H. Solomon, February 26, 1996.) This announcement laid the groundwork for North Korea's decision to sign a nuclear safeguards inspections agreement with the IAEA and to allow inspections in early 1992. It also set the stage for progress in inter-Korean dialogue, leading to the Basic Agreement and the North-South Joint Declaration on the Denuclearization of the Korean Peninsula. The North Korean response aimed to achieve broader objectives by calling for "DPRK-U.S. negotiations to discuss simultaneous inspections and removing the nuclear threat against us" and was consistent with North Korean "matching" (what Sigal calls "tit-for-tat") behavior, as will be discussed in chapter 4. However, the North Korean concession was given in the context of a unilateral U.S. maneuver not taken in response to a demand from Pyongyang and was therefore not a concession to a specific demand by Pyongyang.

17. Some specialists suggest, however, that South Korea and Japan received limited concessions as a result of their food aid, including release of South Korean fishermen in December 1995 and the initiation of visits by Japanese wives who had married North Korean husbands.

18. U.S. government officials, interviews by author, November 1996.

19. Foreign Minister Kang even tried to use threats of noncooperation to put pressure on the U.S. side to reach an agreement in Geneva in September 1994, arguing that President Clinton "needs an agreement for the [mid-term] elections coming up," a rationale for agreement that most people in the U.S. delegation found absurd. Although Gallucci countered that an agreement with North Korea was probably going to hurt the Clinton administration, this bit of North Korean disinformation appeared to work effectively with South Koreans, who were already uncomfortable with U.S.-DPRK negotiations.

20. Nor did Pyongyang bluff in other instances with the IAEA, physically intimidating and "roughing up" inspectors who attempted to go beyond routine maintenance of inspections capabilities in August 1993. The North Koreans also at one time demanded an "entry fee," requesting that the IAEA pay for the privilege of access to certain sites. This is another instance of crude use of threats and intimidation by North Korea in response to perceived threats from the IAEA. Sigal, *Disarming Strangers,* 72.

21. Interview by author, June 1996.

22. Interview by author, August 1996.

23. Interview by author, November 1996.

24. State Department official, interview by author, June 1995.

25. Former State Department official, interview by author, February 1998.

26. State Department official, interview by author, June 1996.

27. Japanese ministry official, interview by author, June 1996.

28. "KCNA Transmits 'Authorized' Statement on Submarine Incident," *FBIS Daily Report,* FBIS-EAS-96-189, September 27, 1996.

29. In addition, there were written assurances between President Bill Clinton and President Kim Young Sam regarding the significance of these announcements for South Korea's involvement in the light-water reactor project envisioned under the Geneva Agreed Framework.

30. See Oberdorfer, *Two Koreas,* 278.

31. The North Korean side had shown unyielding resistance to the concept of "special inspections," which might categorically remove all doubt that North Korea had lied about its nuclear intentions.

32. See Oberdorfer, *Two Koreas,* 308.

33. Interview by author, August 1996.

34. Interview by author, June 1996.

35. North Korean diplomat, interview by author, June 1998.

36. Oberdorfer describes the symbolic significance of the original U.S.-DPRK joint statement in the following way: "Even if it had only described the weather in New York, the statement would have been tangible evidence that the United States had recognized the legitimacy of North Korea and was willing to negotiate." *Two Koreas,* 286.

37. Sigal, *Disarming Strangers,* 111.

38. See ibid., 78.

39. Interview by author, August 1996.

4. COMPARING NORTH-SOUTH AND U.S.-DPRK NEGOTIATING PATTERNS

1. Nancy Anne Abelmann, *Echoes of the Past, Epics of Dissent: A South Korean Social Movement* (Berkeley: University of California Press, 1996); Nancy Anne Abelmann, "The Practice and Politics of History: A South Korean Tenant Farmers Movement" (Ph.D. diss., University of California at Berkeley, 1990); and Scott Snyder, "Patterns of Negotiation in a Korean Cultural Context: Lessons from South Korea," *Asian Survey* 39, no. 3 (May–June 1999).This paper also examines the South Korean labor-management crisis of 1997 and South Korean negotiations with the IMF, among other cases, to determine patterns in South Korean bargaining and conflict resolution.

2. Don Oberdorfer, *The Two Koreas: A Contemporary History* (Reading, Mass.: Addison-Wesley, 1997), 23–27, 30. Details of Ambassador Lee's presentation to the East German leaders are taken from a record of a conversation between Hermann Axen and Lee Chang Su (July 31, 1972), SED Archives, Berlin.

3. Author conversations with staff of the DPRK's Asia-Pacific Peace Committee in July 1995 provided a North Korean view on the "flag flap." A senior North Korean official argued that it had been agreed during negotiations in Beijing that no flag would be flown on vessels within the territorial waters of North Korea, but the details of those instructions had not been passed to the North Korean harbormaster in Chongjin in time as a result of South Korean eagerness to expedite the initial deliveries of rice to the North before the South held local elections.

4. This analysis was stimulated by the discussion found in I. William Zartman and Narushige Michishita, "Two Koreas' Negotiating Strategies Revisited: Focusing on the Nuclear Issue," in *Middle Powers in the Age of Globalization: Implications for Korean Political Economy and Unification,* ed. Hwang Byong Moo and Yoon Young Kwan (Seoul: Korean Association of International Studies, 1996), 395–429. See also Harold Nicolson's classic *Diplomacy* (New York: Oxford University Press, 1964). Zartman and Michishita apply the Warrior and Shopkeeper roles to North Korea and South Korea, respectively. However, my contention is that their application of these roles in the article is erroneous and fails to capture the dynamic or shed light on the Negotiator's Dilemma in a useful way. The application of a more nuanced model in which North and South Korea negotiate as two Warriors, while the United States negotiates as the strongest party and as a Shopkeeper imposes a Shopkeeper's solution on each side, may more accurately reflect the dynamic of the negotiations over North Korea's nuclear program. Certainly, this analogy is also not complete, since the United States, by imposing a solution, exhibits some Warrior characteristics, and indeed there was strong pressure in 1994 for the United States to take a Warrior approach to North Korea. Ultimately, however, the decision to negotiate and North Korea's decision to respond through negotiations show that both sides were willing to take a Shopkeeper's approach for their own reasons.

5. Don Oberdorfer describes the North-South dynamic as one in which "the leaderships and publics of both North and South Korea saw the struggle for influence and supremacy on the peninsula as a zero-sum game, in which any gain for the South was a loss for the North and vice versa. Moreover, for both regimes, considerations of face or prestige were often more important than issues of substance. Thus North-South discussions in the public arena tended to bear fruit only when both countries could credibly claim victory, which was uncommon." *Two Koreas,* 147.

6. Kim Do Tae, "North Korea's Consistent Negotiating Style," *Vantage Point* (Seoul), April 1995, 31–40. Many of these arguments are also presented in an article by Kim entitled "Change and Continuity in North Korea's Negotiating Behavior in the Post–Cold War Era," *Social Science and Policy Research* 17, no. 2 (1995): 277–300.

7. South Korean defense official, interview by author, Seoul, June 1996.

8. Interview by author, Seoul, June 1996.

9. Ibid.

10. Ibid. From the perspective of the Warrior-Shopkeeper negotiating continuum, South Korea, with tactics shaped by a shared historical legacy and cultural influences with the North Korean Warrior, might also be seen as a Warrior. A South Korean Warrior strategy, however, is one that operates under the "disadvantage" of constraints imposed by the need to operate within international norms and within an alliance structure with the United States.

11. The conclusion of the Basic Agreement also raised hopes because the structural environment surrounding the Korean Peninsula appeared to have changed as new diplomatic relationships were established. The ROK was able to establish diplomatic relations with Russia and a rapidly developing economic relationship with China while the DPRK initiated normalization contacts with Japan and, shortly after the signing of the Basic Agreement, achieved its first high-level diplomatic meeting with the United States in January 1992. The DPRK responded to the Bush administration's withdrawal of nuclear weapons from foreign soil, including the Korean Peninsula, by showing a willingness to participate in IAEA inspections of North Korean nuclear sites and the signing of a North-South Joint Declaration on the Denuclearization of the Korean Peninsula.

12. Interview by author, Seoul, June 1996.

13. In the view of some Korean analysts, U.S. pressure on South Korea to push Pyongyang for intrusive reciprocal nuclear inspections crushed a nascent reconciliation process.

14. Chung Won Shik, interview by author, June 1996.

15. Oberdorfer, *Two Koreas,* 264; and General Park Yong Ok, interview by author, June 1996.

16. Interview by author, Seoul, June 1996.

17. See Victor Cha, "Realism, Liberalism, and the Durability of the U.S.–South Korea Alliance," *Asian Survey,* 37, no. 7 (July 1997): 609–622.

18. Studies that have reviewed the U.S.-DPRK nuclear crisis include Michael J. Mazarr, *North Korea and the Bomb: A Case Study in Nonproliferation* (New York: St. Martin's Press, 1995); Mitchell Reiss, *Bridled Ambition: Why Countries Constrain Their Nuclear Capabilities* (Washington, D.C.: Woodrow Wilson Center Press, 1995), 231–321; Chung Ok Nim (in Korean), *588 Days in North Korea's Nuclear Program: The Tactics and Strategy of the Clinton Administration* (Seoul: Seoul Press, 1995); Oberdorfer, *Two Koreas;* Koh Byung Chul, "Confrontation and Cooperation on the Korean Peninsula: The Politics of Nuclear Proliferation," *Korean Journal of Defense Analysis* 6, no. 2 (winter 1994): 53–85; Kihl Young Hwan, "Confrontation or Compromise on the Korean Peninsula: The North Korean Nuclear Issue," *Korean Journal of Defense Analysis* 6, no. 2 (winter 1994): 101–131; and Susan Rosegrant, "Carrots, Sticks, and Question Marks: Negotiating the North Korean Nuclear Crisis" (Kennedy School of Government Case Studies in Public Policy, Harvard University, unpublished manuscript).

19. Lee Sigal describes the dynamic between Washington and Seoul toward North Korea, and the domestic sensitivity of policy toward North Korea, as motivating "Seoul to blow hot and cold about talks between Washington and Pyongyang—warming up whenever the talks sputtered and turning cool whenever they made headway." *Disarming Strangers: Nuclear Diplomacy with North Korea* (Princeton, N.J.: Princeton University Press, 1998), 19.

20. Steve Linton, "Approach and Style in Negotiating with the DPRK" (paper presented at Columbia University Center for Korean Research, New York, April 6, 1995), 5.

21. See Oberdorfer, *Two Koreas,* 286; and Sigal, *Disarming Strangers,* 65. "We didn't realize how much the South Koreans would scream," Sigal quotes one State Department official as saying about the joint statement.

22. See Sigal, *Disarming Strangers,* 35, 180.

23. Ibid., 83.

24. Ibid., 202.

25. Pursuant to the consultations, both sides agreed to take four simultaneous steps on March 1, 1994: (1) The United States announced its decision to agree with the Republic of Korea's suspension of Team Spirit '94 joint military exercises. (2) The inspections necessary for the continuity of safeguards as agreed between the IAEA and the DPRK on February 15, 1994, began and were to be completed within the period agreed by the IAEA and the DPRK. (3) The working-level contacts resumed in Panmunjom for the exchange of North-South special envoys. (4) The United States and the DPRK announced that the third round of U.S.-DPRK talks would begin on March 21, 1994, in Geneva. Each of these simultaneous steps was required for the implementation of the agreed conclusions. See Sigal, *Disarming Strangers,* 105.

26. For more detail on the summit meeting, see Oberdorfer, *Two Koreas,* 293–304; and Sigal, *Disarming Strangers,* 86–88, 107.

27. James Sterngold, "South Korea President Lashes Out at U.S.," *New York Times,* October 8, 1994, 3.

5. THE U.S. NEGOTIATING EXPERIENCE COMPARED WITH KEDO

1. Following the creation of KEDO, negotiations were concluded in 1996 to allow the European Union to join KEDO's executive board in return for a contribution of approximately $20 million per year.

2. Choi Young Jin, "The Korean Peninsula in the Changing Security Context of Northeast Asia: Future Prospects," in *Bringing Peace to the Pacific: Papers from the Tenth Annual Asia Pacific Roundtable,* ed. Mohamed Jawhar Hassan and Sheikh Ahmad Raffie (Kuala Lumpur: ISIS Malaysia, 1997), 155–165.

3. As has been noted, the U.S.–DPRK talks also represented a parallel negotiating process, in which the United States represented the views of Seoul, Tokyo, the United States, and the IAEA.

4. This characterization of policy options toward the North has been frequently offered by Donald Zagoria.

5. KEDO official, interview by author, December 1997.

6. As of the end of 1998, official estimates of the cost of the reactor project stand at approximately $5.18 billion; however, the project cost was revised downward to $4.6 billion as a result of exchange rate adjustments caused by the loss in value of the won during the Asian financial crisis.

7. David F. von Hippel and Peter Hayes, "North Korean Energy Sector: Current Status and Scenarios for 2000 and 2005," in *Economic Integration of the Korean Peninsula,* ed. Marcus Noland (Washington, D.C.: Institute of International Economics, 1998), 77–118.

8. KEDO Annual Report, 1996.

9. It did not help matters that the HFO portion of the Geneva Agreed Framework negotiations was a focal point for political arguments even before the ink was dry in 1994. Foreign Minister Han Sungjoo faced questions at an appearance before a National Assembly committee following the signing of the Agreed Framework in November of 1994; he explained the ROK's commitments to finance its central role in the LWR project but stipulated that ROK responsibilities did not include payment for HFO. Although the Republican assumption of control of Congress following elections in November 1994 made congressional financial support for the agreement less likely, Ambassador Gallucci promised Congress that the Agreed Framework was cost-free for the United States except for the financing of delivery of the initial shipments of HFO. Even this initial cost resulted in a political firestorm on Capitol Hill over "reprogramming" of Department of Defense funds to pay for the first tranche of 50,000 tons of HFO in the winter of 1994. However, the new Republican-led Congress was more concerned with the issue of monitoring, rather than that of paying for, North Korean use of HFO. Administration-led international efforts to raise money for the costs of HFO have been constant but difficult, and the failure to raise such funds had put KEDO severely in debt ($48 million was owed in the HFO account) by mid-1998. Lack of sustained attention to the fund-raising issue among senior members of the Clinton administration allowed debt to mount to levels that have imperiled KEDO's daily operations, but emerging authorizations made from presidential discretionary funding accounts have allowed KEDO's HFO debts to be trimmed by about half to approximately $20 million by early 1999.

10. In previous negotiations between North and South Korea, deficiencies in technical knowledge among North Korean negotiators were frequently sufficient cause for North Korea to break off negotiations and go home (even if the outcome of negotiations might offer Pyongyang tangible benefits). However, the North Korean negotiating team persisted in studying highly technical agreements as part of the negotiating process with KEDO, perhaps because it was acceptable to learn from KEDO officials whereas learning directly from South Koreans might be seen by the North Koreans as undesirable or even threatening.

11. KEDO officials, interviews by author, May 1997.

12. Ibid.

13. The DPRK created a new bureaucratic structure, the General Bureau for the Light-Water Reactor Project, consisting of representatives from relevant ministries to manage their responsibilities under the project.

14. Regarding the technical depth of North Korean negotiators and its past impact on North-South dialogue, see also the observations of Kim Do Tae, "North Korea's Consistent Negotiating Style," *Vantage Point* (Seoul), April 1995, 31–40.

15. KEDO officials, interviews by author, May 1997.

16. Choi Young Jin, "The Korean Peninsula in the Changing Security Context of Northeast Asia," 165.

17. For North Korean attempts to defuse the issue publicly, see Korean Central News Agency, "KCNA Transmits 'Authorized' Statement on Submarine Incident," Foreign Broadcast Information Service, FBIS-EAS-96-189, September 27, 1996.

18. "Address by Ambassador Ho Jong of the DPRK Ministry of Foreign Affairs at the Ground-Breaking Ceremony for the LWR Project," Kumho, DPRK, August 19, 1997 (unpublished text).

19. "Remarks by Ambassador Stephen W. Bosworth, Executive Director, Korean Peninsula Energy Development Organization," KEDO Groundbreaking Ceremony, Kumho, DPRK, August 19, 1997 (unpublished text).

20. Kevin Sullivan and Mary Jordan, "North Korea Initiates Huge Energy Project," *Washington Post*, August 20, 1997.

21. KEDO officials, interviews by author, May 1997.

22. See Kim Do Tae, "Change and Continuity in North Korea's Negotiating Behavior in the Post–Cold War Era," *Social Science and Policy Research* 17, no. 2 (1995): 277–300; and Kim Do Tae, "North Korea's Consistent Negotiating Style."

6. CONCLUSION

1. This is not to say that inconsistency and contradiction in U.S. foreign policy might not themselves be an extraordinarily effective "strategy" in dealing with North Korea. See John Chettle, "The American Way: Or How the Chaos, Unpredictability, Contradictions, Complexity, and Example of Our System Undid Communism and Apartheid," *National Interest* 41 (fall 1995): 3–18.

Selected Bibliography

This bibliography lists selected works used as resources in writing this book. The individuals who provided information through personal interviews are listed in appendix I.

Abelmann, Nancy Anne. *Echoes of the Past, Epics of Dissent: A South Korean Social Movement.* Berkeley: University of California Press, 1996.

Armstrong, Charles King. "State and Social Transformation in North Korea, 1945–1950." Ph.D. diss., University of Chicago, 1994.

Binnendijk, Hans, ed. *How Nations Negotiate.* Washington, D.C.: National Defense University Press, 1987.

Breslin, J. William, and Jeffrey Z. Rubin, eds. *Negotiation Theory and Practice.* Cambridge, Mass.: Program on Negotiation at Harvard Law School, 1991.

Buzo, Adrian. "Stalinism and Traditionalism in the DPRK." *Korea Observer* (autumn 1995): 345–377.

Chen, Jian. *China's Road to the Korean War: The Making of the Sino-American Confrontation, 1948–1950.* New York: Columbia University Press, 1994.

Chettle, John. "The American Way: Or How the Chaos, Unpredictability, Contradictions, Complexity, and Example of Our System Undid Communism and Apartheid." *National Interest* 41 (fall 1995): 3–18.

Choi Young Jin. "The Korean Peninsula in the Changing Security Context of Northeast Asia: Future Prospects." In *Bringing Peace to the Pacific: Papers from the Tenth Annual Asia Pacific Roundtable,* ed. Mohamed Jawhar Hassan and Sheikh Ahmad Raffie, 155–165. Kuala Lumpur: ISIS Malaysia, 1997.

Chung Ok Nim. *588 Days in North Korea's Nuclear Program: The Tactics and Strategy of the Clinton Administration* (in Korean). Seoul: Seoul Press, 1995.

Cohen, Raymond. *Negotiating across Cultures.* Washington, D.C.: United States Institute of Peace, 1991; rev. ed., 1997.

Cold War International History Project, *The Cold War in Asia,* nos. 6–7 (winter 1995–96). Washington, D.C.: Woodrow Wilson Center for International Scholars.

Cumings, Bruce. *Korea's Place under the Sun: A Modern History.* New York: W. W. Norton, 1997.

———. "The Corporate State in North Korea" In *State and Society in Contemporary Korea,* ed. Hagen Koo. Ithaca, N.Y.: Cornell University Press, 1993.

Downs, Chuck. *Over the Line: Dealing with North Korea under the Armistice.* Washington, D.C.: American Enterprise Institute, 1999.

Eckert, Carter J. *Offspring of Empire: The Koch'ang Kims and the Origins of Korean Capitalism.* Seattle: University of Washington Press, 1991.

Em, Henry H. "The Nationalist Discourse in Modern Korea: Minjok as a Democratic Imaginary." Ph.D. diss., University of Chicago, 1995.

Faure, Guy Olivier, and Jeffrey Z. Rubin, eds. *Culture and Negotiation.* Newbury Park, Calif.: Sage, 1993.

Fisher, Glen. *International Negotiation: A Cross-Cultural Perspective.* Yarmouth, Maine: Intercultural Press, 1980.

Foot, Rosemary. *The Wrong War: American Policy and the Dimensions of the Korean Conflict, 1950–1953.* Ithaca, N.Y.: Cornell University Press, 1985.

George, Alexander L. *Bridging the Gap: Theory and Practice in Foreign Policy.* Washington, D.C.: United States Institute of Peace Press, 1993.

Goldhammer, Herbert. *The 1951 Korean Armistice Conference: A Personal Memoir.* Santa Monica, Calif.: RAND, 1995.

Grinker, Richard Roy. *Korea and Its Futures: Unification and the Unfinished War.* New York: St. Martin's Press, 1998.

Habeeb, Mark. *Power and Tactics in International Negotiation: How Weak Nations Negotiate with Strong Nations.* Baltimore, Md.: Johns Hopkins University Press, 1988.

Hayes, Peter, and David von Hippel. "North Korea's Energy Sector." In *Economic Integration of the Korean Peninsula,* ed. Marcus Noland. Washington, D.C.: Institute of International Economics, 1998.

Hunter, Helen-Louise. *Kim Il-Sung's North Korea*. Westport, Conn.: Praeger, 1999.

Jhe Seong Ho. "North Korean Human Rights: A Premise of Unification." *Korea Focus* 3, no. 1 (1995).

Joy, C. Turner. *How Communists Negotiate*. New York: Macmillan, 1955.

Kihl Young Hwan. "Confrontation or Compromise on the Korean Peninsula: The North Korean Nuclear Issue." *Korean Journal of Defense Analysis* 6, no. 2 (winter 1994): 101–131.

Kim Do Tae. "North Korea's Consistent Negotiating Style." *Vantage Point* (Seoul), April 1995, 31–40.

Kim Do Tae and Ch'a Jae Hoon. *Pukhan-ui Hyop-sang Chon-sul Tuksong Yŏngu: Nam-buk Taehwa Salyedul Chungsimulo* (Research on Characteristics of North Korea's Negotiating Strategy: Case Studies on North-South Dialogue). Seoul: Minjok Tongil Yonguso, December 1995.

Kim Il Sung. *With the Century*. Vols. 1–6. Pyongyang: Pyongyang Publishing House, 1991–95.

Koh Byung Chul. *The Foreign Policy Systems of North and South Korea*. Berkeley: University of California Press, 1984.

———. "Confrontation and Cooperation on the Korean Peninsula: The Politics of Nuclear Proliferation." *Korean Journal of Defense Analysis* 6, no. 2 (winter 1994): 53–85.

Lee Dong Bok. "Negotiating with North Korea: Strategy and Tactics." Text of a presentation given at the seminar "Negotiating with the North after Kim Il Sung," American Enterprise Institute, Washington, D.C., August 15, 1994.

Lee, Woo Young. "Northern Defectors in South Korea." *Korea Focus* 5, no. 3 (May–June 1997); originally published in *Shindonga*, May 1997.

Linton, Steve. "Approach and Style in Negotiating with the DPRK." Paper presented at Columbia University Center for Korean Research, New York, April 6, 1995.

Mazarr, Michael J. *North Korea and the Bomb: A Case Study in Nonproliferation*. New York: St. Martin's Press, 1995.

Mansourov, Alexandre Y. "In Search of a New Identity: Revival of Traditional Politics and Modernization in Post–Kim Il Sung North Korea." Paper presented at faculty research seminar, East Asian Institute, Columbia University, New York, January 23, 1995.

McCusker, Christopher Rob. "Individualism-Collectivism and Relationships in Distributive Negotiation: An Experimental Analysis." Ph.D. diss., University of Illinois at Urbana-Champaign, 1994.

Moltz, James Clay, and Alexandre Y. Mansourov, eds. *The North Korean Nuclear Program: Security, Strategy, and New Perspectives from Russia.* New York: Routledge, 1999.

Moon Chung In. *Arms Control on the Korean Peninsula: International Penetrations, Regional Dynamics, and Domestic Structure.* Seoul: Yonsei University Press, 1996.

Nicolson, Harold. *Diplomacy.* New York: Oxford University Press, 1964.

Noland, Marcus, ed. *Economic Integration of the Korean Peninsula.* Washington, D.C.: Institute of International Economics, 1998.

Oberdorfer, Don. *The Two Koreas: A Contemporary History.* Reading, Mass.: Addison-Wesley, 1997.

Reiss, Mitchell. *Bridled Ambition: Why Countries Constrain Their Nuclear Capabilities.* Washington, D.C.: Woodrow Wilson Center Press, 1995.

Robinson, Michael. *Cultural Nationalism in Colonial Korea, 1920–1925.* Seattle: University of Washington Press, 1988.

Rosegrant, Susan. "Carrots, Sticks, and Question Marks: Negotiating the North Korean Nuclear Crisis." Kennedy School of Government Case Studies in Public Policy, Harvard University. Unpublished manuscript.

Roy, Denny. "The Myth of North Korean 'Irrationality.'" *Korean Journal of International Studies* 25, no. 2 (summer 1994).

Schecter, Jerrold L. *Russian Negotiating Behavior.* Washington, D.C.: United States Institute of Peace Press, 1998.

Schmid, Andre. "Rediscovering Manchuria: Sin Ch'aeho and the Politics of Territorial History in Korea." *Journal of Asian Studies* 56, no. 1 (1997): 26–46.

Sigal, Lee. *Disarming Strangers: Nuclear Diplomacy with North Korea.* Princeton, N.J.: Princeton University Press, 1998.

Snyder, Scott. "Patterns of Negotiation in a Korean Cultural Context: Lessons from South Korea." *Asian Survey* 39, no. 3 (May–June).

Solomon, Richard H. *Chinese Negotiating Behavior: Pursuing Interests through "Old Friends"* (Washington, D.C.: United States Institute of Peace Press, 1999).

Song Jong Hwan. "How the North Korean Communists Negotiate: A Case Study of the South-North Korean Dialogue of the Early 1970s." *Korea and World Affairs* 8, no. 3 (fall 1984): 610–664.

Stueck, William. *The Korean War: An International History.* Princeton, N.J.: Princeton University Press, 1995.

Suh Dae Sook. *Kim Il Sung: The North Korean Leader.* New York: Columbia University Press, 1987.

Wagner, Edward, Carter Eckert, Michael Robinson, et al. *A New History of Korea.* Cambridge, Mass.: Harvard University Press, 1990.

Wilhelm, Alfred J., Jr. *The Chinese at the Negotiating Table.* Washington, D.C.: National Defense University Press, 1995.

Yang, Sung Chul. *The North and South Korean Political Systems: A Comparative Analysis.* Boulder, Colo.: Westview Press, 1994.

Yue Daiyun with Carolyn Wakeman. *To the Storm.* Berkeley: University of California Press, 1985.

Zartman, William I., and Narushige Michishita, "Two Koreas' Negotiating Strategies Revisited: Focusing on the Nuclear Issue." In *Middle Powers in the Age of Globalization: Implications for Korean Political Economy and Unification,* ed. Hwang Byong Moo and Yoon Young Kwan, 395–429. Seoul: Korean Association of International Studies, 1996.

Index

Abelmann, Nancy, 97
Ackerman, Gary, 89–90
action, military, danger of provoking the U.S. to, 72
agenda
    control of, 150
    hidden, 12
    loading, 11, 44, 146
    North Korean, 43, 72–73
    side issues on, 95
Agreed Conclusion between the United States and North Korea, 71, 89, 91–92, 93, 110–111, 186 *n.* 25
Agreed Framework. *See* Geneva Agreed Framework
Agreement on Reconciliation, Non-aggression, Exchanges and Cooperation (the Basic Agreement), 69, 181 *n.* 16, 184 *n.* 11
    negotiation of, 102
    South Korean assessment of, 103–106

suspension of, 75
agreements, joint, preoccupation with equivalency in, 91–92
ambassadors
    North Korean, signals from, 50
    South Korean, as observers, 109
ambiguity, importance of avoiding, 151
An Chang Ho, 175 *n.* 20
analysts, limitations of North Korean, 51
Anderson, Desaix, 178 *n.* 11
APEC. *See* Asia-Pacific Economic Cooperation Group
apologies
    negotiations over, 133–134
    subcontexts of, 75, 100–101, 133
    unprecedented, 75
armistice, Korean War, 11–12, 13
Armistice Agreement, 10, 13, 134, 143
Armstrong, Charles, 26–27, 29, 38, 40

Asia Society, 178 *n.* 10
Asia-Pacific Economic Cooperation
    Group (APEC), 110, 114, 133
Asia-Pacific Peace Committee, 101,
    183 *n.* 3
axe murder in the DMZ, 5, 12, 134,
    169 *n.* 3

Basic Agreement. *See* Agreement
    on Reconciliation
behavior, matching, in negotiations,
    98–103
benefits to North Korea
    acknowledgment of and negoti-
        ating behavior, 122, 127, 140–
        141, 147, 151, 154, 156–157
    forgone to spite South Korea, 9,
        12–13, 85, 177 *n.* 1
blackmail, importance of avoiding
    appearance of, 150
blame, as a tactic, 86–88
bluff
    calling, 62, 80–81, 82–83, 181
        n. 19
    as a counterstrategy, 152–153
    as a tactic, 62, 76, 77, 79, 80–81,
        146, 148–149
bone rank, 33, 176 *n.* 30
border incursions, 12, 73–74
Bosworth, Stephen, 118, 120, 121–
    122, 124, 129, 135
breakdown (walking away)
    protocol and, 54
    as a tactic, 44, 83–88, 144, 146,
        153
    to avoid admission of ignorance,
        188 *n.* 10
brinkmanship, 9, 144

avoidance of, 104–105
credibility and, 81, 127, 154
dangers of, 78
effects of, 77, 83–85, 143, 156–
    157, 181 *n.* 14
Geneva Agreed Framework
    and, 62
and the guerrilla tradition, 22,
    66
KEDO negotiations and, 122,
    123, 139
limitations of, 147
limiting, 151
long-distance, 76–77
retaliatory, 84
as a signal of progress, 44
South Korea's, 98, 110, 113
and U.S.-ROK relationships,
    107
usefulness of, 146
bureaucracy, socialist, in North
    Korea, 32, 45, 143
Buzo, Adrian, 26

Carter, Jimmy, 72, 80, 111, 180 *n.* 8
Center for Strategic and Interna-
    tional Studies, 70
chaebol (industrial conglomerate),
    South Korean, 105
Chang Chong U, 130
Chang Sun Sop, 135
ch'emyon. See "face" saving
Chiang Kai-shek, 23
China
    and Korea, 20, 34
    Ming dynasty in, 176 n. 27
    National Salvation Army of, 23
    negotiating practices of, 31

China *(cont.)*
  Qing dynasty in, 176 *n.* 28
  Song-dynasty Confucianism
    of, 31
  T'ang dynasty in, and Korea, 20
China, People's Republic of (PRC)
  and the Korean War armistice,
    10, 13
  Nixon's visit to, 75, 99
  and North Korea, 13, 24, 26, 27
  South Korea and, 184–185 *n.* 11
Cho Man Sik, 29, 175 *n.* 20
Choi Young Jin, 118, 119, 130
Chollima movement, the, 27
Chun Doo Hwan, 5
Chun Geum Chol, 100–101
Chung Won Shik, 105
Clinton, Bill
  condolences from, on the death
    of Kim Il Sung, 111
  and the Four Party Talks, 52, 79,
    114, 119, 134
  and the North Korean subma-
    rine incident, 114, 133
  and North Korea's nuclear
    facilities, 71, 112, 181 *n.* 17,
    182 *n.* 29
  and the summit conference with
    Kim Young Sam, 110–111
Cohen, Raymond, *Negotiating
  across Cultures*, 9–10
Cold War
  and North Korean negotiating
    behavior, 9, 12, 13, 76, 143
  North Korea's foreign policy
    during, 24
  and North Korea's relative posi-
    tion of power, 14, 106

and the partition of the Korean
    Peninsula, 29
  and U.S. relations with South
    Korea, 107
collaboration, punishment of, by
    the DPRK, 29, 175 *n.* 18
collectivism, and negotiation,
    170 *n.* 12
collectivization, models for, 27
colonialism. *See* Japan, occupation
    of Korea by
commitments, North Korean per-
    ceptions of, 11
Communist Party, in North Korea,
    25, 38, 49
compromise
  circumstances for, 42, 57
  deadlines and, 83
  informal meetings and, 56, 95
  rejection of, 99
  signals about, 49, 95–96
concessions, 98
  demanding unilateral, 78–79,
    86, 181 *n.* 16
  the end game and, 61, 62
  KEDO and, 128–129
  masking, 59, 145, 148
  pocketing, 11, 25, 78–79, 103,
    181 *n.* 16
  as precedent, 128
  reciprocated, 155, 181 *nn.* 16, 17
  reneging on, 130–131
  uses of, 23
  see also behavior, matching
conditionality
  South Korean demands for, 110
  unpalatability of, for North
    Korea, 92–93

confidentiality, to mask concessions, 90, 148
conflict, escalation of, and brinkmanship, 78
Confucius, influence of, on Korean
   culture, 19, 31–34, 38, 98,
   145, 176 n. 28
consensus, importance of, 118,
   126, 139, 149
consultation
   management of internal KEDO,
      125, 126–127, 128–129
   recess for, 60, 61
contact
   informal, 45, 51, 52, 53, 95, 133,
      145, 148–149
   working-level, 71, 110, 186 n. 25
costs
   of the Geneva Agreed Frame-
      work, 157
   of light-water reactors for North
      Korea, 123–124, 136, 137,
      187 nn. 6, 9
counterproposals, North Korean
   reluctance to make, 59
counterstrategy, 147–153
crisis
   negotiation oriented by, 7, 43, 84,
      98, 150, 151, 153–154, 157–158
   nuclear, 3–6
   permanent, North Korean
      nationalism as, 40
   unexpected, negotiation and,
      75–76, 131
   see also deadlines, fabricated
crisis diplomacy, 9, 66, 68, 69–76,
   144, 146, 147, 154
   penalties for using, 150

Cultural Revolution (China), 39
culture
   Chinese, 13
   defined, 9–10, 170 n. 11
   Korean, 13, 19
   and negotiating behavior, 7, 13
Cumings, Bruce, 23

deadlines, fabricated
   as a counterstrategy, 152–53
   as a negotiation tactic, 66, 69–
      70, 81–83, 94, 122, 136, 146
deadlock, 57, 84
   see also stalemate
deal making, 44, 58–59
decision making, North Korean
   hierarchical, 28
delay, as a negotiating tactic, 11, 31,
   54, 60, 61, 83, 146, 172 n. 16
   in KEDO talks, 120, 122
demands, maximal, 11, 85, 146, 149
Demilitarized Zone (DMZ), 5, 84
deniability, usefulness of, 149
dialogue, inter-Korean
   agreement in principle on, 96
   concessions and, 93
   dual-track negotiations in, 45
   effects of, 184–185 n. 11
   face-saving and, 90
   and future negotiation, 154, 155
   initiation of, 99
   one-upmanship in, 14
   patterns in, 98–103
   prenegotiations for, 51, 178 n. 9
   as probing for weakness, 100
   Red Cross and, 12
   resumption of, 10–11, 75,
      155–156, 181 n. 16

dialogue, inter-Korean *(cont.)*
  South Korean demands for,
    109–110
  ulterior motives in, 102
  as a zero-sum game, 14, 99, 111-
    112, 143, 146, 154, 155, 9,
    98, 119, 184 *n.* 5
dilemma, Toughness (Negotiator's),
    7, 98, 101, 107, 109–110, 146,
    183–184 *n.* 4
diplomat, North Korean. *See*
  negotiators
disinformation, for South Korea,
    48, 181–182 *n.* 19
DMZ. *See* Demilitarized Zone
Dole, Robert, 111
Downs, Chuck, 11
DPRK. *See* North Korea (Demo-
    cratic People's Republic
    of Korea)
draft
  South Korean, of the Basic Agree-
    ment, 105–106
  as a working document, 58–59
dynasty, Korean
  Koryo, 18
  Shilla, 33, 176 *n.* 30
  Yi, 18, 31, 34, 176 *nn.* 27, 28
  see also China

Economist, The, 37
emotion, display of, as a negotia-
    tion tactic, 66, 94–95, 152
end game, North Korean tactics
    for, 44, 59, 61–62, 146, 148
equivalency
  as an issue of protocol, 53,
    91–92

demands for, as a negotiating
    tactic, 9, 23, 34, 66, 145,
    146, 148
ethics, negotiation, 101
European Union, as a member of
    KEDO, 137, 186 *n.* 1

"face" saving (*ch'emyon*)
  allowance for, as a strategy, 152
  as extrication from a predica-
    ment, 90–91
  inter-Korean dialogue and,
    184 *n.* 5
  manipulation of the concept
    of, as a tactic, 86, 89–91
  as a metaphor, 91
  protocol and, 54
  significance of, 89–90, 92, 170
    n. 12, 172 *n.* 20
"flag flap," the, 100–101, 183 *n.* 3
food aid, for North Korea
  as demands, 79, 80–81, 86
  donations of, 78–79, 100–101,
    112, 155, 181 *n.* 17
  need for, 75, 113, 134
foreigners, Korean perceptions
    of, 20, 24
Four Party Talks
  North Korea and, 114, 152
  and North Korea's internal
    crises, 75, 86, 157
  objective of, 134
  preliminary negotiations about,
    43, 52, 79
  proposal for, 113, 119, 150
fuel oil, heavy (HFO)
  benefits of, and negotiation
    stance, 122, 127

fuel oil, heavy (HFO) *(cont.)*
  political significance of, 124–125,
    187 *n.* 9
  supplies of, 6, 45, 117, 118, 132
  see also Korean Peninsula
    Energy Development Orga-
    nization
fuel rods, issues over, 43, 71–72,
    80–81, 82, 84–85, 122, 151

Gallucci, Robert L., 97, 111
  KEDO and, 187 *n.* 9
  U.S.-DPRK nuclear negotiations
    and, 4, 5–6, 10, 54, 62, 94–95,
    169 *n.* 5, 181 *n.* 19
General Sherman, USS, 18, 32
Geneva Agreed Framework, 74,
    79, 82
  and appearances of equivalency,
    91–92
  confidential minute attached
    to, 90
  costs of, 187 *n.* 9
  crisis diplomacy and, 150
  described, 6, 118–119
  draft of, 58
  end game of, 61–62, 89
  implementation of, 36, 113, 131,
    138, 157
    see also Korean Peninsula
      Energy Development
      Organization
  and the North Korean spy sub-
    marine incident, 132–133
  South Korean compromising
    of, 112–113, 114
  technical negotiations and, 47
  time pressures and, 94

German Democratic Republic, 99
Graham, the Reverend Billy, 67
Great Leap Forward, the, 27
guerilla, partisan, as a cultural
    influence, 21–25, 172 *n.* 5

Habeeb, Mark, *Power and Tactics in
    International Negotiation,* 69
Hall, CWO Bobby, 73, 84
Han Sungjoo, 187 *n.* 9
HFO. *See* fuel oil, heavy
Hideyoshi, and Korea, 20
hierarchy, traditional Korean, 33,
    176 *n.* 30
history, nationalist definition
    of, 35
Ho Chi Minh, 21
Ho Jong
  KEDO and, 122, 129, 134, 135
  lobbying by, 53–54, 178 *nn.* 10, 11
  relationship building by, 51
hospitality, uses of, 56–58
How Communists Negotiate (Turner
    Joy), 11
Hubbard, Thomas, 68, 73–74, 82,
    83, 84, 89, 109
Hunziger, Evan, 133
Hyland, William, 5
Hyojong, King, 176 *n.* 28
Hyun Hong Choo, 109

IAEA. *See* International Atomic
    Energy Agency
IDP. *See* Institute of Disarmament
    and Peace
implementation, negotiation
    about, 62–63, 149, 151
incentives, limitations on, 103

individualism, and negotiation, 170 *n.* 12

Institute of Disarmament and Peace (IDP), 51, 52, 178 *n.* 10, 179 *n.* 12

insults, North Korean sensitivity to perceived, 37, 40–41, 136–137, 145

interdependence, global, 35

International Atomic Energy Agency (IAEA), inspections of North Korean facilities by, 6, 85

the Agreed Conclusion and, 186 *n.* 25

concessions on, 93

and crisis diplomacy, 69–70

"face" saving over, 90

negotiations about, 71

North Korean agreement to, 181 *n.* 16, 184–185 *n.* 11

refusals of, 81, 82, 104, 105, 182 *n.* 20

wording of agreements on, 92, 93

International Security Council, 178 *n.* 10

intimidation, by North Korea, 143, 182 *n.* 20

Japan

and KEDO, 117, 123, 137

legacy of, 30

Liberal Democratic Party, 46

normalization negotiations and, 46, 55, 184–185 *n.* 11

and North Korean dual-track negotiations, 45, 46

as object of North Korean vituperation, 30

occupation of Korea by, 17, 19, 20, 23, 27–30 passim, 34, 144–145

rice from, for North Korea, 78–79, 181 *n.* 17

Joint Denuclearization Declaration. *See* North-South Joint Declaration

joint statements

as empty symbol, 100, 108

language of, 57

reactions to, 108, 186 *n.* 21

juche (self-reliance), philosophy of

as definitive, 32, 34–37, 145

and national self-identity, 18, 20, 21, 27, 123, 144

juche-ui chongsin (autonomous spirit), 35

Kanemaru, Shin, 46

Kang Sok Ju, 10

anger displayed by, as a facilitating tactic, 94–95

bluffing by, 62

protocol and, 3, 4, 54

signals from, 60

threats made by, 83, 181 *n.* 19

Kanter, Arnold, 4, 70

KCNA. *See* Korean Central News Agency

KEDO. *See* Korean Peninsula Energy Development Organization

KEPCO. *See* Korean Electrical Power Company

kibun (feeling), in negotiations, 66–67, 68, 146

Kim Byong Hong, 52
Kim Dae Jung, 104, 154, 155
Kim Dal Hyun, 105
Kim Do Tae, 12, 102
Kim Hyong Jik, 32
Kim Il Sung
    apologies by, 134
    autobiography of, 23, 27, 29,
        30, 32, 35–36, 175 nn. 19, 20
    biography of, 173 n. 22
    and the Chinese nationalists,
        23, 173 n. 6
    as the Eternal President, 37
    family of, 17–18, 31–33
    as the Great Leader, 17, 38
    as a guerrilla patriot, 21–22, 144,
        173 n. 5, 175 n. 20
    infallibility of, 37, 90
    and Jimmy Carter, 72, 80, 180
        n. 8
    nationalism of, 29, 175 n. 8
    personality cult of, 26, 32–33,
        37–41, 145
    political philosophy of, 20,
        175 n. 19
    on reciprocity, 92
    and South Korea, 10, 75,
        99–100, 111
    Soviet influences on, 25–26
    Soviet perceptions of, 36, 174
        n. 8
    support for, from fellow guerrilla
        partisans, 174 n. 7
    U.S. condolences on death
        of, 111
    With the Century, 23
Kim Jong Il, 31, 33, 39–40, 41, 112,
    136–137, 176 n. 28

Kim Jong U, 45, 54, 60, 81, 82, 89,
    179 n. 17
Kim Ku, 175 n. 20
Kim Kye Gwan, 81–82, 83, 89
Kim Song Ju. See Kim Il Sung
Kim Yong Chul, Major General,
    105, 106
Kim Yong Nam, 40, 53
Kim Yong Sun, 4, 70
Kim Young Sam
    and the Four Party Talks, 52,
        79, 114, 119, 134
    on the Geneva Agreed Frame-
        work, 112–113, 182 n. 29
    and inter-Korean dialogue, 113
    and the North Korean subma-
        rine incident, 88, 114, 131,
        132, 133, 134
    reaction of, to the death of Kim
        Il Sung, 111–112, 119
    and summit meeting with Clin-
        ton, 71, 110–111
Koh Byung Chul, 20, 36
kojip (stubbornness), 66, 67–68, 146
    see also kosaeng
Korea
    China and, 34
    foreign policy in, 20, 49
    international position of, 20
    self-perceptions of, 20
    social order of, 19
    see also North Korea; South
        Korea
Korea Air Lines (KAL), 5
Korea Asia-Pacific Peace Commit-
    tee, 52
Korea Institute of National Uni-
    fication, 12

Korea Times, 110
Korean Central Intelligence Agency
(KCIA), 37
Korean Central News Agency
(KCNA), 30, 36, 48, 87, 134
Korean Communist Party, 29
Korean Electrical Power Company
(KEPCO), 118
Korean Peninsula Energy Development Organization
(KEDO), 43
acceptance of, by North Korea,
117, 120–125, 140
as a bridge between North
and South Korea, 119, 131,
135, 147
delays in, 89, 125, 126
implementation of, 113, 114,
135–136, 137
internal negotiations within,
136–138
multilateral composition of,
117–118, 119, 121–122,
125–129, 139, 147
and the North Korean spy submarine incident, 132–133,
134, 137
politics and, 137, 138
protocol of, 120, 121–124,
125–131, 132, 134
purpose of, 117
subcontractors to, 137
technicalities of, and North
Korea's bargaining stance,
125, 127, 129–130, 139–140,
147, 188 *n.* 10
time pressures in, 94
Korean People's Army, 26, 47

Korean War, 4, 5, 10, 11, 111, 140
see also prisoners of war, negotiations over
Korean War Memorial, 113
Korean Workers Party, 4
kosaeng (suffering), displays of, as
a tactic, 86, 88–89

landownership, study of negotiations over, 97
language, importance of details
of, 46, 56, 57, 58–59, 62, 92,
95, 110, 121
Lee Chang Su, 99
Lee Hu Rak, 37
legitimacy
North Korea's quest for, 12, 28
South Korea's competition for,
102–103, 108
leverage
from a position of weakness, 51,
66, 68, 70–71, 85–91, 157
maximizing, 144
li (righteousness), 31, 34
Lim Dong Won, 104–105
Linton, Stephen, 45, 67
Lord, Winston, 132, 133, 169 *n.* 5
LWRs. *See* reactors, light-water

MAC. *See* Military Armistice
Commission
Manchuria, Japanese occupation
of, 23
Mangyongdae, mandatory pil-
grimage to, 17–18
Mansourov, Alexandre, 33
Mao Zedong, 21, 26, 27, 37, 39
March First Movement, 174 *n.* 19

masses, propaganda for, 48
Mazarr, Michael, 70
media, North Korean
 analysis of, as useful, 48–49,
  149
 hierarchy in, and audiences
  for, 48, 50
 international outlets of, 48–49
 rhetoric of blame in, 87
 signals in, about negotiation,
  44, 47–50, 148
meetings
 informal, 56–58
 sidebar, 56, 129
 technical, 56
 working-level, 56
 see also contact
middle game, 58–59
Military Armistice Commission
  (MAC)
 crisis diplomacy and, 69, 73, 74,
  180 *n.* 9
 durability of agreements under,
  96
 negotiation and, 11–12, 73, 100,
  143
 technical contact with North
  Korea and, 10, 12
 and UNC, 73, 180 *n.* 9
Minju Chosun (newspaper), 48
missiles, North Korean
 development of, 84, 148, 156
 testing of, as a diplomatic crisis,
  74, 81, 158
missing-in-action, issues of Americans. *See* prisoners of war
mistakes, North Korean silence
  on, 87–88, 89

Mount Myohyang, museum at, for
  gifts to Kim Il Sung, 34–35
mourning period, political importance of, 32, 33, 176 *n.* 28
mythology, national, in North
  Korea, 17–18, 22, 31

Namkung, K. A., 67
nationalism
 and the cult of personality, 38
 and *juche*, 35, 36–37
 Kim Il Sung's manipulation of,
  29, 175 *n.* 18
 and the liberation from Japanese colonialism, 28–31
 metaphors of, 38
 South Korean, 36
 as a state of permanent crisis, 40
negotiation
 assessment of preliminary, 60
 bilateral, 118
 communication in, 170 *n.* 12
 counterstrategies for, 147–153
 culture and, 13, 125, 130, 170
  n. 12
 cyclicality of, 44, 56, 62–63, 149
 differences between North and
  South Korea and, 106–115
 dual-track. *See* negotiation,
  parallel
 future, 153–157
 guerrilla tradition and, 22, 66, 69
 Kim Il Sung's shadow over, 40
 linear, as a U.S. perception, 44,
  62, 149
 multilateral, 9, 151–152
 objectives in, 12–13, 73, 102,
  150–151

negotiation *(cont.)*
  "package (basket)" approach
    to, 59, 110, 124, 148
  parallel (dual-track), 45, 60–61,
    113–114, 119, 187 *n.* 3
  preliminary contacts for, 23
  process of, 44, 50–63
  realistic expectations and, 149
  as ritual competition, 99, 100,
    156
  as self-defense, 99–100
  strategy for. *See* strategy
  structural factors in, 106–107,
    170–171 *n.* 12
  style of North Korean, 43, 66–68,
    141
  tactics in. *See* tactics
  as "tit-for-tat," 180 *n.* 5, 181 *n.* 16
  as unrealistically aggressive, 79–80
  as war by other means, 13
  see also end game; middle
    game; U.S.-DPRK nuclear
    negotiations
Negotiator's Dilemma. *See* dilemma
negotiators, North Korean
  influences on, 41–42, 45–47
  informal contacts and, 57–58
  for the KEDO project, 127,
    188 *n.* 13
  private and public behavior of,
    179 *n.* 19
  as reshapers of DPRK percep-
    tions, 46–47
  training for, 51
Neutral Nations Supervisory Com-
    mission (NNSC), North
    Korea's dismantling of,
    180 *n.* 10

New York Times, 112, 114
Nicolson, Harold, 101
Nixon, Richard, visit of, to China,
    as a shock, 75, 99
NNSC. See Neutral Nations Super-
    visory Commission
Nodong Sinmun (newspaper), 48
noninterference, as an inviolable
    principle, 31
North Korea (Democratic People's
    Republic of Korea; DPRK)
  as an unknown quantity, 3–5
  anniversary of, and negotiation
    deadlines, 94
  Bureau of Atomic Energy, 47
  Committee for External Eco-
    nomic Affairs, 105
  culture of, and negotiation, 21–
    42, 125, 130, 170–171 *n.* 12
  distinguished from the Commu-
    nist Party, 48
  economic decline of, and rela-
    tive power, 9, 75, 127, 154,
    156
  External Economic Affairs
    Commission, 45, 60, 101
  family ties in, 33
  former guerrilla partisans as
    leaders of, 174 *n.* 7
  General Bureau for the Light-
    Water Reactor Project, 188
    n. 13
  and KEDO, 117, 120, 128, 138,
    140
  legal system of, 30
  Mangyongdae as the national
    shrine of, 17–18
  Marxism-Leninism in, 25–26

North Korea (Democratic People's
Republic of Korea; DPRK)
(cont.)
Ministry of Foreign Affairs, 45,
47, 49–50, 51, 52, 94
objectives of, 12
Observer Mission to the United
Nations, 51, 178 *n.* 10
and the People's Republic of
China, 24
propaganda war on South
Korea by, 175 *n.* 18
revisionist history of, 22, 35
as a revolutionary state, 25–28
rhetoric of, as bluffing, 148–149
sensitivity of, about North-South
relations, 125
and South Korea. *See* dialogue,
inter-Korean
South Korean images of, 103,
104–106
and South Korean personnel of
KEDO in, 120, 128, 132, 136
sovereignty of, as a prime concern, 9, 30
and the spy submarine incident,
131–132, 133–134
statecraft of, and the guerrilla
tradition, 23–25, 174 *n.* 7
structure of, 25–26, 69, 87–88,
144, 145
technology for, 138–139
see also Korean Peninsula
Energy Development
Organization
traditionalism in, 26–27, 31
United States and, 5, 24, 65, 70–
71, 106, 107, 128, 147–153

and the U.S.S.R., 13, 24, 25, 27,
36, 174 *n.* 8
North-South Joint Declaration on
the Denuclearization of the
Korean Peninsula, 104, 181
n. 16, 184–185 *n.* 11
NPT. *See* Nuclear Non-Proliferation
Treaty
Nuclear Non-Proliferation Treaty
(NPT), negotiations over
North Korea's threat to withdraw from, 3, 57, 58–59,
69–70, 80, 81
nuclear program, North Korean
bluffing about, 81
crisis diplomacy and, 4, 43, 107,
151, 156
discrepancy in reporting, 69
dismantling of, 6, 132
reciprocal inspection and, 104,
185 *n.* 13
see also fuel rods, issues over

Oberdorfer, Don, *The Two Koreas,* 38
oil. *See* fuel oil
omissions, as signals, 49, 55
one-upmanship, as a negotiating
tactic, 14, 100, 102–103,
146, 149

Park Chung Hee
and national self-identity, 20, 36
and North Korea, 10, 99–100
and reunification, 75
the Yusin reforms and, 36,
177 *n.* 39
Park Yong Ok, Major General,
105, 106

patience, 83, 153
Patriot missiles, 72
pattern of negotiation, 68–96, 97–98
    as a code, 55
    predictability of, 43, 143, 145–146
    using, as a counterstrategy,
        147–148
Perry, William, xiii, 72
personality, cult of, in North Korea,
    26, 37–41, 145
philisophy, neo-Confucian. *See*
    Confucius, influence of
piety, politics of filial, 32–33
plenary sessions, 49, 54–55, 87, 145,
    148, 179 *n.* 18
Politburo, East German, 99
politics, KEDO and, 137, 138
*Power and Tactics in International
    Negotiation* (Habeeb), 69
PRC. *See* China, People's Repub-
    lic of
preconditions, North Korean anti-
    pathy toward, 93
prenegotiation, 23, 50–53, 148
press
    North Korean. See media
    South Korean, 133
press conference, ambassadorial,
    as a signal, 50
press statement
    and considerations of equiva-
        lency, 92, 182 *n.* 36
    to save face, 90, 148
pride
    brinkmanship and, 77–78
    see also "face" saving
prisoners, political, North Korea's
    demands for release of, 73

prisoners of war, negotiations over,
    43, 47, 52, 79, 84, 86, 151,
    179 *n.* 13
propaganda, North Korean
    against Japan, 30
    against South Korea, 80, 184 *n.* 8
    blame as, 86–87
    by the media, 47, 48
    negotiation as, 28, 100, 102
    protocol and, 54
    and the spy submarine incident,
        132–133
protocol, 3, 4, 53–54, 100, 179
    nn. 16, 17
    KEDO negotiations and, 120–
        121, 124, 125–131, 134
pseudonegotiation, 12
Public Security Bureau, DPRK, 26
Pueblo, USS, capture of, 5, 12, 24
punuigi (atmosphere), influence
    of, on negotiation, 66, 68,
    146, 147–148

Quinones, C. Kenneth, 3, 4, 53–54,
    179 *n.* 16

reactors, light-water (LWRs), 6, 117
    costs of providing, 123, 124,
        136, 137, 187 *nn.* 6, 9
    groundbreaking for, 135
    repayment for, 123–24
    South Korean provenance of,
        45, 79, 81, 82, 89, 113, 118,
        119, 122–123, 182 *n.* 29
    stalemate in, 54, 60, 95
    wording of agreement on, 92
    see also Korean Peninsula Energy
        Development Organization

recess, uses of, 57, 60, 84
reciprocity
  deal making and, 110
  North Korean insistence on, 23,
    101, 123, 145, 146
  uses of, 9, 149, 155–156
Red Cross
  humanitarianism, as a meta-
    phor, 100
  negotiation by, 12, 112,
    151–152
relationships
  building, 23, 53, 67, 129, 130
  personal, 53, 67, 148
religion, Kim Il Sung's cult of personality as, 39
reporting back
  considerations for North
    Korean negotiators, 54–55,
    60, 145, 179 n. 19
  to South Korea, 109
Republic of Korea (ROK). See
    South Korea
resistance, Kim Il Sung as a leader
    of, 172 n. 5
reunification, 10, 37, 75, 99, 171
    n. 14
Ri Gun, 52
Ri Hyong Chol, 52, 132, 133–134
Ri Jong Hyok, 52
rice. See food aid
Richardson, Bill, 52, 73, 86, 133
risk, brinkmanship and, 77
ruler, role of, 31, 32

sadaejuui ("serving the great"), as
    a survival tactic, 34, 35
Samore, Gary, 45, 54, 81, 82, 89

sanctions, economic, against North
    Korea, 3, 70, 71, 72, 76, 80,
    81, 111
Scalapino, Robert A., 178 n. 10
self-preservation, as a guiding
    principle, 42
self-reliance, Mao's doctrine of, 27
  see also juche
Shanghai Communiqué, 75
Shevardnadze, Eduard, 179 n. 19
Shopkeeper, as negotiator, 101,
    115, 183–184 nn. 4, 10
Shtykov, T. F., 25
siege mentality, in North Korea, 40
signals, North Korean
  about negotiations in progress,
    44, 48–50, 55, 60–61, 122,
    148, 153
  crisis diplomacy and, 73
  see also media
simultaneity, preoccupation with
    appearances of, 91, 92–93, 135
Sin Chae Ho, 35
social position, as a determinant in
    North Korea, 31–32
Solomon, Richard H., 181 n. 16
South Korea (Republic of Korea;
    ROK)
  assassination of cabinet mem-
    bers of, 5
  authoritarianism in, 20
  and direct DPRK-U.S. negotia-
    tions, 107–115, 185 n. 19
  effect of democratization in,
    173 n. 4
  food from, for North Korea,
    78–79, 86, 90, 100–101, 155,
    181 n. 17

South Korea (Republic of Korea; ROK) *(cont.)*
Geneva Agreed Framework and, 58
and KEDO, 117, 136, 137, 187 *n.* 9
Ministry of National Unification, 106
North Korea as a standing threat to, 106
as an object of North Korean vituperation, 88, 134
patterns of negotiation by, 97–103, 115
perceptions of North Korea's negotiating strategy by, 103
reaction of, to the North Korean spy submarine, 131, 133–134
social structure of, 33
Sunshine Policy of, toward North Korea, 154, 155
and the U.S., 107–108, 113–114, 146, 147
U.S.S.R. and, 111, 179 *n.* 19, 184–185 *n.* 11
see also dialogue, inter-Korean
South-North Joint Communiqué (1972), 10
sovereignty, importance of, 29, 30, 36–37, 144–145
Soviet Union. *See* U.S.S.R.
spy ring, North Korean, 105
stalemate, as a result of toughness, 102, 113–114, 144, 146
Stalin, Joseph, 13, 21, 26, 37
stalling. *See* delay
Stillwell, General Joseph W., 178 *n.* 10

strategy
brinkmanship, 78–85
dual-track, 45–46
importance of detail in, 152
irrationality in, 5, 43, 143, 189 *n.* 1
North Korea's, vis-à-vis South Korea, 99, 103
in plenary sessions, 54–55
South Korea's, 184 *n.* 10
stupidity in, 85
unchanging, 157–158
see also dilemma, Toughness
submarine, North Korean, in South Korean waters, 52, 75, 87
and U.S.-South Korean relations, 61, 114, 131–135
summit conferences, 110–111
Sunshine Policy, 154, 155
"Super Tuesday," 110
Syngman Rhee, 175 *n.* 20

tactics, negotiation, 11, 23, 170 *n.* 12
blame as, 86–88
brinkmanship, 77–78
evolution in, 140–141, 144
"face" saving as, 86
facilitating, 93–96
fundamental choices in, 68
guerrilla, 9, 23–24, 44, 70, 85, 144, 156
and the importance of sovereignty, 31
inflexibility as, 44, 113
patterns of, 66, 68–96
reciprocity, preoccupation with, 91

tactics, negotiation, *(cont.)*
  showing *kosaeng* (suffering), 86,
    88–89
  as signals, 44
  simultaneity, preoccupation
    with, 91
  Stalinist "salami-slicing," 28
  Turner Joy on communist, 11,
    172 *n.* 16
  unspecified threats as, 80–81
talking points, South Korea's need
    to approve, 108
Tan'gun, 18, 33
Team Spirit (military exercise), 93,
    186 *n.* 25
telephone, as a means of informal
    contact, 57, 84, 179 *n.* 16
threats, 24, 110, 132, 182 *n.* 20
  as counterstrategy, 152–153
  KEDO negotiations and, 122
  to gain leverage, 85–86
  to walk away. *See* breakdown
  unspecified, as a negotiating
    tactic, 80–81
  see also bluff
Three Principles for Korean
    Unification, 99
time pressure. *See* deadlines,
    fabricated
toughness, show of, 54, 88, 98, 128,
    130, 154, 156
Toughness Dilemma. *See* dilemma
trade-offs, North Korea's incompre-
    hension of, 59
tradition, neo-Confucian. *See* Con-
    fucius, influence of
traditionalism

and the Japanese occupation,
    29–30
  and nationalism, 26–27, 38
  and negotiating style, 68
trial balloon, 45, 49, 59, 66, 95–96,
    145, 148
Triandis, Harry, 170 *n.* 11
tribute, traditional precedent for,
    and the DPRK, 34–35
troops, U.S., in South Korea, 72,
    75, 93, 99
trust, lack of, between North and
    South Korea, 98–101
Turner Joy, C., *How Communists
    Negotiate*, 11, 13, 172 *n.* 20
Two Koreas, The (Oberdorfer), 38
Two-Plus-Two negotiations, 113

Umezu, Itaru, 118
United Nations Command (UNC),
    11, 51, 69, 73, 178 *n.* 10, 180
    n. 9
United Nations Organization, 57,
    70, 151
United States (U.S.)
  counterstategies for, 147–153
  culture of, and negotiation,
    170 *n.* 12
  Department of Energy, 132, 151
  Department of State, 52
  and KEDO, 117, 137, 138, 187
    n. 9
  military escalation in, 72
  neglect of North Korea by, 150
  negotiating style of, 112, 115,
    149, 180 *n.* 5, 183 *n.* 4,
    189 *n.* 1

United States (U.S.) *(cont.)*
  North Korean informal contacts
    with, 51–52
  perceptions of North Korea in,
    5, 11, 12
  relationship of, to North Korea,
    106, 107
  South Korea and, 107–108,
    113–114, 146, 147
  U.S.-DPRK nuclear negotiations,
    45, 54, 96, 186 *n.* 25
  compared with KEDO negotia-
    tions, 138–141
  initial, 3–4, 5–6, 184 *n.* 11
  as parallel negotiations, 113,
    187 *n.* 3
  results of, 6
  tactics used in, 60, 61
U.S.S.R.
  and North Korea, 13, 24, 25, 27
  perceptions of Kim Il Sung in,
    36, 174 *n.* 8
  recognition of South Korea by,
    111, 179 *n.* 19, 184–185 *n.* 11
  Soviet Council of Ministers, 13

venues, for negotiation, 47, 54, 55,
    178 *n.* 5
veto, as a negotiating tactic, 11
victory, symbolic, and negotiation,
    24, 54, 73, 74, 100

walking away. *See* breakdown
war
  negotiation as, 13
  North Korean perceptions of
    acts of, 3, 76, 80, 111

warfare, psychological, as a negoti-
    ation tactic, 11
Warrior, as negotiator, 101, 105,
    115, 183–184 *n.* 4, 10
weakness
  inter-Korean dialogue and,
    100, 106
  leverage and, 7, 85–91
  North Korean exploitation
    of, 24, 51, 55, 58, 68, 79,
    120–121, 144, 146, 149
weapons
  North Korean threats about,
    154, 156
  withdrawal of U.S. nuclear, 181
    n. 16, 184–185 *n.* 11
With the Century (Kim Il Sung), 23
Wold, James, 84
Wolfowitz, Paul, 5
Wu Yi Cheng, 23, 173 *n.* 6

Yang Sung Chul, 27, 109
Yi Kwang Su, 13, 131
yi (principle), 31, 34
Yusin reforms, in South Korea, 36,
    177 *n.* 39

zero-sum
  and inter-Korean dialogue, 9,
    14, 98, 111–112, 119, 143,
    146, 154, 155, 184 *n.* 5
  as a North Korean approach to
    negotiation, 12–13, 177 *n.* 1
Zhou Enlai, 75

Scott Snyder has been an Asia specialist in the Research and Studies Program of the United States Institute of Peace since 1994. During 1998–99, he conducted independent research in Tokyo and Seoul as an Abe Fellow of the Social Sciences Research Council. He has written on the political and security implications of the Asian financial crisis and on regional island disputes in Asia. A former acting director of the Contemporary Affairs department of the Asia Society in New York, Snyder received a B.A. from Rice University and an M.A. from the Regional Studies East Asia Program at Harvard University. He was the recipient of a Thomas G. Watson Fellowship in 1987–88 and attended Yonsei University in South Korea.

UNITED STATES INSTITUTE OF PEACE

The United States Institute of Peace is an independent, nonpartisan federal institution created by Congress to promote research, education, and training on the
peaceful management and resolution of international conflicts. Established in
1984, the Institute meets its congressional mandate through an array of programs,
including research grants, fellowships, professional training, education programs
from high school through graduate school, conferences and workshops, library
services, and publications. The Institute's Board of Directors is appointed by the
President of the United States and confirmed by the Senate.

Chairman of the Board: Chester A. Crocker
Vice Chairman: Max M. Kampelman
President: Richard H. Solomon
Executive Vice President: Harriet Hentges

Board of Directors

Chester A. Crocker (Chairman), James R. Schlesinger Professor of Strategic
    Studies, School of Foreign Service, Georgetown University
Max M. Kampelman, Esq. (Vice Chairman), Fried, Frank, Harris, Shriver and
    Jacobson, Washington, D.C.
Dennis L. Bark, Senior Fellow, Hoover Institution on War, Revolution and
    Peace, Stanford University
Theodore M. Hesburgh, President Emeritus, University of Notre Dame
Seymour Martin Lipset, Hazel Professor of Public Policy, George Mason University
W. Scott Thompson, Professor of International Politics, Fletcher School of Law
    and Diplomacy, Tufts University
Allen Weinstein, President, Center for Democracy, Washington, D.C.
Harriet Zimmerman, Vice President, American Israel Public Affairs Committee,
    Washington, D.C.

Members ex officio
Phyllis Oakley, Assistant Secretary of State for Intelligence and Research
Daniel H. Simpson, Vice President, National Defense University
Walter B. Slocombe, Under Secretary of Defense for Policy
Richard H. Solomon, President, United States Institute of Peace (nonvoting)

NEGOTIATING ON THE EDGE

This book is set in New Baskerville; the display type is Twentieth Century. Hasten Design Studio designed the book's cover, and Day Dosch designed the interior. Pages were made up by Helene Y. Redmond. David Sweet copyedited the text, which was proofread by Karen Stough. Frances Bowles prepared the index. The book's editor was Nigel Quinney.